egory

D0427354

Theory and History of Literature
Edited by Wlad Godzich and Jochen Schulte-Sasse

The Structural Allegory

Reconstructive Encounters with the

New French Thought

Edited and with an Introduction
by John Fekete

Theory and History of Literature, Volume 11

University of Minnesota Press, Minneapolis

Copyright © 1984 by the University of Minnesota
All rights reserved.
Published by the University of Minnesota Press,
2037 University Avenue Southeast, Minneapolis MN 55414
Printed in the United States of America

Library of Congress Cataloging in Publication Data
Main entry under title:

The structural allegory.
    (Theory and history of literature; v. 11)
    Includes bibliographical references and index.
    1. Structuralism—Addresses, essays, lectures.
2. Philosophy, French—20th century—Addresses,
essays, lectures. I. Fekete, John. II. Series.
B841.4.S84 1984   149'.96   83-19878
ISBN 0-8166-1271-4
ISBN 0-8166-1270-6 (pbk.)

Translated excerpts from *L'Institution imaginaire de la société*,
by Cornelius Castoriadis, © Éditions du Seuil 1975, used with
permission of Éditions du Seuil, Paris, and Georges Borchardt,
Inc. Translated excerpts from *L'Échange symbolique et la mort*,
by Jean Baudrillard, © Éditions Gallimard 1976, used by
permission of Éditions Gallimard, Paris. "The Paradigm of
Language: Wittgenstein, Lévi-Strauss, Gadamer," by György
Márkus, originally appeared, in somewhat different form, as
"Positivismus und Hermeneutik als Theorien der Objektivation"
in Ernst Bloch, ed., *Marxismus und Anthropologie: Festschrift
für Leo Kofler* (Bochum: Germinal, 1980).

The University of Minnesota
is an equal-opportunity
educator and employer.

For Raymond
  *whose integrity, intelligence, and commitments continue
  to inspire*

                              and

For Susan
  who has stood by me these many years

Contents

Acknowledgments

I will always remember the three years 1980-83 as a time of intense intellectual exchange and excitement. From the conception to the production of this book, over a wide range of communications related to conceptual design, solicitation of commitments and materials, review, revision, and editing, the genesis of this text has been associated for me with the warm interest, friendly cooperation, and intellectual stimulation volunteered by a considerable number of active, busy colleagues. I believe that this book can serve as a link among individuals closely engaged with the issues it encounters, indeed with the intellectual and historical destiny of our times.

I wish to record my appreciation to all the contributors to this volume, as well as to all the many others who took an interest, including Ioan Davies, Pamela McCallum, Eve Tavor, Peter Beilharz, Elie Noujain, Paul Heyer, Jon Bordo, Ágnes Heller, Ferenc Fehér, Costas Boundas, Alan Orenstein, Wodek Szemberg, and Tom McCarthy. Special thanks are due to my good friends Andrew Wernick and Charles Levin, whose continuous generosity with time, encouragement, and advice made the preparation of this text immeasurably easier and more rewarding. I am grateful to Susan Wheeler, who developed the index, and to Pat Saunders for her bibliographical assistance, as I am to Lindsay Waters and his editors at the University of Minnesota Press for all their efforts to improve the copy and to make it widely available.

Last but, as everyone in a similar position well knows, not least, I would like to thank Marg Tully for her invaluable secretarial work which, from the first letter to a potential contributor to the final technical detail, through seemingly endless typing, reorganizing, and retyping, often beyond the call of duty, has seen this book through to its publication. A Leave Fellowship from the Social Sciences and Humanities Research Council of Canada was most helpful in supporting the first stages of this project, as was a research grant from Trent University in supporting its late stages.

Descent into the New Maelstrom: Introduction
John Fekete

Our present is like being lost in the wilderness, when every pine and rock and bay appears to us as both known and unknown, and therefore as uncertain pointers on the way back to human habitation.

George Grant, *Time as History*

The metaprogramming circuit of the nervous system allows the brain to become aware of its programming, to choose which circuit will be operating, to edit and orchestrate experience. This was traditionally the Great Work of the Alchemists. Those who fall into it accidentally and un-prepared to handle the new freedom are called 'schizo-phrenics.'

Robert Anton Wilson, *Schrödinger's Cat*

We live in a post-Kantian world where the shifting of paradigms disorients our attempts to come to terms with experience. In this context, successive waves of what I call the structural allegory have swept over the widening spaces between concept and action. The "classical" intellectual disciplines, already unstable, have thus come under the assault of a series of invading ideas: "Kantism without a transcendental subject" (Lévi-Strauss), "process without a subject" (Althusser), "structure without a center" (Derrida), and "power/knowledge" without a localized base (Foucault). The cumulative effect of these new organizing concepts has been to erode traditional disciplinary foundations further and to repattern the field of intellectual attention.

The structural allegory, with its configurational logic, reprocesses all the antinomies we associate with the dimmed Enlightenment vision of rational, efficacious human agency—for example, culture and nature, subject and object, thought and history—and presents them as merely contingent effects. In this articulation, the conceptual grid has been so reorganized that no pole of the familiar dualities remains stable or autonomous. Instead, both poles are reduced to mere functions in a structural relationship, always already coded in a system of differences.

The structural allegory is now in its second stage, having passed through "structuralism" proper to the currently dominant model of "post-structuralism." Although certain differences and antagonisms between the two stages have been highlighted polemically among insiders, the second stage may be seen as a series of attempts to carry out uncompleted tasks of the structuralist program. In many cases the same individuals play important roles in these efforts. In the "human sciences," over and above divisions touching on general ideology, the structural allegory continues to be one of the most powerful forces in our intellectual world, building upon a firm base in a variety of disciplines (linguistics, anthropology, and psychoanalysis) and gaining strength in others (literary and cultural studies, philosophy, and history, for example). All these fields, through structuralist efforts, increasingly share a set of metatheoretical parameters and a common method of formalization.

Happily, the first series of expositions, accolades, and critical revisions is behind us. It is time to come more fully to terms with what is at stake in the structural allegory, especially in the influential version that has become so prevalent in French thought. All the essays in this volume mean to engage critically this mode of intellectual representation and to evaluate its role as a mediation of contemporary human practices and possibilities.

What is at stake in the encounter with the structural "turn" is the Western mind itself, although it is still a matter of dispute whether the structural tradition is its protagonist or antagonist, heir or mortician. It may be, paradoxically, both at once. We still cannot be sure

whether the new French thought offers an epistemological breakthrough or whether it should perhaps be seen as part of the wider
development of structural approaches since Marx and Freud. No matter how such an evaluation is settled, the new structural allegory can,
on the positive side, be recognized as the first broad-gauged development in the humanities and the social sciences that is an analogue to
the paradigm shifts of modern biology and quantum physics. The
transition from earlier paradigms of mechanical causality and evolutionary reproduction to the various metaphors of regulation through
formalized media—to Lévi-Strauss's "combinative, categorizing unconscious," Foucault's "technologies of power and strategies of normalization," Barthes's libidinal, literary body, or Derrida's orgasmic
surrender to the "seminal adventure of the trace"—is as decisive as
the shift to the model of the genetic code or Schrödinger's equations.

The strategic move effected in the language paradigm is the refusal
of conscious, intentional sources of meaning. The language paradigm
is in a position to rest its strategy on the analogy of genetic indetermination, or the (paradoxical) requirement in quantum theory that
the sources of energy and order must function nonlocally and with
nonlocal effects in space and time. "The medium," as Marshall
McLuhan was the first to say, "is the message"; it is the main player
on the structural stage.[1] In other words, the worlds of quantum
mechanics, genetic variation, and semiotic play form a single major
family of regulative metaphors that face us as an unavoidable modality of the contemporary scientific mythos.

In this context, a decisive contribution of the new French thought
has been its antiempiricist impulse. The structural allegory knows no
"things." It introduces between "words" and "things" a structural
relation—the language of thought (Derrida), the language of custom
(Foucault), and the language of production (Althusser). It dissolves
"meanings" into "prior" regularities and processes of signification. It
decenters and deconstructs articulations. It proposes that historical
and institutional particularities are effectively functions of their
(re)textualization.[2] In other words, the structural allegory directs
attention to a combinatory dimension (codes, conventions, traces,
genealogies) in the formation of objects: it both denaturalizes and
demythologizes, on a methodological principle (notwithstanding the
new features of dogmatism that accrete to the practical sedimentations
of a new tradition). By virtue of the structural method, the classical
intellectual inquiry into the "reality" of "things" is becoming transformed across the range of professional discourse.

At another level, the attention to configurational repetitions (whether in the combinatorial regularities of structuralism proper or the dynamic free play of the post-structuralist "trace" and genealogy) serves to reinsert a pattern of intersubjective/objective relations into the social sciences and humanities. The priority assigned to language entails the recovery of collective social categories, even if only in their methodological dimensions. The structural allegory thus challenges attempts to explain human activity along the lines of individual psychogenesis. In this respect, we should not forget, of course, that this critique of the Cartesian approach is indebted to a tradition that goes back to Durkheim and his notions of collective representations, or that, at its best, the structural allegory has much in common with Hegelian theories of social objectivation and institutionalization.

Indeed, it is to the credit of the new French thought that it provides the most powerful modernization of theories of reification, theories central to Western Marxism. From a transformist[3] point of view, the structural allegory may be flawed insofar as its articulations flatly duplicate the instituted domination of both achieved structural codes and indeterminately decentered structural processes in the contemporary world. Nonetheless, there is accuracy in the analysis thus afforded us. Seen from one point of view, we are provided a stunning intellectual reminder that the power of structures is more effective today than any individual or associated human agency. The structural allegory renders problematical all the (ultimately) self-betraying affirmations of the effective subjectivity of the human individual or the progress of history, and thus it serves as a valuable critique of sentimental humanism and evolutionary historicism. In this sense, again, the structuralist/post-structuralist tradition inscribes itself as a necessary horizon of contemporary intellectual life.

It is fair to say, then, that we are inescapably called upon to face up to the power of the structural allegory and to accept the admirable intellectual achievements that its deployment has brought. And yet, at the same time, we are entitled to have reservations about it that are just as strong as the admiration it deserves, because the structural allegory has not proved more sufficient in and of itself than any other master code. Moreover, it presents special problems when one asks what practical implications it has in its capacity as an active intellectual and ideological intervention. It may have succeeded in dissolving some of the inadequate answers provided by the classical traditions, but, on the negative side, it has also tended to bracket away some questions of enduring importance and in doing so to break faith with the hopes of the past. Ironically, because its biases and priorities have excluded or preempted the exploration of novel practical possibilities, its own program to dissolve rigidified antinomies in a new articulation may be threatened. In some disturbing respects, the evolution in the form of the structural allegory up to the current moment of post-structuralism appears to bind this intellectual tradition—as its antinomic otherness—to the entropic rationalism that has increasingly consumed the Enlightenment heritage.

The structural tradition begins with the critique of identity theory, any theory that allows the concept to dominate particulars of life. In this it resembles the Frankfurt School. But, by contrast, the critique is here coupled with an uncompromising formalism. Irony comes to be the dominant trope of the post-structuralist formulations used to deconstruct romantic organicism (known pejoratively as "logocentrism"). Catachresis becomes hypostatized as the universal rhetorical feature of language, and this development has far-reaching ramifications.[4] In this view, the notion of language as "representation," as something binding signifier to signified, is regarded as abusive and in danger of misapplication. The effort is no longer to liberate particular objects from subordination to the tyranny of the transcendental signified—the Frankfurt School project; but rather to liberate the free play of signifiers (viewed as the process of signification proper) from the transcendental signified in the sense of concept, stable meaning, the "presence" of thought to itself. The critical impulse is thus formalized in a way that approaches all forms of achieved meanings, values, and coherence—no matter how provisional a resting place they may offer in the adventures of culture—as decisive violations. The demythologizing impulse, using language as the structural model for all forms of human activity from literature and philosophy to politics, comes to address all articulated activity as inscribed within discourses of power and domination and thus the fitting targets of a transgression that would restore the play of contingency.

The post-structural formalization is thus programmatically committed to seeing all increases in the measure of satisfaction, all forms of human coherence and attempts to achieve plenitude, in a negative light. In other words, it cannot tell if a cup is half empty or half full, cannot differentiate between the positive values of any relatively successful social forms and the negative values of any relatively unsuccessful social forms. In short, it cannot adequately conceptualize either communication or community. The post-structuralist position suggests a number of things—in psychoanalytic terms, the revenge of desire against its satisfaction; in political terms, the vengeful anarchism and nihilism of impatience and desperation; in sociological terms, the revenge of the marginalized "other" against the individual and xvi □ JOHN FEKETE

associated selves and their capacities for quasi-autonomous, quasi-efficacious self-articulation; and in psychological terms, the *ressentiment* of the defeated who have no values to affirm. This is not a position to be condemned or dismissed without sympathy. Nor is it, however, a position fit to be widely embraced in a collective drama.

The post-structuralist critique ends in a paradoxical situation. On the one hand, post-structuralism set out methodologically to make dynamic and fluid the synchronous invariances emphasized by classic structuralism. Propelled by a formalizing momentum, made all the more far-reaching and autonomous by the language paradigm, post-structuralism is nonetheless led by its sense of structurality to recover-reconstitute a recurring structure of structures wherever it focuses on the infinite variations of common and intellectual life. Post-structuralism is drawn, in spite of its rejection of representation, to the presupposition of a synchronous macrostructure, now characterized as the untranscendable horizon of total domination articulated through the media of power and knowledge. A poignant pathos marks the post-structuralist adventure each time it reaches the self-canceling terminus of its itinerary. The untranscendable horizon where it arrives, when analyzed, displays the very logocentrism and features the same discourse of normalization that were the putative objects of deconstruction. The deconstructor might reply that this conclusion was to be expected all along, but we are not compelled to endorse the desperation that motivates such a claim of fatality.

The skeptical formalizations of post-structuralism founder on at least four types of difficulties. The first concerns the logic of modeling the relations between two structural levels. A wall built of bricks from a faulty mold, such that every brick tends to crumble on the left, may or may not be flawed; if flawed, it may or may not tend to crumble on the left; and even if it does, this is still not the same flaw as the flaw in any given brick or in the mold.[5] The point is that the relationship between microflaws (e.g., in mental structures, or norms) and macroflaws (e.g., in politics or social organization) cannot be assumed to be direct. This distance between the micrological and the macrological may offer space and time for creativity and novelty.

The second difficulty concerns the openness of structural development. Topological geometry (catastrophe theory) suggests that, as far as we know, determinate systems may, in a stable process, emerge into indeterminacy.[6] This means that the permeation of cultural structures with flawed relations does not necessarily resolve into an ultimate fatality.

The third difficulty for post-structuralism is caused by its failure to recognize the limits of structurality. The resulting constipation is characteristic of the structural allegory. The inflation of contingency and diacritical (inter)textuality as ideal values within the finitude of a structure disguises the intellectual practice whereby a synchronous presupposition is being simultaneously inflated in order to provide the boundaries of free play. Ultimately, the post-structuralist project is short-circuited by its structuralist beginnings in determinacy, by its unquestioned attachment to the formal logic of a discontinuous configuration of distinct, determinate "differences" (however much these are extended serially in the structure of trace or genealogy). Post-structuralism has failed to go far enough in dynamizing the structural theory of language. In challenging representation, it has severed the logic of semiosis from the logic of the symbolic (which Baudrillard laments) and also from the imaginary logic of signification, which (as Castoriadis argues) is an indeterminate *magma*, not a structure. In so doing, it has become captive in the structural closure of multiplied binary relations without theorizing the topological complexity of the relations between regions of determinacy and indeterminacy, and, hence, without breaking through the inherited (Cartesian and Kantian) binary polarity of sign and action.

A fourth difficulty for post-structuralism is posed by the nature of the social and cultural world. If the nature of that world is to be understood in terms that admit of ambivalence and not just "difference" —of yes-no-maybe—then where the frontiers are placed in the play of determinate and indeterminate regions is not a matter of formal prediction. It is rather a matter of substantive rationalities at play. A problem complex centering itself in substantive rationality and concerning itself with how the modern world is instituted and how it might be reconstructed calls for an intellectual address that lies beyond the frame of post-structuralist method and sets in sharp relief the solipsism of self-referentiality in which the structural allegory has tended to become trapped.

We should remember that there are voices from both premodernist and postmodernist quarters that lament the loss of normative constraints on how human beings may behave to one another. Thus George Grant sees in the endless freedom of the will to remake the world a mark of the demonism of modernity, just as Baudrillard sees the sign of evil in the collapse of a communicative rationality of reciprocal symbolic exchange.[7]

Meanwhile, this demonic triumph of will for the sake of itself finds general support in the nihilism evident in the post-structuralist's refusal of any substantive praxis and in the post-structuralist's affirmation of free space for the play of language and the will, affirmation granted on the condition that language and will abrogate their symbiotic ties to communicative meaning and value. Today we find simultaneously the absence of a hierarchy of goals along with the proliferation of norms in microcultural forms. This situation makes for a paradoxical combination in society of anomie and hypernormalization, a paradox that has become more pronounced in its cultural impact since Durkheim first observed the one and championed the other. The paradoxical social combination finds its intellectual analogue in the Derridean embrace of contingency in a structural configuration. The critical impulse that devotes itself solely to resistance against the stabilization of coherent concepts is unable to think of proposing a new table of values and is thus defenseless against the demonism of the "will-to-will" that Heidegger identified and that Grant takes to be "the very signature of modern man"—namely, "to deny reality to any conception of good that imposes limits on human freedom."[8]

If we are to move past these contradictions, we must reconceptualize reality in such a way that structurality comprises only a shifting region of determinacy, *beyond* which—and not just within which—there is indefinite space and time for creative and transformist praxis. We must, accordingly, reconceptualize the process that leads to the formation of efficacious agency on the individual and social levels within these determinate regions of fluid frontiers. The challenge that faces us is to rediscover the place for substantive rationality. We can credit the structural tradition with having convincingly shown the need to separate substantive rationality from a metaphysical, universal teleology. Now it remains for us to consider how a substantive rationality can be articulated with principles of appropriateness that are context-sensitive and decentralized.

Such a project of rethinking would benefit from a theory of predication that would be satisfied neither with Ernst Bloch's arguably eschatological "s is not yet p" (the subject is not yet predicate, man is not yet human, not yet a plenitude), nor with its variants in the structural allegory: "s is already p" (structural causality) and "p is not p" (difference, trace, structure). It might explore "s is never yet p" in order to translate the dynamic, utopian quality of the Blochian conception into a nonlogocentric form that does not betray its aspirations by implying certitude and that can be read as a complex of romantic, comic, tragic, and ironic modalities.

Consequently, it should be possible to articulate a less one-sided analogue of the natural scientific paradigms, drawing, for instance, on the *nonskeptical* implications of quantum mechanics. Quantum theory, after all, metaphorically transposed, suggests not only an anarchist picture of the universe, but specifically one in which Schrödinger's cat shows that it is not Pavlov's dog and that there are always alternatives open to *decisions* on which life and death hang in the balance. We should be able to draw from the antiobjectivist implications of the new physics a *participatory* theory of the universe in order to promote self-conscious reprogrammings of social and individual life and to reimprint the radical imagination. Many of the major competing interpreters of quantum mechanics (the Copenhagen School, the nonobjectivists, Herbert, Walker, Sarfatti and the California Physics/Consciousness group, Robert Anton Wilson) emphasize the fundamental role of intelligence-consciousness-information in their pictures of the universe. A stress on consciousness properly fits a reconstructed intellectual project. That such a stress on conscious participation should have become a taboo subject for the critical intelligentsia at this moment — a moment when even biological frontiers are opening on an era of evolutionary leaps in the extension of life and intelligence — is a sign of a most profound crisis of the Western mind, a most profound loss of nerve.

In this context, the structural devaluation of conscious agency appears especially short-sighted. The structural argument against a master code, against the centralized domination of a master program, has great merit. Yet it needs a supplement. For now Foucault, and others such as Baudrillard, have also elucidated the microcontrols of normativity, and pointed to the totalitarian operation of decentralized power. In consequence, it becomes strategically vital — contrary to the new taboos of the structural polemic — to reconceptualize the place of singularity in the new era. In effect, we must try to provide a charter of rights for a materialized *cogito*. The structural allegory constructs the place of the individual only negatively, as an absent otherness, a faded trace in the problematization of the human. A long tradition of civilization, however, from Aristotle to the modern variants of praxis theory, has strived in one way or another to provide a place for individual autonomy in its basic constructs. The hopes of the Western heritage and the threats and promises of the present demand that we think again of how autonomy can be rearticulated and valued positively as we work on the contemporary projects of human reconstruction. I state here the other side of the transformist orientation, the necessary complement to rethinking the place of community and of the collective-social.

Finally, if we wish to move past the aporias of the structural allegory, we are called on to rethink the problem of domination and history—not in terms of the linear unfolding of some originary sociology but in terms, perhaps, of a poetics of history, of a narrative theory of the social imaginary that could convincingly identify domination (as we know it) as a determinate regional configuration, an island in an ocean of human possibilities: a poetics of history that could hold out intimations of something better. Insofar as the structural allegory has been unable to situate itself in connection with a project of human reconstruction, the revolution in thought that it proclaims—if the terminology of "revolution" may serve for the moment—is linked with a broader (counter)revolution of lowered expectations that is shamefully prominent in our times. In this sense, the structural allegory bears the marks of an ethos, an ethnos, and a pathos of disenchantment.

Against a lowering of expectations, a "revolution" of *rising* expectations is the major competing dynamic in this century. We must reconnect the project of human reconstruction to the revolution of rising expectations. The sciences already suggest that we can turn the traditional metaphysical fantasies—immortality, accession to another world (indeed worlds), etc.—into material realities. At the same time the sciences present us with a dark, malignant side that, wedded to a global misadventure, threatens to lay waste the earth and its planetary life. The project of achieving at least some elementary, local progress in the never-ending "humanist" reconstruction of our personal and associated lives is, therefore, more urgent than ever. Judged from this standpoint, the structural allegory, in spite of all its illuminations, is not good enough. My emphasis falls on the adverb "enough." We cannot dismiss the structuralist program; but what it lacks as a strategy of decipherment and affirmation we must supplement and rearticulate. Going beyond the structural allegory does not mean closing the book of the structural tradition, but rather reading it in a certain way: as a valuable but ambivalent effort to retextualize the human adventure in such a way as to render it problematical.

What is needed, then, against this general background, is a dialogue with the structural tradition, a conversation of many voices. The selections in this book draw on a range of disciplinary and interdisciplinary complexes—literary, philosophical, cultural, and sociological —in order to provide a perspective on the symbolic life. The essays are meant to comment on one another and on the traditions of the structural allegory. One piece (Márkus) has been previously published in German; two others (Castoriadis, Baudrillard) are original translations from the French, selected and prepared for this volume; the two introductions to these translations (Singer, Levin) and the seven other essays were solicited, prepared, and edited specifically for this book with the aim of making a contribution to the debates that define contemporary understanding of these issues. In spite of the prevailing uncertainty in our day about intellectual positions and models, these essays display a certain confidence in intellectual life and a commitment to its mission, along with a cautious transformist impulse and a strategic ecumenicism. Several of these essays argue for such ecumenicism—that is why they are here: to try to make the fragments of the Western mind intelligible to one another, and to render themselves more intelligible at a new level by engaging in this dialogue.

The essays variously bring to the foreground different dimensions of the structural allegory. They seek to reconstruct and engage the traditions of the new French thought and several of its major figures (Saussure, Lévi-Strauss, Althusser, Barthes, Derrida, and Foucault), with specific attention to Anglo-American connections and general attention to the complex Western heritage. Cornelius Castoriadis, having elaborated since the second World War the most thoroughgoing internal critique of Marxism that we have, in the essay printed here moves on to propose a theory of the radical imaginary, in its relations with the institution of society, with the goal of providing a strategic perspective on the symbolic dimension and an account of the autonomization of symbol and institution. He resituates the relation of identity and difference within a logic of the social-historical and its significations. Of particular interest in this text from the mid-1960s is that Castoriadis's social ontology makes possible a critique of Lévi-Strauss that has significant points of contact with Derrida's critique of early structuralism. At the same time, Castoriadis's argument moves in a different direction to provide an alternative treatment of logocentrism, the limitations of reason, and the place of radical imagination.

The excerpts from Jean Baudrillard's later writing juxtapose what might be called an expressionist element—an expression of pain that marks the experience of forcing the structural allegory to yield a social revelation—with a systematic presentation of the genealogy of successive orders of signification. The result is a periodization of accelerating social disintegration. Baudrillard's inspired vision of the social body technocybernetically regulated on the model of the genetic code and his reconstruction of the Freudian death principle as a challenge to autonomized formalization, as the ambivalent return of the repressed social-symbolic, offer a darker complement to Castoriadis's placement of semantic evolution. Both of these responses from within the French debate, subverting the comforting commonplaces of Marxian, Freudian, and semiological discourses, may be found illuminating in their polemical as well as their theoretical facets.

Arthur Kroker's Baudrillardian study of Foucault and Parsons shows the continuities of a Parsons-Foucault tradition within the post-Newtonian epistemic universe of established sociology, modeled on the regulative paradigm of genetic biology. He describes an articulation constructed from the interfaces of genetic biology, cybernetic theory, and linguistic theory as the organizational schema of the new structural horizons of Western knowledge. The operations of power, described as a normalizing, regulatory language in contemporary "disciplinary society," are analyzed acutely in the light of recent paradigm shifts—the shifts effected by the dislocation of the political-economic objectivations of production and power in favor of the knowledge/power circuit born of the objectivations of language and custom. Like Baudrillard's, Kroker's challenges to what he regards as the obsolete Marxian models of production and power are likely to prove provocative and stimulating.

Although Marx's work and traditions are in the background of all these essays, their arguments invite not only a revision of received notions about the intellectual value of Marxism but a general reflection on models and their ramifications as well. Like Baudrillard's *Mirror of Production*, the work of the post-Lukácsian Budapest School has most lucidly and extensively reconsidered the implications of a paradigm of production[9] (which precedes the language paradigm as the hegemonic form in the social sciences and today is frequently recycled as analogy or metaphor in a variety of non-economic discourses, e.g., "literary production," "the productive unconscious," and so on). Here, György Márkus shows what is at stake in paradigm shifts, and particularly in the shift to the language paradigm itself (as opposed to other theories of objectivation). He does so by exploring critically the hegemonic dispersion today of the language paradigm in discourses as disparate as those of Wittgenstein, Lévi-Strauss, and Gadamer. The analytic narrative Márkus provides starts off from an implicitly problematical production paradigm and makes explicitly problematical the language paradigm in order to reveal the ineluctably practical dilemmas of one's orientation.

Márkus's post-Enlightenment humanism is complemented by Andrew Wernick's transformist pursuit of rational supports for both humanism and science. Wernick reviews and addresses the demolition of the radical Enlightenment's deepest faiths and the self-destruction of the French rationalist project to conjoin faith and reason. He reconstructs the intellectual history of this dislocation from the Middle Ages to the contemporary crisis of epistemology and the social sciences, paying specific attention to the Western epistemological project and the final aporias to which an autonomized configurational logic of cultural objectivations leads. Of particular interest in Wernick's efforts to deconstruct and reconstruct the history of the European metatheoretical traditions so as to situate within it the French Marxist/structuralist moves is his sensitivity to national traditions and *epistemes*.

Marc Angenot, in a discussion of the institutionalization of Saussure, likewise distinguishes French intellectual life, to argue provocatively that it has been inferior to the great intellectual movements of the twentieth century elsewhere. On this account, in the 1960s French structuralism did not exist as an epistemic formation or even a regulating hegemony, but rather as a factitious amalgamation of incompatible elements, a label for a syncretic simulacrum that was to substitute for Marxism as the encompassing frame for the social sciences. Angenot is equally provocative when discussing the penetration of structuralism into literary studies, especially when he describes literary scholarship as a syncretic recycling plant.

The three essays that follow analyze the major figures in the post-structuralist stage of the structural allegory in French thought: Derrida, Foucault, and Barthes. Each essay attempts to set out the strategic moves made by these writers in the formation of intellectual models. D'Amico examines the text of an early Derrida-Foucault debate over a reading of Descartes to tease out a deeper understanding of textuality from this confrontation than has been proposed either in structuralism or in interpretation theories. Charles Levin's thoroughgoing critique of the entire Derridean corpus exposes the relation of the deconstructionist project to its Enlightenment forebears and to the metaphysical baggage of Heidegger's ontology. In a closely worked retextualization of Derrida, Levin reconsiders the Derridean project as an extension of configurational logic, overdetermined as a formulation of the "cupidity of the text": a solipsistic "desire of desire," analogous to the "will-to-will." Levin's discussion of this autonomization of the formal principle uncovers through an analysis of Derrida the dominant cybernetic paradigm in the structural allegory. Of related interest is John O'Neill's presentation of Barthes. O'Neill traces Barthes's self-critical intellectual trajectory from structuralism to post-structuralism, from Marxism to semiology to critical play, where it comes to rest in the pleasures of the text, locked into the trope of revolutionary sexuality. From a critical consideration of the polytextuality of the libidinal literary body, with its analogue, a polymorphous life, O'Neill arrives at a reflection on other types of body structures at the levels of social reproduction and hence at a more complex theory of a resurrected body politic.

Finally, my own closing essay, aiming to supplement *The Critical Twilight*, discusses the North American literary institution, from Ransom, Frye, and McLuhan through Stanley Fish, in connection with the matrix of French theory and its impact on a tradition laced with Germanic, Romantic, and pragmatic elements. The essay braids together and then distinguishes three strands—formalization, language paradigm, and anti-foundationalism—of literary modernity. Its concluding propositions are both openly ecumenical and strategically directed to renewed axiological concerns that may help to reorient the study of signs, the radical imagination, and those relationships between the symbolic and the imaginary that we know as the signs of the times.

Notes

1. For an extensive discussion of McLuhan's strategic place in the structural turn of Anglo-American literary/cultural theory, see John Fekete, *The Critical Twilight: Explorations in the Ideology of Anglo-American Literary Theory from Eliot to McLuhan* (London and Boston: Routledge & Kegan Paul, 1978), pp. 135-96.

2. For the argument that, as a matter of historical fact, the structuralist "revolution" has had as its hegemonic form a model of decipherment "of which literary and textual criticism is in many ways a strong form," see Fredric Jameson, *The Political Unconscious: Narrative as a Socially Symbolic Act* (Ithaca: Cornell University Press, 1981), pp. 297-98.

3. See Fekete, *The Critical Twilight*, pp. 196-97.

4. For a discussion of the strategic role of the rhetorical trope of catachresis in Foucault's writing, see Hayden White, "Michel Foucault," in John Sturrock, ed., *Structuralism and Since: From Lévi-Strauss to Derrida* (Oxford: Oxford University Press, 1979), pp. 81-115.

5. Samuel R. Delany offers this example in a brilliant science-fiction text whose theoretical dimensions draw extensively on the new French thought. See *Triton: An Ambiguous Heterotopia* (New York: Bantam, 1976), pp. 358-59.

6. See, for example, René Thom's writings over the past two decades on catastrophe theory and the mathematics of structural models; in particular "Topological Models in Biology," *Topology*, 8 (1969), 313-35: "a deterministic system may exhibit in a 'structurally stable way' a complete indeterminacy in the qualitative prediction of the final outcome of its evolution" (321). For a general discussion of catastrophe theory and its appropriation for social science, in the context of which Thom is cited, see Michael Thompson, *Rubbish Theory: The Creation and Destruction of Value* (Oxford: Oxford University Press, 1979).

7. See George Grant, *Lament for a Nation: The Defeat of Canadian Nationalism* (Princeton: D. Van Nostrand, 1972); Jean Baudrillard, *The Mirror of Production*, trans. Mark Poster (St. Louis: Telos Press, 1975), and *For a Critique of the Political Economy of the Sign*, trans. Charles Levin (St. Louis: Telos Press, 1981).

8. Grant, *Lament for a Nation*, p. 56. The point about the will can be made without following Grant in emptying the category of "freedom."

9. For a recent example, see Ágnes Heller, "Paradigm of Production: Paradigm of Work," *Dialectical Anthropology*, 6 (1981), 71-79.

The Structural Allegory

Chapter 1
Introduction to Castoriadis
Brian Singer

The following translation is taken from the major work of Cornelius Castoriadis to date, *L'Institution imaginaire de la société*. This work is composed of two parts written during two different periods, under dissimilar circumstances, and with evident differences in language, organization, and style. The first part, written and published in the middle sixties (1964-65), must be related to the disintegration of *Socialisme ou Barbarie*, a small political group with a journal of the same name, in which Castoriadis was the major "animateur" and leading author.[1] The group's collapse, its cause and consequences, both theoretical and political, are clearly legible in this text: the critique of Marxism from within Marxism, which had always been *Socialisme ou Barbarie*'s hallmark, finally touches bottom with the discovery that Marxism itself has to be rejected, not simply in terms of its specific claims, but as a general mode of theorizing.

This "final" critique of Marxism opened up a series of more general and fundamental questions. Castoriadis moved beyond the "traditional" concerns of political economy into linguistics, psychoanalysis, and, above all, philosophy.[2] In the last third of the first part of this book, in the section "L'Institution et l'imaginaire: premier abord," the first fruits of this reflection are sketched out. By the time the second part was written a few years later, the ideas had developed to the point where their expression could be refined and

3

elaborated in a manner that, without ever being "complete" or "total," eliminated much of the scrappiness suggestive of a "work under construction." The first four sections of the translation are drawn from this "first approach," and the last two from the second part proper.

The interest in the selection for the present volume lies less with the scores settled with a Marxist past than with Castoriadis's relation to structuralism. The text reveals that the author has appropriated and assimilated certain structuralist concerns and motifs; indeed, the piece is unthinkable without such an assimilation. But attention is redirected to questions of meaning, reason, and history in contrast to a structuralism that treats meaning as epiphenomenal, rationality as essentially a problem of form, and history as an accumulated jumble of combinations and their ruptures. Behind the frequent attacks on "inherited thought," there is something classical about Castoriadis's interrogation; the seemingly odd vocabulary proves to have very familiar, though imperfect, correlates: "the first natural stratum" corresponds roughly to nature, "institution" to culture, and "identitarian-ensemblist thought" to reason. However, let there be no mistake: the responses to this interrogation, the very method of posing the questions, are anything but traditional—the critique of Marxism had gone too far for that.

There is, for example, no attempt to establish in yet another guise a social teleology whereby the meaning of history would be borne by reason. Reason is not made to explain the meaning of history; rather the question is asked: what in society, in its most elementary and fundamental gestures, bears the imprint of reason, if only in germinal form; and what is the latter's relation to the constitution of social meanings, to the problem of signification? A "social ontology" is immediately substituted for a "social teleology," but reason is only situated in society (and not as the end of society) in order to delimit reason from what in society is not "rational"—the symbolic, the imaginary—and yet is equally elementary and fundamental. In this way reason is separated out from the problem of signification and denied any possible equivalence with society as it is or should be. From the outset, and without lapsing into irrationality, the analysis is placed within the horizons of a comprehension of the limitations of reason. And as if by epistemological rebound, the same strategy checks our own surreptitious "logocentrism," forcing us to confront the limits of our own possible knowledge of society. Only then can we place ourselves on the threshold of history and its creation.[3]

The term *ensemble* has been translated as "ensemble," to which have been added such barbarisms as "to ensemblize," "ensemblizable," and so on. The term could have been alternately translated as "set" in the mathematical sense (at several points Castoriadis refers at length to Bourbaki's formulations of set theory) and refers to a "totality" whose elements are distinct and determinate, and which therefore is easily denotable. The term should be contrasted with what Castoriadis calls a "magma," a sort of inchoate totality whose moments (one can hardly speak of elements) are indistinct and indeterminate, and whose definition can only be connoted. Magmas belong—though not exclusively—to the "logic" of signification, as opposed to an "identitarian-ensemblist" logic.

The term *"étayage"* can be translated, particularly with reference to a specifically psychoanalytic context, as "anaclitic relation." Since Castoriadis is using the term in the context of the relation between nature and culture, I have preferred the more familiar word "grounding." In psychoanalytic discourse, the term refers to a relation that, while necessary, excludes any form of determination. Society is grounded in nature without being determined by nature—a point of particular importance when it is realized that nature is appropriated by society as meaningful, as responding to "the question of signification."

NOTES

1. Castoriadis wrote in *Socialisme ou Barbarie* under the pseudonyms Pierre Chaulieu and Paul Cardan. His works of this period, along with various conjunctural pieces and several long introductions of more recent vintage, have been collected in eight volumes and published by 10/18. Two of the introductions can be found in English translation: "On the History of the Workers' Movement," *Telos*, 30 (Winter 1976-77), 3-42, and "Socialism and Autonomous Society," *Telos*, 43 (Spring 1980), 91-106.

2. Concerning Castoriadis's theoretical itinerary, see "An Interview with C. Castoriadis" and the introduction by Dick Howard, *Telos*, 23 (Spring 1975), 117-55, as well as my own "The Early Castoriadis: Socialism, Barbarism, and the Bureaucratic Thread," *Canadian Journal of Political and Social Theory* 3:3 (Fall 1979), 35-56.

3. For a more extensive discussion of *L'Institution imaginaire de la société*, see Dick Howard's chapter on Castoriadis in *The Marxian Legacy* (New York: Urizen, 1977), pp. 262-301, and my own "The Later Castoriadis: Institution under Interrogation," *Canadian Journal of Political and Social Theory*, 4:1 (Winter 1980), 75-101. See also *Les Carrefours du labyrinthe* (Paris: Éditions du Seuil, 1978), a collection of Castoriadis's most recent essays. An English version of this book is scheduled to appear from The Harvester Press.

Chapter 2
The Imaginary Institution of Society
Cornelius Castoriadis

Institution and the Symbolic

All that exists within the social-historical world is indissociably entwined with the symbolic without, however, being exhausted in it. Real acts, individual or collective—work, consumption, war, love, childbirth—and the innumerable material products without which no society could live for an instant, are not (not always and not directly) symbols. But their existence is impossible outside a symbolic network.

We first encounter the symbolic, of course, in language. But we also encounter it, to another degree and in another manner, in institutions. Institutions cannot be reduced to the symbolic, but they can only exist in the symbolic. Outside a second-order symbolic their existence is impossible, for each institution constitutes its own symbolic network. A given organization of the economy, a system of law, an institutionalized power or religion exist socially as sanctioned symbolic systems. They attach symbols (signifiers) to signifieds (representations, orders, incentives, or injunctions to act or not to act, as well as their consequences—significations in the loose sense of the term)[1] and validate them as such; that is, they render these attachments

Translation by Brian Singer. The text is drawn from *L'Institution imaginaire de la société* (Paris: Éditions du Seuil, 1975), pp. 162-63, 175-204, and 311-24.

more or less compulsory for a given society or group. A property title or deed of sale is a socially sanctioned symbol of the proprietor's "right" to engage in an indefinite number of acts relative to the object of his property. A paycheck is the symbol of the wage earner's right to demand a certain quantity of bills which, in their turn, are symbols of their possessor's right to purchase a variety of goods, each of which will have, again, a symbolic dimension. The labor for which the paycheck is given, though eminently real for its subject and in its results, is constantly traversed with symbolic acts (in the thoughts of the person working, in the instructions he receives, and so on). And this labor becomes itself symbolic when, having been reduced to hours and minutes calculated according to certain coefficients, it enters into the computation of the enterprise's payroll or "results of exploitation"; or when, in the case of litigation, it fills the blank spaces in the premises and conclusions of a juridical syllogism. The decisions of economic planners are symbolic (with and without irony). The tribunal's decrees are symbolic, and their consequences are almost entirely so, right up to and including the actions of the executioner which, though real *par excellence*, are immediately symbolic at another level.

Every functionalist view is aware of and must recognize the role of symbolism in social life. But only rarely do such views recognize its importance—and then they would limit it. Either symbolism is seen as a simple lining, a neutral instrument perfectly adequate to the expression of a preexisting content (the "true substance" of the social relations), neither adding to nor subtracting from the latter. Or else symbolism is recognized as having its "own logic," but this logic is seen exclusively in terms of the symbolic's insertion in a rational order with its own consequences, both desired and undesired.[2] In both cases the form is at the service of the content, and the base is "real-rational." But this is not how it is in reality, which undercuts the interpretive pretensions of functionalism. . . .

The reverse claim is equally invalid: one cannot say that institutional symbolism "determines" social life. We have here a relation *sui generis*, one that is misconstrued and deformed when grasped as either sheer causation or pure association, absolute liberty or complete determination, transparent rationality or a simple succession of brute facts.

Society constitutes its symbolism, but not in total liberty. Symbolism cleaves to the natural and the historical (to what already exists), and partakes of the rational. As a result, connections and consequences emerge from the association of signifiers, and from the relation between signifiers and signifieds, that were neither intended nor expected. Neither freely chosen, nor forcibly imposed on society; neither a neutral instrument or transparent medium, nor an impenetrable opacity or irreducible vicissitude; neither society's master, nor the supple slave of its functionality, nor the means for directly and fully participating in a rational order, symbolism determines certain aspects of social life (and not only those that it is supposed to determine), while simultaneously being full of interstices and degrees of liberty.

These characteristics of symbolism, while indicating the *problem* constituted for society by the symbolic nature of its institutions, do not render the problem insoluble. Nor do they account, by themselves, for the autonomization of institutions relative to society. The autonomization of symbolism, for all that it is present in history, is not an irreducible fact, and is not self-explanatory. There is an immediate utilization of the symbolic where the subject lets himself be dominated by the latter, but there is also a deliberate and lucid utilization. And although the latter can never be guaranteed a priori (one cannot construct a language, or even an algorithm, in which mistakes are "mechanically" impossible), it does occur nonetheless; and this fact alone points to a relation in which the symbolic is no longer autonomized, and can be rendered adequate to its contents. It is one thing to say that one cannot choose one's language in absolute liberty, that each language encroaches on what "there is to say." It is quite another to believe that one is fatally subject to language, that one can say only what it makes one say. We can never leave language, but our mobility within language is limitless, allowing us to question everything, including language and our relation to it.[3]

And the same applies to institutional symbolism—except, obviously, that the latter's complexity is incomparably greater. There is nothing intrinsic to the symbolic that necessitates the domination of an autonomized symbolism over social life; nor is there anything in institutional symbolism that excludes its lucid utilization by society —it being understood, once again, that institutions cannot be so constructed as to prevent "mechanically" the enslavement of society to its symbolism. In this regard, there has been real historical progress in our Greco-Occidental culture, as much in its relations with language as in its relations with institutions. Even capitalist governments have finally learned how to use—in certain respects, and with some degree of accuracy—the "language" and symbolism of economics to say what they want to say with credit, fiscal policy, etc. (the *content* of what they say is obviously something quite different). This is not to suggest that just anything can be expressed in any language; the musical ideas in *Tristan* cannot be stated in the language of the *Well-Tempered Clavier*, and even a simple mathematical theorem is undemonstrable in everyday language. In all likelihood, a new society will create new institutional symbolism, and the institutional symbolism of an autonomous society will have little relation with what we have known until now.

The mastery of institutional symbolism would not, therefore, seem to pose problems very different from those involved in the mastery of language (abstracting for the moment from the former's material "heaviness"—its embodiment in classes, arms, objects, etc.) if this were all there was to it. Symbolism can be mastered—except insofar as it refers, in the last instance, to something that *is not* of the symbolic. For what goes beyond any simple "rational progress," what allows the autonomization of institutional symbolism to be more than just a passing deviation to be set straight again (as with a lucid discourse), what, lastly, provides symbolism with its essential supplement of determination and specification, does not depend on the symbolic.

The Symbolic and the Imaginary

There still remains an essential, and for our purposes, decisive dimension to every symbol and symbolism, at whatever level they are situated. We are referring to the imaginary dimension.

Consider the term "imaginary" in its everyday meaning (which for the moment will suffice): we speak of the imaginary when we wish to speak of something "invented"—be it an "absolute" invention ("a story invented from scratch") or a slippage or displacement of meaning in which already existing symbols are invested with significations other than their "normal" or orthodox significations ("What are you imagining there?" says the woman to the man chiding her for a smile exchanged with a third person). In both cases, it is understood that the imaginary is distinct from the real, whether it claims the latter's position as its own (a lie) or simply claims its own position (a story).

The profound and obscure nature of the relation between the symbolic and the imaginary becomes apparent as soon as one reflects on the following: the imaginary must utilize the symbolic, not only in order to be "expressed"—this is self-evident—but in order to "exist," to move beyond a merely virtual state of existence. The most elaborate delirium, like the vaguest and most secret phantasm, consists of "images," but these "images" are present as representations of something else, and so have a symbolic function. But inversely, symbolism presupposes an imaginary capacity. That is to say, it presupposes the capacity to see in a thing what it is not, or to see it other than it is. And insofar as the imaginary can be resolved into a first and fundamental faculty for posing, in the form of representation, things and relations that do not exist (that are not, and have never been, given in perception), we shall speak of an ultimate or radical imaginary as the common root of the positive imaginary and the symbolic.[4] In the last analysis we are dealing here with the elementary and irreducible capacity for evoking images.[5]

The imaginary's decisive hold on the symbolic can be understood in terms of the following consideration: symbolism supposes the capacity to establish a permanent connection between two terms such that the one "represents" the other. But it is only in the more advanced stages of rational thought that these three elements (the signifier, the signified, and their connection *sui generis*) are maintained as simultaneously united and distinct in a relation that is both firm and supple. Otherwise the symbolic relation (which, when "properly" used, supposes the imaginary function *and* its mastery by the rational function) slips back to, or rather remains from the start, where it first emerged—with the rigid connection (usually in the form of identification, participation, or causation) between signifier and signified, symbol and thing, that is to say, in the positive imaginary.

If we have said that the symbolic presupposes and depends on the radical imaginary, this does not mean that the symbolic is simply the positive imaginary considered in terms of its contents. For the symbolic almost always bears a "real-rational" dimension (that which represents the real, and is indispensable for thinking about or acting in the real). But this dimension is inextricably entwined with the positive imaginary dimension—and this poses a major problem for both politics and the theory of history.

It is written in Numbers (15:32-36) that the Jews, having caught a man who, contrary to the Law, was working on the Sabbath, brought him before Moses. The Law did not set a fixed penalty for the transgression, but the Lord manifested himself unto Moses and demanded that the man be stoned to death—and he was.

One cannot help but be struck—as often happens when perusing Mosaic Law—by the excessive character of the penalty, the apparent absence of any necessary relation between the fact (the transgression) and its consequence (the penalty). Stoning, after all, is not the only way to have the Sabbath respected; the institution (the penalty) clearly exceeds any rational connection of causes to effects, or means to ends. If reason is, as Hegel said, an action in conformity with an end, were the Lord's actions in this case reasonable? But the Lord, one will say, is imaginary. Behind the Law—which is "real," a positive social institution—stands an imaginary Lord who exists as its source and ultimate sanction. But is the Lord's imaginary existence to be supposed reasonable? One may claim that, at a certain stage of the evolution of human societies, the institution of an imaginary endowed with more reality than the real itself—God, or more generally, a religious imaginary—is "in conformity with the ends" of society, stems from its real conditions, and fulfills an essential function. One may try to show from either a Marxist or Freudian perspective (and here they do not exclude each other, but are complementary) that such a society produces this imaginary of necessity, that it needs this "illusion," as Freud said in reference to religion, for its functioning.

These interpretations are valid and valuable. But their limitations become evident when faced with the following sorts of questions: Why must society seek the necessary complement to its order in the *imaginary*? Why does one always find within this imaginary, and in all its expressions, something irreducible to the functional, something akin to an initial investment by society of itself and its world with meaning—meanings that are not "dictated" by real factors (since it is this investment that provides these factors with their place and importance in the universe constituted by a given society) and that can be recognized in both this society's style and contents (they are not all that far removed from what Hegel called "the spirit of a people")? Why, for example, of all the pastoral tribes wandering the desert between Thebes and Babylon during the second millenium B.C., did only one choose to set a severe and vindictive, unnamable Father up on high, and make him the sole creator and foundation of the Law, thereby introducing monotheism into history? And why, of all the peoples who built cities in the Mediterranean basin, did only one decide on the existence of an impersonal law applicable even to the gods, claim that it was consubstantial to rational discourse, and seek to establish men's relations on the basis of this Logos—thereby inventing with one fell swoop both democracy and philosophy? How is it that three thousand years later we are still experiencing the effects of what was dreamed up by the Jews and ancient Greeks? Why, and how, does this imaginary, once established, lead to consequences that go beyond its functional "motifs" and may even oppose them, which survive long after the circumstances responsible for its emergence—and which reveal the imaginary as an autonomized factor of social existence?

Let us consider the Mosaic religion. Like every religion, it is centered on an imaginary. As a religion it must establish rites, and as an institution it must surround itself with sanctions. But it can exist neither as a religion nor as an institution if it does not begin developing a *second imaginary* around the *central imaginary*. God created the world in seven days (six plus one). Why seven? One can interpret this number in Freudian terms; and one can relate it to any number of facts or customs. But however it be interpreted, this terrestial determination ("real" perhaps, but perhaps already imaginary), once exported to the heavens, is reimported in the form of the *week* and its sanctification. The seventh day is now a day of rest and worship. Consequences, innumerable consequences, begin to proliferate. First there was the stoning of one unfortunate wretch for collecting tinder in the desert on the Lord's day. And among more recent consequences we might mention at random the frequency curve of sexual intercourse in Christian societies with its periodic maximum every seven days, the rate of surplus value,[6] and the mortal boredom of English Sundays.

Take as another example the "rites of passage," the ceremonies of initiation or confirmation that mark the entry of adolescents into adulthood, ceremonies that play such an important role in archaic societies, and whose not inconsiderable remnants subsist in modern societies. Whatever their context, these ceremonies evidence an important economic-functional dimension, and are meshed in a thousand ways with the "logic" of the society in question (a largely nonconscious "logic," of course). It is necessary that the accession of a group of individuals to full enjoyment of their rights be publicly and solemnly proclaimed (in the absence of a written, public register, a pedestrian functionalist would say); it is imperative for the adolescent's psyche that this crucial stage of his maturation be marked by festivities and tests, that, as it were, a "certification" take place. But around this nucleus—one is almost tempted to say, in analogy with pearl oysters, around this impurity—one finds crystallized an immense sedimentation of rules, acts, rites, and symbols full of magical, and more generally, imaginary elements, whose justification relative to the functional nucleus becomes increasingly mediated and, in the end, null. The adolescents must fast for a certain number of days, eat only certain foods as prepared by a certain class of women, undergo certain tests, sleep in a certain hut or remain awake for a certain length of time, wear specific crests and ornaments, and so on.

The ethnologist, with the aid of Marxist, Freudian, or other conceptions, will try to provide a complete interpretation of the ceremony in all its details. It is immediately apparent, however, that one cannot interpret the ceremony by directly reducing it to its functionalist dimension (no more than one can interpret a neurosis by saying that it has to do with the subject's sexual life); the function is the same almost everywhere and cannot therefore explain the improbable luxuriance of details, their complications and differentiation. So the interpretation will engage in a series of *indirect* reductions where one will again find a functional element—*and* something else. (For example, the composition of the adolescents' meal, or the class of women that prepares it, will be related to the clan structure or the tribe's alimentary regime, which in their turn will be related to certain "real" elements, but also to totemic phenomena, alimentary taboos, and so on.) These successive reductions eventually come up against two limitations. First, the last elements are symbols, from whose constitution the imaginary can be neither separated nor isolated. And second, the successive synthesis of these elements, the "partial totalities" that make up a society's life and structure, the "figures" that render society visible to itself (the clans, ceremonies, moments of religion, and forms of authority relations) themselves possess an indivisible meaning, as if this "totalized" meaning were the result of some founding act that constituted it all at once. This meaning, henceforth operative as such, is situated at a level other than that of any possible functional determination.

This double movement can be easily seen in the most "integrated" cultures, whatever their mode of integration. It is evident in totemism, where an "elementary" symbol is both the world's organizational principle and the foundation of the tribe's existence. It is apparent in Greek culture, where religion (which is inseparable from the city and its sociopolitical organization) overlays every natural element and human activity with its symbols *and* simultaneously bestows a global meaning on the universe and man's place in it.[7] It even appears in Western capitalist societies, where the "world's disenchantment" and the destruction of all anterior forms of the imaginary have paradoxically been accompanied by the constitution of a new imaginary that is centered around the "pseudo-rational" and that bears on both the world's "ultimate elements" *and* its total organization.

We have been speaking about what might be called a culture's central imaginary, as situated at the level of either its elementary symbols or global meaning. There also exists what one might term the peripheral imaginary, which, though no less important in its effects, will not occupy us here. It corresponds to successive layers of sedimentation, to the second, third, nth degree imaginary elaboration of symbols. An icon is a symbolic object of a certain imaginary—but it is invested with a different imaginary signification when the faithful scrape off its paint and drink it as medication. A flag is a symbol with a rational function, a sign of reconnaissance and a rallying point, which quickly becomes something for which one can and must die, and which sends shivers down the spine of patriots when military parades march by.

The modern approach to institution, the one that reduces its signification to the functional, is only partially correct. For though it presents itself as *the* truth about institution, it is but a projection. It projects on all history an idea taken from the Western capitalist world —though not from the reality of the latter's institutions (which, in spite of the enormous trend to "rationalization," have always been, and will always be, only partially functional) but rather from how this world would like them to be. Even more recent views that attempt to conceptualize institution in terms of *only* the symbolic (and identify the latter with the rational) represent an equally partial truth, and their generalization is just as much a projection.

Ancient views about the "divine" origin of institutions were, under their mythical shell, closer to the truth. When Sophocles spoke of divine laws as more compelling and durable than those made by the hands of men[8] (and, as if by chance, the law in question here was the incest taboo violated by Oedipus), he was pointing to a source of institution beyond man's lucid consciousness as a legislator. It is the same truth that underlies the story of the Law given to Moses by God—an invisible and unnamable *pater absconditus*. Beyond all conscious attempts at active institutionalization, institutions have their source in the *social imaginary*. This imaginary must intersect with both the symbolic (otherwise society would be unable to "pull itself together") and the economic-functional (otherwise it would be unable to survive). It can also, and indeed must, place itself in their service; the imaginary of institution has a *function*, though here again the imaginary's effects *go beyond* its function. It is not an "ultimate factor" (and we are not looking for one). But without the imaginary, the determination of the symbolic and the functional, the specificity and unity of the first, the orientation and finality of the second, would remain incomplete, and in the end, incomprehensible.

Alienation and the Imaginary

Institution is a socially sanctioned symbolic network in which the functional and imaginary dimensions are combined in a variable relation, and in varying proportions. Alienation involves the autonomization and dominance of the imaginary moment of institution, and this in turn entails the autonomization and dominance of institution relative to society. This autonomization of institution is expressed and incarnated in the materiality of social life. But it also supposes that society lives its relation with its institutions in the form of the imaginary; i.e., that it does not recognize the institutional imaginary as its own product.

Marx was aware of this. He knew that "in the life of the Greeks, the Apollo of Delphi was as real a power as any other." When he spoke of commodity fetishism, and demonstrated its importance for the functioning of the capitalist economy, he moved beyond a merely economic viewpoint to a recognition of the imaginary's role.[9] When he stated that the memory of dead generations weighs heavily on the minds of the living, he was pointing to a particular type of imaginary where the past is lived as the present, ghosts are more powerful than men of flesh and blood, and the dead seize hold of the living. And when Lukács, in another context, and following Engels, said that the mystified consciousness of the capitalist is necessary for the adequate functioning of the capitalist economy, i.e., that only by "using" people's illusions can its laws become effective, he showed how a specific imaginary fulfilled one of the conditions of functionality.

But Marx saw the imaginary has having a limited, or more precisely, a functional role, that of the "noneconomic" link in an economic chain. For Marx thought he could chalk it up to a provisional deficiency (provisionally lasting from prehistory to communism) of history as economy, i.e., to humanity's present technical immaturity. He was ready to recognize the power of man's imaginary creations— both supernatural and social—but only as a reflection of man's real impotence. It would be shallow and schematic to say that for Marx alienation was just another term for scarcity, but in the last analysis, it nonetheless remains true that, in his conception of history as formulated in his mature works, scarcity is the necessary and sufficient condition of alienation.[10]

This conception cannot be accepted, for reasons exposed at greater length elsewhere:[11] in brief, because one cannot define a threshold of technical development or economic abundance beyond which the division of classes or alienation would lose their "raisons d'être"; because the achievement of such technically induced abundance is at present already socially blocked; because the "needs" in terms of which a state of scarcity can alone be defined are not at all fixed, but express a social-historical state.[12] But, above all, because such a conception entirely misjudges the role of the imaginary—the fact that it lies at the root, not only of alienation, but of creation in history.

For creation, like alienation, presupposes the capacity to pose things that are not (not given in perception, or in the symbolic connections of an already established rational system of thought). And one cannot distinguish the imaginary active in creation from the imaginary "pure and simple" by claiming that the former "anticipates" a reality whose existence will later be verified. For one would first have to explain how this "anticipation" can occur without an imaginary, and what prevents the latter from ever going astray. And then one must consider that creation does not, in its essentials, involve a "discovery" but the constitution of something new. Art does not discover, it constitutes; and the relation of what it constitutes to the "real," while certainly very complex, is not one of verification. Again, with regard to the social plane—our main concern—the emergence of new institutions and life-styles does not involve "discovery" but active constitution. The Athenians did not find democracy among the flowers growing wild on the Pnyx, and the Parisian workers did not unearth the Commune while digging up the flagstones of the boulevards. Nor did either of them "discover" these institutions in the sky of ideas, after having inspected all the possible forms of government neatly displayed from all eternity. They invented something that certainly proved viable in the circumstances, but which also, once it was established, modified these circumstances, and indeed continues, twenty-five centuries or a hundred years later, to be "present" in history. This sort of verification has nothing to do with Magellan's verification of the idea that the world is round—an idea which, if it did not first exist in perception, nevertheless referred to an *already constituted* reality.[13]

When one affirms, with regard to institution, that the imaginary only plays a role because of "real" problems that men have not yet managed to solve, one forgets that, to the extent that men do solve these problems, they do so only *because* of their imaginary capacities. What is more, these problems are only problems, are only constituted as problems, as *those* that a given period or society must try to solve, as a function of this period or society's central imaginary. This does not mean that these problems are invented from scratch or pulled out of thin air. But what for each society forms a problem (or emerges as such at a given level of specification or concretization) is inseparable from its general mode of being, from that "totalized" and, indeed, problematic meaning with which it invests the world and its place in the latter—a meaning that as such is neither true nor false, neither verifiable nor falsifiable by reference to "true" problems or their "true" solutions, except in one very specific sense to which we shall return.

Consider the case of an individual, any individual. Does it make any sense to say that his imaginary formations have an important role to play only because "real" factors—instinctual repression, traumas—had already created a conflict? Certainly, the imaginary acts on a terrain where instinctual repression exists, and works on the basis of one or more traumas. But such instinctual repression is always there; and what constitutes a trauma? Outside of certain extremes, an event is traumatic only because it is "lived as such" by the individual, which in these circumstances is to say, because the individual imputes to it a signification that is not its "canonical" signification, or is not in any case ineluctably imposed as such.[14]

Similarly in the case of society, the idea that its imaginary formations "form an independent kingdom in the skies" because the society in question has not solved its problems "in reality" may be true at a secondary level, but not at a fundamental level. For such a claim would make sense only if one coud say *what* the problem is that society is temporarily incapable of solving. Now, a response to this question is impossible, not because of the insufficient advancement of our inquiries or the relativity of our knowledge, but because the question makes no sense. *The* problem of society does not exist. There is no particular "thing" that men want deeply but until now have been unable to get because their technical skills were insufficiently developed or because society remained divided into classes. Men have individually and collectively wanted, needed, and acted, but each time with a different object in mind, and as a consequence, to the extent that men are composed of these needs and actions, with a different "definition" of themselves.

To say that the imaginary only emerges—or comes into operation—because men are incapable of solving some real problem supposes that one can know and state what this problem is, and that it will always remain the same (for if the problem changes one will have to ask why, and one then returns to the preceding question). Such a claim supposes that one knows, and that one can say what humanity *is*, what it *wants*, and where its *tendency* lies, in the manner in which one speaks (or believes one can speak) of objects.

To this question Marxists have a double and contradictory response, one whose confusion no dialectic can mask, and which, at its limit, involves a good dose of bad faith.

Humanity, it is claimed, *is* hungry.

And humanity *wants* freedom—not freedom from hunger, but that freedom about which everyone agrees that it neither has, nor can have, any determinate "object."

Humanity is hungry, true enough. But what does it hunger after, and how? Half of its members are still hungry in the literal sense, and this hunger must certainly be satisfied. But is its hunger only for food? How then does it differ from sponges and corals? And why does this hunger, once satisfied, always seem to lead to other questions and other demands? Why has the life of the privileged strata, which have always been able to satisfy their hunger, or of entire societies that can now do so, not become free? Why has the security, satiation, and copulation *ad libitum* of Scandinavian societies, and increasingly of all modern capitalist societies (a billion individuals), not resulted in the emergence of autonomous individuals and collectivities? What is this *need* that these populations are unable to satisfy? Should one claim that humanity remains unsatisfied because of technical progress, which makes new objects arise, or because of the existence of privileged strata, which places other manners of satisfaction before the eyes of the less privileged, one will have admitted what we have been trying to say. For one will have conceded that this need does not have an object that could satisfy it, as say the need to breathe has its object in the atmosphere's air; that it emerges historically, and that no determinate need is equivalent to *the* need of humanity. Humanity hungered and still hungers for food, but it also hungered for clothes, and for fashions unlike those of last year; it hungered for cars and televisions, for power and holiness, asceticism and debauchery, mysticism and rational knowledge; it hungered for love and fraternity, but also for its own corpses; it hungered for festivals and tragedies, and now it seems that it has begun to hunger after the moon and planets. And it would require a good dose of cretinism to claim that humanity invented all these hungers just because it had not managed to eat enough or fuck enough.

Man does not consist of some need that bears its complementary "good object," like a keyhole with its key (which one either finds or makes). Man can exist only by continuously defining himself as a set of needs with corresponding objects, but he constantly transcends these definitions. And if he is capable of transcending them (not just as a permanent potentiality, but in the actuality of historical movement), it is because they issue from himself, because he constitutes them (not arbitrarily, of course—there is always nature, history, and the minimal coherence required by rationality), because, therefore, he *makes* them in his acts and in the act of making himself, because, lastly, they cannot be fixed permanently by any rational, natural, or historical definition. "Man is he who is not what he is, and who is what he is not," as Hegel said.

Imaginary Social Significations

As we have seen, one cannot understand institutions, and even less, all social life, as a simply functional system, an integrated series of measures for the satisfaction of society's needs. For every such interpretation immediately raises the question: functional in relation to what and to what end—a question that cannot be answered from within a functionalist perspective.[15] True, institutions are functional in that they have to ensure the survival of the society in question.[16] But what one calls "survival" varies widely between societies; and what one calls "functional" is in relation to ends that have little to do with either functionality or its opposite. No society—whether a theocratic society, one where a class of lords is allowed to wage wars without end, or a society like that of modern capitalism, which creates a continuous stream of new "needs" and exhausts itself in their satisfaction—can be either described or understood *in its functionality* except relative to the designs, orientations, and chains of signification that not only escape functionality, but to which functionality is largely subordinated.

Nor can one understand institutions as simply a symbolic network.[17] Institutions form a symbolic network, but this network refers by definition to something other than its symbolism. Every purely symbolic interpretation of institutions immediately opens onto the following questions: (a) Why was *this* system of symbols chosen, and not another? (b) What do these symbols convey; what are their *significations*, the system of signifieds to which the system of significers refers? and (c) Why, and how, do symbolic systems manage to become autonomized? Already one suspects that the answers to these questions are profoundly related.

(a) In order to understand (inasmuch as one can understand) the "choice" a society makes with regard to its symbolism, one must go beyond all formal or even "structural" considerations. When one says in connection with totemism that certain animal species are chosen not because they are "good to eat" but because they are "good to think,"[18] one is no doubt disclosing an important truth. But it must not lead one to neglect the questions that then follow: why are some species "better to think" than others; why is one pair of oppositions chosen over all the other possible pairs offered by nature; who thinks these pairs, when and how? In short, this truth must not serve to eliminate considerations of content, the reference to the signified. When a tribe designates two clans as homologous to the pair eagle-hawk/crow, the question immediately emerges: why, of all the pairs capable of connoting a difference in kinship, was this one chosen? It is clear that this sort of question appears with infinitely more insistence in historical societies.[19]

(b) To comprehend, or even simply to apprehend, a society's symbolism is to grasp the significations that it conveys. These significations appear only by way of signifying structures; but this does not mean that they can be reduced to these structures, that they are determined by or, in some univocal manner, result from the latter. When one teases out of the Oedipus myth a structure composed of two pairs of oppositions,[20] one is probably pointing to a necessary condition (like the phonematic oppositions in language) for the *saying* of something. But what is it that is being said? Is it just anything, that is to say, nothing? Does it not matter that this structure, this particular organization of signifiers and signifieds, with all its various levels, ultimately transmits a global signification or articulated meaning—in this case, the prohibition and sanction of incest? Is it a matter of indifference that the latter is constitutive of a world of human co-existence, one where the other is not just an object of my desire, but has an existence of his own and engages in relationships from which I am excluded? And when structuralist analysis reduces an entire set of primitive myths to an attempt to signify, by means of the opposition between the raw and the cooked, the passage from nature to culture,[21] is it not clear that what is being signified by the contents possesses a fundamental meaning, that it indicates an obsession with the question of origins, a form and part of the obsession with identity, with the being of the group in question? If the structuralist analysis is correct, it would seem that men ask themselves what constitutes the specifically human world, and answer with a *myth*: the human world is one that causes natural givens to undergo a transformation (where foodstuffs are cooked). Ultimately we are dealing here with a rational response given in the imaginary by symbolic means.

Meaning can never be given independently of *all* signs, but is not necessarily tied to *any particular signifying structure*. For meaning is, as Shannon said, what remains invariable when a message is translated from one code to another, and, it might also be added, what allows the definition of an identity (however partial) among different messages in the same code. One cannot maintain that meaning simply results from the combination of signs.[22] One might just as well say that the combination of signs results from meaning. After all, the world is not just made up of those who interpret the discourses of others. In order for the former to exist, the latter must first have spoken, and to speak they must have chosen signs, hesitated, collected their thoughts, rectified signs that they had already chosen—and all as a function of meaning. The structuralist musicologist is a most respectable person as long as he does not forget that he owes his existence (from an economic, but also an ontological point of view) to someone who traveled the same path before him, though from an opposite direction. He is dependent on the creative musician who, guided by a musical signification that he was seeking to express (either consciously or unconsciously, it hardly matters), chose "these signs and their oppositions," placed them on a score, enriched or impoverished a certain harmony, gave the woodwinds a phrase initially confided to the brass (while, of course, never ceasing to be influenced throughout the composition by the signs available in the code used, in the musical language that he had adopted—though a greater composer modifies this language and constitutes his own signifiers *en masse*). The same applies to the structuralist anthropologist or mythologist, except that here, the creator being an entire society, the reconstruction of the codes is much more radical, and much more covert; in short, the constitution of signs as a function of meaning is an infinitely more complex affair.

To consider meaning as simply the "result" of the difference between signs is to transform the necessary conditions for the *reading* of history into the sufficient conditions of its *existence*. And while these conditions of "reading" are intrinsically conditions of existence, since history exists only because men communicate and cooperate in a symbolic milieu, this symbolism is itself *created*. History exists only in and by "language" (all sorts of languages), but history gives itself this language, constitutes it, transforms it. To ignore this side of the question is to describe the multiplicity and succession of symbolic (and therefore institutional) systems as brute facts about which nothing can really be said (let alone be done). It is tantamount to dismissing the historical question par excellence, the question of meaning's genesis, the production of new systems of signifiers and signifieds. And if this holds true for the historical constitution of new symbolic systems, it is equally true of the utilization of established symbolic systems. Here again one cannot say that meaning is either the "result" or the "cause" of the opposition between signs; for one would be suggesting relations of causality, or at the very least, of rigorous bi-univocal correspondence, which mask and efface the symbolic's most profound trait—its relative indetermination. This indetermination is clearly indicated at the most elementary of levels by the overdetermination of symbols (several signifieds can be attached to the same signifier)—to which should be added the inverse phenomenon, what might be called the oversymbolization of meaning (the same signified is borne by several signifiers; within the same code there are equivalent messages, and within every language "redundant" features, and so on).

The extremist tendencies of structuralism are a result of its complicity with "the utopian ideal of the day," which is not "to construct a system of signs on a single level of articulation,"[23] but to *eliminate meaning* (and in another form, to eliminate man). And so, to the extent that meaning cannot be identified with a combination of signs (as the latter's necessary and univocal result), it is reduced to a non-transferable interiority, or a "certain flavor."[24] Thus one seems incapable of conceiving meaning except in its most limited psychological-affective sense. But the prohibition of incest is no flavor; it is a law, i.e., an institution with its own signification, symbol, myth, and rule. As such it refers to a meaning that organizes an infinite number of human actions; one that erects within the field of the possible, and in its center, a wall separating the licit from the illicit; and that creates a value that rearranges the entire system of significations, conferring on consanguinity, for example, a content it never had "before." The difference between nature and culture is not just a simple difference in flavor between the raw and the cooked, but a world of significations.

(c) And lastly, one cannot avoid the question: how and why does the symbolic system of institutions manage to become autonomized? How and why does the institutional structure become a factor to which the actual life of a society is subordinated, seemingly enslaved? To answer that it is symbolism's nature to become autonomized is to perpetrate more than an innocent tautology. It is equivalent to saying that it is in the subject's nature to alienate himself in the symbols he employs; it is thus to invalidate all discourse, dialogue, and truth by claiming that everything we might say is borne by the automatic fatality of symbolic chains.[25] We know, however, that symbolism's autonomization in social life is a secondary phenomenon. When religion confronts society as an autonomous factor, religious symbols have value and independence only because they incarnate a religious signification; their luster is borrowed—as is further demonstrated by the fact that religion can invest new symbols, create new signifiers, and extend the sacred into new regions.[26]

One need not fall into the traps of symbolism in order to recognize its importance. Discourse is not independent of symbolism, and symbolism is far from being simply its "external condition"; rather, discourse is held in symbolism's embrace. This does not mean that it is fatally enslaved to symbolism. After all, what discourse strives for is not symbolism but *meaning*—meaning that can be perceived, thought, or imagined. And it is this relation to meaning that makes it into either a discourse or a delirium (which can be grammatically, syntactically, and lexically impeccable). The distinction, which we cannot avoid making, between someone who, on seeing the Eiffel Tower, says: "There is the Eiffel Tower," and someone else who, in the same circumstances, says: "Look, there's Grandma"—this distinction is specific to the relation of the discourse's signified with the canonical signified of the terms used, and with a sort of nucleus independent of all discourse and symbolization. This independent nucleus that comes to expression (and which, in this example, is "the real state of things") is the discourse's meaning.

We can therefore posit that significations exist that are relatively independent of their signifiers, and that play a role in the choice and organization of the latter. These significations correspond to the *perceptual*, the *rational*, or the *imaginary*. The fact that intimate relations practically always exist among these three poles should not cause us to lose sight of their specificity.

Consider, as an example, God. Whatever the support his representation may find in the perceptual, whatever this representation's rational efficacy as an organizational principle for certain cultures, God is not a signification of either the real or the rational; nor is he a symbol of something else. But what then is God—not as a theological concept or philosophical idea—but for us, when we try to imagine what he is for those who believe in him? They can evoke him, they may refer to him, but not without the aid of symbols, be it only his "name"—and yet God for them, and for us when considering the historical phenomenon constituted by God and by the faithful, indefinitely transcends this "name." God *is* this something else; he is not the name nor the images a people give themselves of him, nor anything similar. Conveyed and indicated by all these symbols, he is what in each religion makes these symbols into religious symbols. He is a central *signification*, one that organizes signifiers and signifieds into a system, upholds their intersecting unity, and allows their extension, multiplication, and modification. And this signification, which corresponds to neither something perceived (real) nor something thought (rational), is an imaginary signification.

Take the phenomenon Marx called reification, and more generally the "dehumanization" of the exploited classes during certain historical periods, where the slave is perceived as an *animal vocale*, and the worker as a "cog in the machine," or a simple commodity. It is of little concern here that this assimilation is never fully realized, that the human reality of the slaves or workers constantly places it in question, and so on.[27] Our concern is with the nature of this signification, which, far from being just a concept or representation, has an operative significance with heavy historical and social consequences. A slave is not an animal, and a worker is not a thing; but reification is neither a false perception of the real nor a logical error—nor can it be made into a "dialectical moment" in a totalized history of the human essence, where the latter would first have to be radically negated in order for its truth to be positively realized. Reification is an imaginary signification (and we need hardly stress that the social imaginary, as we understand it, is more real than the "real"). From a narrowly symbolic or linguistic perspective, reification appears as a displacement of meaning, as a combination of metaphor and metonymy. The slave can only "be" an animal metaphorically, and this metaphor, like all metaphors, is based on metonymy, the part being taken for the whole (for the animal as well as the slave), and this pseudo-identity being extended to the entirety of the object under consideration. But this slippage of meaning—which is, after all, only symbolism's perpetual *modus operandi*—the fact that under one signifier another signified slips in, while describing what has occurred, does not account for either the genesis or the mode of being of the phenomenon in question.

For what is at issue here—in the case of either the slave or the proletariat—is the constitution of a new *operative signification* where one category of men is held by another to be assimilable, for all practical purposes, to animals or things. Reification is an *imaginary creation*, and cannot be explained by reality, rationality, or the laws of symbolism (even though it does not "violate" the real, the rational, or the symbolic). It need not be explicitly proclaimed in concepts or representations in order to exist; as meaning, it actively organizes human behaviors and social relations in a given society independently of whether or not this society is "conscious" of its existence. In actual social practice, the slave was metaphorized into an animal, and the worker into a commodity, long before Roman jurists, Aristotle, or Marx came onto the scene.

What makes this problem so difficult—and probably explains why it has for so long been viewed in such a partial fashion, and why even today one notes, in both anthropology and psychoanalysis, immense difficulties in distinguishing the symbolic from the imaginary—is not just the "realist" and "rationalist" biases (of which the most extreme tendencies of present-day "structuralism" represent a curious mixture) that prevent acknowledgment of the imaginary's role. The difficulty is that in the case of the imaginary one can hardly lay hold of the signified to which the signifier refers, for its "mode of being" is by definition a mode of nonbeing. In the register of the perceptual (the real), whether "interior" or "exterior," the physically distinct existence of signifier and signified is immediately evident. No one confuses the word "tree" with a real tree, or the word "anger" or "sadness" with the corresponding emotions. In the register of the rational, the distinction is no less clear. We all know that the word (the "term") designating a concept is one thing, whereas the concept itself is another. But in the case of the imaginary, things are less simple.

True, we can distinguish here, at a first level, words from what they designate, signifiers from signifieds. "Centaur" refers to an imaginary being that is distinct from this word, and that can "be defined" by words (and thereby assimilated to a pseudo-concept) or represented by images (and thereby assimilated to a pseudo-perceptual).[28] But even in this rather facile case (the imaginary centaur being only a collage of pieces taken from real beings), such considerations are not exhaustive, since the being of centaurs, for a culture living their mythological reality, is something quite different from any verbal description or sculptural representation one might give them. But how is this a-reality to be seen? Like "things in themselves," it is really only given in terms of its consequences, results, and derivatives. How is one to grasp God as an imaginary signification, if not in terms of the shadows (the *Abschattungen*) he projects on the screen of actual social activities? But at the same time, how can one not see that God, like something perceptible, is a condition for the possibility of an inexhaustible series of such shadows, even though, in contrast to perceptible objects, he is never there "in person"?

Consider someone living a scene in the imaginary, either by giving himself over to reverie or by reliving a scene in his mind. The scene consists of "images" in the widest sense of the term. These images are made of the same material as symbols are sometimes made of. But are they symbols? Not explicitly in the subject's consciousness, since they are not there for something else, but are "lived" for themselves. The problem, however, does not end here. For they may represent something else, and in particular, unconscious phantasms—and this is how psychoanalysts generally see them. Such images then are symbols—but of what? To answer this question, one must enter the labyrinth of the imaginary's symbolic elaboration in the unconscious. And at the end of this labyrinth one finds something that does not exist *in order to represent* something else, but is instead the operative condition of all ulterior representation, and yet itself already exists in the mode of representation: the subject's fundamental phantasm, his nuclear schema (not the "primal scene"), where that which constitutes the subject in his singularity is to be found.

This fundamental schema structures its own structure; it organizes and is organized, constituting itself into images. It exists not in symbolization, but in an imaginary "presentification" which for the subject is already signification, both incarnate and operative, and the first appropriation and constitution of an articulated relational system that establishes, separates, and conjoins "interior" and "exterior." Through this "presentification" are posited the rudiments of action and perception; the distribution of the archetypal roles and the first imputation of a role to the subject himself; the first valuations and devaluations. It is the source of all ulterior symbolic significance, and the origin of the specific privileged investments of the subject. At the individual level, the production of this fundamental phantasm proceeds from what we called the radical imaginary (or the radical imagination); this phantasm exists as both a moment in the positive imaginary (the imagined), and as the first signification and core of all ulterior significations.

It is doubtful whether one can directly take hold of this fundamental phantasm. At best it can be reconstructed from its manifestations. For it appears as the basis of the possibility and unity of all that makes the subject's singularity more than a purely combinatory singularity, and of everything in the subject's life that points beyond the specifics of his reality and history. Indeed, it appears as the ultimate condition for this reality and history actually to *occur for* the subject.

When shifting to the societal level—and, needless to say, we are not about to transform society into a "subject," not even metaphorically—we encounter the same difficulty in aggravated form. For we can, starting from the imaginary as it immediately swarms to the surface of social life, penetrate the labyrinth of the imaginary's symbolization. And by pushing the analysis, we can arrive at significations that do not exist *in order to* represent something else, but appear as the ultimate articulations imposed by society on itself, its needs, and world—as the "organizing schemas" that constitute the condition of representability for everything society gives itself. But by their very nature, these schemas do not themselves exist in the form of representations that one could, with the aid of analysis, put one's finger on. One cannot speak here of "images," however vague and indefinite the meaning one gives this term. God may be, for each believer, an "image"—or even a "precise" representation—but as an imaginary signification, God is not the "sum" of these images, their "average," or what they have "in common." God is their condition of possibility; he allows these images to be images "of God." Nor can one consider the imaginary core of the phenomenon of reification as an "image."

Imaginary social significations do not, properly speaking, exist in the form of representations; they are of a different nature, for which no analogy can be drawn from other domains of our experience. Compared with individual imaginary significations, they are infinitely larger than any phantasm (the schema underlying the Jewish, Greek, or Occidental "world image" is infinite in its extension), and do not have any precise place of existence (if one can call the individual unconscious a precise place of existence). They can be grasped only in an oblique and derivative manner: like the difference (which, while obvious, is impossible to delimit exactly) between a society's actual life and organization, and (what is equally impossible to define) the same life and organization conceived in strictly "functional-rational" terms; like a "coherent deformation" of the system of subjects, objects, and their relations; or like the curvature specific to each social space; like the invisible cement holding together the immense bric-a-brac of the real, rational, and symbolic that constitutes society; or the principle that chooses and shapes the bits and pieces that will be admitted into society. Imaginary social significations—or at least those that are truly "ultimate"—do not *denote* anything, though they *connote* well-nigh everything. This is why they are so often confused with their symbols, not only by those who use them, but by "scientists" who analyze them and, in so doing, conclude that their signifiers (since they do not refer to anything one can *designate* as real or rational) signify only themselves, and thereby attribute to these signifiers, and to symbolism as such, a role and efficacy infinitely superior to what they actually possess.

But is it not possible to "reduce" this social imaginary to the individual imaginary—and thereby provide these signifiers with a *denotable* content? Could one not say, for example, that God can be derived from the individual unconscious, that he signifies an essential phantasmic moment of the unconscious, and in particular the imaginary father? Such reductions—like the one Freud attempted for religion, or like those one might attempt for the imaginary significations of our own culture—contain an important if partial truth. It is incontestable that an imaginary signification must find points of support in the individual unconscious. But this condition is not sufficient—and one may even legitimately wonder whether it is not the result rather than the condition. In certain respects the individual and his psyche seem, especially for us living today, to possess an eminent "reality" that the social lacks. But in other respects this conception is illusory, "the individual being an abstraction." The fact that one cannot take hold of the social-historical field as such, but only of its "effects," does not prove that this field is any less real, but rather the opposite. Weight is a property of a body, but it is also a property of the surrounding gravitational field (which can only be perceived by "mixed" effects of this type). What a body possesses "in its own right," its mass in classical terms, is not, to believe certain modern cosmological conceptions, one of its "properties," but an expression of the action on this body of all other bodies in the universe (Mach's principle)—in short, it is a property of "coexistence" appearing at the level of the totality. That we meet with something in the human world that is both more and less than a "substance"—the individual, subject, or for-itself—should not lead us to diminish the reality of the "field."

Even if one grants the existence of "a place to be filled" within the individual unconscious, as in the Freudian interpretation of religion, and even if one accepts the latter's understanding of the processes resulting in the necessity of religious sublimation, it still remains true that the individual cannot fill this space with his own productions, but must use signifiers that he does not freely dispose of. The individual can produce private phantasms, not institutions. Sometimes a junction does occur, in a way one can date and situate, among the founders of religions and other "exceptional individuals." Their private phantasms manage, at the right moment and in the right place, to plug the holes in the unconscious of large numbers of people; and these phantasms have enough functional and rational "coherence" to prove viable once symbolized and sanctioned, i.e., once institutionalized. But these considerations do not imply a "psychological" solution to the problem, not just because of the rarity of these cases, but because even here the irreducibility of the social is still quite visible. In order for such a junction to occur among the unconscious tendencies of many different individuals, in order for the prophet's discourse to be more than a personal hallucination or the credo of an ephemeral sect, favorable social conditions must have shaped unconscious leanings over an indefinite area, and prepared them for the "good news."

The prophet himself works in and by established institution (*l'insti-tué*), and even when subverting the latter, he draws support from it. All religions about whose genesis we know are transformations of former religions or contain an enormous syncretic component.

Only the myth of origins formulated by Freud in *Totem and Taboo* escapes these considerations in part. And this is because it is a myth —and because it refers to a hybrid, and in truth, incoherent state of affairs. The primitive horde is not a fact of nature; even it supposes institution. Neither the castration of male children nor the preservation of the last-born is the result of biological "instinct" (with what finality, and how could it "disappear" afterward?); they already express the action of the imaginary (without which, moreover, the submission of the descendants is inconceivable). The murder of the father is not the inaugural act of society but a response to castration (and is not the latter a sort of anticipated counterresponse?); and thus the community of brothers that succeeds the father's absolute power amounts to revolution rather than to the pristine establishment of society. What is not yet present in the "primitive horde" is that institution, all of whose elements are otherwise present, is not symbolized as such.

Outside of a mythical postulation of origins, every attempt at an exhaustive derivation of social significations from the individual psyche is doomed to failure because it fails to realize that one cannot isolate the psyche from a social continuum which, in order to exist, must already be instituted. And for imaginary social significations to exist, collective signifiers, but above all, signifieds—which do not have the same form as individual signifieds (as perceived, conceived, or imagined by an individual subject)—must be available.

Functionality draws its meaning from outside itself; and symbolism necessarily refers to something that is not of the symbolic—and that is not simply real-rational either. This something, the element that provides the functionality of each institutional system with its specific orientation, and overdetermines the choice and connections of the symbolic networks; this creation specific to each historical period, its singular way of constituting, perceiving, and living out its existence; this primary and active structuration, this central signifier-signified; the source of meanings that are given as beyond all discussion and dispute; the support for the articulation of and distinction between what does and does not matter; and the origin of that excess of being attached to practical, affective, or intellectual objects of investment (whether individual or collective)—this element is none other than a society or period's *imaginary*.

No society can exist without organizing the production of its material life and its reproduction as society. But neither production nor reproduction is, or can be, ineluctably dictated by natural laws or rational constraints. And within what thus appears as a margin of indetermination must be situated that which is essential from the point of view of history. For what is essential from this point of view is not the fact that men have always eaten or have always begotten children, but that they have done so in an infinite variety of ways; that everything given to a society is *apprehended* in a determinate manner, in practical, affective, and mental terms; that *articulated meanings* are imposed on the given; and that distinctions are made between what is and is not of value (in all senses of the word, from the most economic to the most speculative) and between what ought and ought not to be done.[29]

This structuration certainly finds points of support in corporeality, insofar as the world present to the senses is necessarily an articulated world, but also because corporeality supposes need. Within the hollow of this need, material and human objects, food, and sexual coupling are immediately inscribed, so that a relation to objects and other human beings, and therefore a first "definition" of the subject as need and as a relation to what satisfied this need, is immediately borne by the fact of his biological existence. But this universal presupposition, in its invariable sameness, is absolutely incapable of accounting for either the variation or evolution of the forms of social life.

The Social Institution of Ensembles

The very existence of society, as anonymous and collective activity/representation (*faire/representer*) is impossible (or at least inconceivable for us) without the institution of the *legein* (the capacity to "distinguish-choose-pose-assemble-count-speak") and the implementation of the identitarian-ensemblist logic incorporated in the latter.

Social activity always presupposes, and social representation always refers to, distinct and definite objects. These objects can be brought together to form wholes; and these wholes, which are defined by determinate properties and serve as a support for the latters' definition, can be further composed or decomposed in accordance with other properties and definitions. This is true of a society's institution whatever the type and contents of the global and detailed organization of itself and its world, whatever the forms of thought accompanying this organization, and however inaccessible the imaginary significations underlying it. A visible object might possess invisible properties; an animal or stone may be a god; or a child may be the reincarnation of an ancestor, or even the ancestor himself in person. These attributions, properties, relations, and manners of being might be lived, spoken, thought, and acted out in sincerity, duplicity, or (in our eyes) the most complete confusion. But whatever the case, it will always be with absolute necessity that each and every cow is an instance of the category "cows," that it is not a bull (or not in just any manner), and that it gives birth, with practically absolute certitude, to calves. Likewise, it is of necessity that a certain ensemble of huts forms a certain village, in this case *our* village, the one to which we *belong*, and to which those of another or any other village do not belong. Knives must cut, water flow, and fire burn. Society is neither an ensemble, nor a system or hierarchy of ensembles (or structures); it is a magma and magma of magmas. Nonetheless, social activity/representation, social life and organization, society's institution, admits of an indispensable dimension which is, and can only be, congruent with identitarian or ensemblist logic. For it is in and by this logic that institution is established and, in the end, simply "is."

It would be a most serious error, a crime equivalent to the object's murder—structuralism's crime—to claim that this logic exhausts the life, or even logic, of society. One would have to give up thinking if one were to refrain from asking how and why a society distinguishes, chooses, poses, assembles, counts, and speaks certain terms and not others, in one manner and not another. And as a result one would have to act as if one believed that the ensembles of elements posed by different societies were given in perpetuity and in and of themselves; as if they corresponded to the given's organization of itself, while being in the complete possession of the knowing subject (when even the terms "masculine"/"feminine," as social and not as biological terms, are socially, and thus variably, instituted). In such a situation, one remains a naive and complete prisoner not only of the ensemblist logic, but of its specific material content as instituted in one's own society and period.

Such simplistic notions should not prevent us from observing that the institution of society necessarily includes the institution of the *legein*, in and by which the identitarian-ensemblist logic is deployed. Why? This is the sort of question that will always have its hold on us, even as we will never be able to get a firm hold on it. For we would be unable either to think or to speak if we abandoned identitarian logic entirely. We can question this logic, but only by employing it; when doubting it, we confirm it in part. In effect, this "why" is the why of the *legein*, and, as a consequence, it is also that of language (for if language cannot be reduced to the *legein*, neither can it do without the *legein*—without, here again, our ever being able to say why). Since we can only respond to this "why" in and by language, we are unable to theorize it. But this does not prevent us from being able to elucidate it, in the sense given here to this term.

In summary, then, the ontological decision exposed in the above discussion is well-founded in part. For the ontological creation represented by the institution of society is grounded in a preexisting stratum, in which it can find partial support and stimulation. To say that all known societies require the institution of an identitarian logic is to say that there is a layer or stratum of existence, of what is or is actually present, that is amenable to ensemblist organization. In this, the first natural stratum, the given always lends itself to its constitution into distinct and definite elements which, conforming to the principles of identity and the excluded third, and possessing sufficient properties for the definition of classes, can be grouped into specifiable sets, and classed into hierarchies and clear-cut crossings and juxtapositions of hierarchies. This stratum possesses a formidable representative in the person of the living, whether vegetable or animal, with which society must immediately and necessarily concern itself, and which indeed comprises its own raw material. *Anthropos anthropon genna*, Aristotle tirelessly repeated; it is a man that begets man, and it is a man that man begets. There are species, and there are individuals, specimens of a genus, different instances of the same category. Not only are stable properties, or the decisory characteristics, necessary for the existence of living beings, and for man, who lives off the living; but living beings, in and for themselves, immediately appear as the expression of an Aristotelian ensemblization-hierarchization. Of themselves, they are grouped into species and genera that can be fully defined by the union, intersection, or disjunction of their properties or attributes.

The Grounding of Society on Nature

How is this grounding of society on the ensemblizable dimension of the first natural stratum to be understood? In society there are men and women; they can be unambiguously classified as (biologically) male or female. And they beget boys and girls who, independent of time or place, are incapable of surviving unless taken under adult care for a fairly long period of time. None of this results from either the legislation of a transcendental consciousness or the institution of society. The ensembles of males and females, or of children below a certain threshold of biological maturation, are, when considered strictly as such, given in nature—as are the attributes most likely to affect them. The division of the collectivity (viewed as an ensemble of heads) into male and female subensembles cannot be ignored by the institution of society. But if the latter *must* allow for the *natural fact* of being-male and being-female, institution involves the transformation of this fact into an *imaginary social signification* of being-a-man or being-a-woman (which refers to all the significations of the society considered). Neither this transformation as such, nor the specific tenor of the signification in question, can be deduced, derived, or generated from the natural fact, which invariably remains the same.

True, natural facts place embankments or limits on the institution of society; but reflection on these limits produces only trivia. When a certain archaic society compels its men, for weeks after the birth of a child, to mime a woman in childbirth and take over her role, one can triumphantly point to the fact that it cannot force the men actually to give birth to children. But to reach this conclusion we did not have to examine a society; we could have simply looked at a herd of goats. What interests us, obviously, is how and why a society forces its men to mime the situation of the other sex, and what this practice means. Similarly, a society cannot institute men and women in a way that makes them absolutely undesirable to each other. But to say that a minimal heterosexual desire has to be tolerated on pain of the collectivity's rapid extinction tells us nothing about the interminable alchemy of desire observable in history—and it is the latter that is worth considering.[30] A natural fact can provide support or stimulus for this or that institution of signification; but an abyss separates a support or stimulus from a necessary and sufficient condition. Supports and stimuli may be taken into account, neglected, canceled out, or even counteracted, but, in any and all such cases, they are taken up, transformed and transubstantiated by their insertion into a network of imaginary social significations. One need only consider what happens in different societies to such natural givens as the male's superior physical force or female menstruation.

One can perhaps better illustrate the significance of the grounding on the first natural stratum by considering the difference between children and adults. It is not just that the signification being-a-child is always instituted in a different manner and with a different tenor, or that it is rarely unitary, but that the institution, with the supports and stimuli it finds in the natural facts of maturation, can do practically anything. The only natural invariant comes down to one rather distressing commonplace: someone must take care of the child for a certain period of time. It is false, in both logical and real terms, that this someone has to be the child's mother or biological family. Those who look after the child may be adults or, after a certain age, other children; they might have familial or blood ties with the child, and they might not; the successive changes in the child's status may be related to stages of biological maturation or to arbitrarily instituted criteria and tests; children's sexual activities may be repressed, tolerated, ignored, encouraged, or instituted with utmost solemnity; children may participate in the collectivity's labors at a very early age or only long after they have acquired the necessary physical capacities; they may contract marriages at birth, before their sexual maturity, or long after . . . and so on.

In these examples, the grounding of institution in the natural stratum "internal" to society appears, and in effect is, rather vague and distant. It is almost nonexistent when we consider the tenor of instituted imaginary significations as such. Nonetheless, it cannot be eliminated. Not only is it the physical and biological condition of society's existence (a trivial point); it is the logical support and point of anchorage for the ensemblization implied by society's institution and entails the fixation of the indicative terms (*termes de repérage*) without which the imaginary significations would not find points of references. For example, whatever the tenor of the imaginary social signification being-a-child, its articulations or ramifications, one still has to know at any given moment *who* is a child, to what class he belongs, and so on. Whether the passage from one age class to another is fixed by the first menstruation, initiation rites, entry into high school, or age as a function of the official registers—the *legein* has to be able to fix the indicative and referential terms in a univocal manner, so that one can, in both word and deed, distinguish and reassemble the different elements of the instituted classes. In other words, it must be possible to designate these elements without ambiguity. But this possibility only exists because the first natural stratum is "ensemblizable"—because singular events can be isolated from the flux of becoming, because the natural periodicity of certain phenomena provides support for the ensemblist and measurable demarcation (*repérage*) of instituted time, and so on.

An essentially analogous situation exists relative to the grounding of institution in the natural stratum "external" to society. (Needless to say, the expressions "internal" and "external" to society are a gross abuse of language.) One might be tempted to claim that the first natural stratum that society immediately encounters—and from which society emerges—not only is ensemblizable, but is of itself already ensemblized. After all, the different living species, the varieties of soils and minerals, the sun, moon, and stars did not wait for their prolation or institution in order to be distinct and definite, possess stable properties, or form classes. But from what point of view are they distinct and definite? In what respect do they possess stable properties? And in whose eyes do they form classes? The seemingly obvious assumption of a given, assignable organization of nature which society has only to take up, by means of the progressive conquest of this organization's logic, the arbitrary appropriation of certain of its elements to form a structure or system, or the determination by nature itself (including the nature of man) of the timetable of its own discovery—this illusory assumption shared by innumerable authors from Marx to Lévi-Strauss, when examined closely, proves to be based on a most peculiar idea. For it supposes that the first man was both a pure animal and a nineteenth-century scientist suffering from partial and temporary amnesia.

Why a nineteenth-century scientist? Because the representation of nature underlying discussions about the relation of nature and society (or culture), the idea that the organization of nature is out there, given, assignable (and essentially, that is, ontologically, simple), that it can be gradually and progressively appropriated by society—this incoherent fantasy is specific to a certain stage of Western science. How did the Neanderthals go about reconciling general relativity with quantum theory? When we speak of nature, we are speaking only of those aspects deemed relevant to man's existence—but which man's existence? And as a function of what? Are petroleum deposits or the fusion of hydrogen relevant to man's existence? And the naming of flowers or the stars? And what about the properties of vibrating columns of air?

There is but one perspective from which one could effectively try to get hold of the aspects of nature that *ne varietur* remain relevant to man, and do so within the framework of identitarian logic. This is the perspective that considers man as pure animal, or as a mere living being. One can, in effect, describe living beings as identitarian automatons[31]—though such a description is undoubtedly insufficient. All living beings, it can be said, possess a first "filter-transformer" that transforms "objective" events into events *for* the living being, i.e., into information *for* him. A second filter-transformer differentiates this information into a subensemble of relevant information, and a subensemble of irrelevant information or noise. A series of mechanisms then elaborates elements of the relevant information, endowing them with weight, value, univocal "interpretations," etc., in terms of which response mechanisms (or programs) can be activated. (For any given type of living being, catastrophes define the limit of relevant events, beyond which it does not possess any response programs.) Thus, radio waves have no existence for terrestrial beings; they are not elements in the ensemble of information defined for and by these automatons. Solar rays, on the other hand, do exist for the majority of these beings, though they are one thing for plants, and quite another for sea turtles. It is probable that a good part of the sensorial information received by the higher animals is of no relevance.[32] The configuration of the starry sky (barring the sun, moon, and exceptional phenomena) is probably irrelevant to most of the mammals capable of seeing it.

And so it can be said that every living being constitutes a part of the "objective" world for itself; that in this part it makes a division between relevant and irrelevant subensembles; that within the first it establishes new subdivisions, defining classes of events according to their properties, thereby "recognizing" an event as an individual instance of a given class; and that, taking into account all the other relevant information over which it disposes, it responds to the event in accordance with fixed programs which in their specifics may, of course, be extremely complex.[33]

By adopting this language (which, it should be remembered, not only is without any absolute privilege, but is simply the expression of our identitarian logic at a certain stage of its explication and application), we can say that living beings exist by ensemblizing parts of the world (distinguishing therein elements that are valid as instances of classes, that possess stable properties, and so on). Although, once again, we ought to say (somewhat tautologically) that this happens only because what exists is, at a certain level, ensemblizable. But at no time can it be claimed that what exists is in actuality only a single, orderly hierarchy of ensembles. We just do not know whether or not this is true (though we suspect that it is not). Within the limits of our present understanding, all we can say is that living beings come into existence as establishing ensembles, and as establishing themselves in and by ensembles. For a dog, a rabbit is an instance of a class defined by stable properties, i.e., it is an adequately determined "thing." But what in general is a "thing"? At this point biologists as well as sociologists tend to forget not only their philosophy but their physics as well. For according to physics, "what there is" (*today*) is a dance of electrons or other elementary particles, or force fields, local torsions of space-time, and so on. Within the latter, living beings constitute "things" and are themselves constituted as "things"; out of the infinite number of the characteristics of what there is, they produce translations whose character is also dependent on the character of the filter-transformers that beget them.

A thing's "reality" for living beings—including man as just a living being—is contingent on the filter-transformer and its mechanisms of "temporal regulation." For a living being "tuned" to another temporality, the configuration of earth's mountains and continents might be as changeable as clouds on a windy day; as, also, what appears to us as the universe's expansion may be only the diastole of the heart of an animal on which we are parasites. And what things would we see if the differentiating powers of our retina were equal to those of an electronic microscope? All of this brings us back, once again, to the fact that what exists is, throughout its successive strata, organizable, and cannot therefore be just anything, nor exist in just any manner. But it also suggests that what appears organized is inseparable from what organizes it. And though we can seemingly expand this circle without limit, we can never get outside it.

Hence, to speak of nature as a given organization or system of ensembles, subject to a certain particularization of identitarian logic (one that, for example, "sees" physical existence in terms of "material things" rather than local torsions of space-time) is to conceive of man as a pure animal or living being, for whom there is an established "universe of discourse" homologous to the organization of all the mechanisms that allow him to be a living being, the living being man. Conversely, it is only insofar as one conceives of man as pure animal that one can say that there must be for him a fixed stable organization of nature, an ensemblist categorization or classification of what exists for him—or of what he constitutes—as a living being. And it could not even be said that he cannot, except by placing his own life in danger, ignore or transgress this fixed and stable organization. Such a transgression would be absolutely out of the question, for by definition, a living being, whatever its type, cannot ignore or transgress what for it is the organization of nature corresponding to its own organization.

This fixed and stable organization of a part of the world, homologous to man's organization as a living being (and these are but two complementary sides of the same system, at least for the meta-observer, e.g., for man when he tries to theorize it), constitutes what we have referred to as the first natural stratum on which the institution of society is grounded, and which society can neither disregard nor force at will.

By saying that the institution of society *is grounded* on the organization of the first natural stratum, we mean that institution does not reproduce or reflect this stratum, that it is in no way *determined* by the latter. Instead, institution finds here a series of conditions, points of support and stimulation, dikes, and obstacles. In the language of the preceding pages, society, like all automatons, defines its own universe of discourse; and to the extent that society is not to be reduced to the animal being of the human species, this universe of discourse is of necessity different from that of the animal man. What is more, each society is an automaton of a different type, because (or insofar as) each society establishes a different universe of discourse, that is to say, because the institution of society establishes what, for the society in question, is and is not, what is and is not relevant, the weight, value, and "translation" of what is relevant—and the corresponding "response."

But if one examines this language more closely, one sees that the metaphor of the automaton is almost vacuous. In more exact terms, one realizes that society is not an identitarian or ensemblist automaton, no matter how complex the automaton one has in mind. This is already evidenced by the fact that in a society the weight, value, and "translation" of the relevant information, and the corresponding "response," are not fixed in a univocal (or finitely multivocal) manner. But the point can be demonstrated by means of an even more elementary consideration.

As already noted, an identitarian automaton supposes the division of the objective world (the world as it exists for a meta-observer, i.e., for someone who can treat both the automaton and its world as objects of its own world) into a part that exists for the automaton and a part that does not; and a division of the former into a subensemble of relevant information and a subensemble of irrelevant information or "noise." These divisions, however, have very different meanings for society (when considered as society and not as a concourse of two-legged animals).

In the first place, what *exists* for society need not correspond to an organization (identitarian or otherwise) of the natural stratum. Thus the existence of spirits, gods, myths, etc.—to cite only a few obvious examples. And what *does not exist* for society is not necessarily, and not always, pure nonbeing, i.e., nonbeing so absolute that it can never enter the universe of discourse, even if just to be denied.

THE IMAGINARY INSTITUTION OF SOCIETY □ 39

On the contrary, the being of nonbeing, or nonbeing as such, always exists for society; it enters the universe of discourse in the form of entities whose being must be denied, or in the form of positions that are affirmed only by being explicitly negated, or established only in order to be repudiated. The possibility that "that doesn't exist" or "it's not like that" is always explicitly posed in the institution of society.

In the second place, irrelevant information does not exist for society; the irrelevant is only a limiting case of the relevant. In other words, "noise" does not exist for society as noise; it always exists as something, and at its limit is explicitly posed as noise, or as irrelevant information. This brings us, by way of a seemingly minor route, to a point that lies at the very heart of the social. Everything that, in one way or another, is apprehended or perceived by society must *signify* something or be invested with a signification, and what is more, it not only signifies, but is always apprehended in advance in and by the possibility of signification. Ultimately it is only in and by this possibility that something can be qualified as devoid of signification, as insignificant or absurd. The absurd can only appear—even, and above all, when it is irreducible—by reason of the absolute demand for signification.

For an identitarian automaton (or for what amounts to the same thing, a completely formalized calculus), a term exists only if it has a recognizable, determinate, and predetermined form (i.e., if it is an instance of a particular *eidos*). And a term "has meaning" (an abuse of language) only if its form determines its insertion into a syntax of determinate and predetermined operations. (Needless to say, what does not exist or have meaning *for* the automaton can still act *on* it, and may, for example, partially or totally destroy it.)

For a society, a term exists only if it signifies something (if it is a signification, is posed as a signification, is tied to a signification). And once a term exists, it *always* has meaning, in the narrow sense indicated above; it can always be inserted into a syntax or can constitute a syntax into which to enter. The institution of society involves the institution of a world of significations—and this world is, as such, creation, and in each specific case, a particular creation.

Within this world, an important place must always be found for the first natural stratum, whose being (for the living being man) is, both generally and concretely, the very condition of society's existence. But this stratum is not, and can never be, taken up simply as such. Its contents are appropriated in and by the magma of significations instituted by society, and as such are transubstantiated or ontologically altered. They are altered in their mode of being, in that they now exist and exist only by way of their investment by signification. They are also altered, and cannot but be altered, in their mode of organization. For not only is the organization of a world of significations different from the ensemblist organization of the first natural stratum; but once everything has to signify something, this ensemblist organization no longer responds to the question of signification, and even ceases to exist as an organization, even an ensemblist one.

That the ensemblist organization does not respond to the question of signification is sufficiently indicated by the fact that contemporary formalists, whether mathematicians, linguists, or ethnologists, feel compelled to deny the question's very existence. And it is not very difficult to see why the ensemblist organization ceases to be an organization, even an ensemblist one, once the demand for signification appears. For this organization, as given in its immediacy, exists (and coheres) as such only in certain respects and from one point of view, that of the animal man—precisely that perspective from which the question of something's significance cannot be posed.

Let us suppose, for example, that the question of signification is precluded or eliminated by the regularity of the given. (Although this is by no means true, and cannot but be a naive projection of modern scientism. The corroboration or establishment of regularity still raises the question of its significance. All societies must account for and interpret the regularities that they note—not to mention the fact that one must know what is meant by regularity, what objects it covers, and how far it should extend.) Now, the existence of such regularity is as much denied as affirmed by the first natural stratum. Game is scarce, the rains late, a child stillborn, and there is an eclipse of the moon. What then do these different events signify? It would be false to claim that they suggest even that the organization of the first natural stratum, as "naturally" given, is incomplete, deficient, or lacunary. From the perspective of the animal man, it is neither complete nor incomplete; it is simply what it is—it is (after the event) both necessary and sufficient for the animal man's existence, homologous and consubstantial to this existence. From the perspective of signification—the perspective adopted by society from its very first day—the natural ensemblist organization is as such almost nonexistent. And if one (incorrectly) defines signification in terms of coherence and regularity, it is more than simply lacunary, or even fragmentary, since the part that appears irregular and incoherent is no less extensive than the part that appears rational and coherent. Now it is true that

THE IMAGINARY INSTITUTION OF SOCIETY □ 41

this latter part both conditions society's biological existence and provides institution with its grounding, particularly with regard to its identitarian-ensemblist dimension. But an immense distance separates this claim from the idea that society creates a world of significations either as a way to fill several lacunae in a rational (or identitarian-ensemblist) organization that would of itself be present with nature, or as a sort of substitute that will be gradually reduced with the progressive discovery of this supposedly rational organization.

At this point we can sort out the constituents of the idea—still so widespread—that imaginary significations are merely a substitute or compensation. The Western scientist is possessed by two fantasies: first, that the world is rationally organized (when, in fact, he knows nothing about it), and second, that his science is on the point of fully disclosing the world's rationality (while it creates more enigmas than it resolves). By transporting these fantasies ten thousand years back in time or ten thousand kilometers forward in space, he then interprets the representations of primitive peoples as attempts to fill up the holes that they *should have* discovered in *their* world's organization *if* they were possessed by *his* fantasies. Now, here is a tautology worth stating: lacunae within the organization of the natural stratum only appear as lacunae of a *rational* organization once it has been decided that the only valid explanation is a rational one, and the only true organization an identitarian-ensemblist organization.

This decision, however, is particular to a rather recent social-historical institution. And this is why another current idea is also naively ethnocentric—the idea that mythical thought is essentially classificatory, and so can be reduced to the rudiments of ensemblist logic (imaginary significations as flavors, will-o'-the-wisps, or illusions to be shared by noble savages and bad ethnologists). To paraphrase the father of this idea: to say that savages classify is a truism (otherwise they would not speak); but to say that they do nothing but classify is an absurdity. What might appear to the contemporary Western scientist as lacunae in the natural stratum's organization, lacunae that should serve to stimulate research into ways to fill them, appear as lacunae only by virtue and as a function of the institution of unlimited interrogation within the horizons of identitarian logic. The given is logically or rationally incomplete only when completeness has been posed as logical or rational completeness.

But the idea that everything must respond to the demand for logical or rational completeness (*logon didonai*, to give an account of and reason for—Hegel's "all that is real is rational") is just a particular avatar of the idea that everything must respond to the demand for signification—if one can call that an idea which is at the basis of every idea. The institution of society institutes both this demand and the response that it receives in each particular case. To be sure, between the demand and its response tension can always appear—this is part and parcel of the very possibility of history understood as society's auto-alteration. Nevertheless, for the vast majority of known societies, i.e., mythical societies, the given does not appear to be *logically* incomplete, not because they have classified all that is classifiable, nor because their classifications are logically watertight or complete, but simply because this criterion is foreign to them. In fact, in such societies the given does not appear incomplete in any manner whatsoever. For the mythical response to the question of signification *saturates* everything with meaning—something that a logical or rational response can never do (which is why it is irresistibly borne toward the myth of rational completeness, of the integral rationality of the given, the myth of being as determinacy).

NOTES

Notes marked (a) have been added by Castoriadis to the 1975 edition of the initial text.

1(a). "Signifier" and "signified" are understood here and in what follows *latissimo sensu.*

2. "In a modern state, law must not only correspond to the general economic position and be its expression, but must also be an expression which is consistent in itself, and which does not, owing to inner contradictions, look glaringly inconsistent. And in order to achieve this, the faithful reflection of economic conditions is more and more infringed upon." Friedrich Engels's letter to Conrad Schmidt, October 27, 1890, reprinted in *The Correspondence of Marx and Engels* (London: Lawrence and Wishart, 1934), p. 481.

3(a). See the second part of *L'Institution imaginaire de la société* (Paris: Éditions du Seuil, 1975); also "Le Dicible et l'indicible" in *L es Carrefours du labyrinthe* (Paris: Éditions du Seuil, 1978), pp. 125-46.

4. One could try to distinguish what we have called the ultimate or radical imaginary (the *capacity* to establish, in the form of images, something that is not, and has not been) from its *products* by designating the latter as the *imagined.* But the grammatical form of this term may be rather confusing, and so we prefer to speak of the positive imaginary.

5. "Man is this night, this vacuous nothingness that contains everything in its simplicity; an infinite wealth of representations and images, none of which emerge within the mind in a precise manner, none of which were always present. Here is night, the interiority of nature—the *pure Self.* In fantastic representations it is night all around; here a head stained with blood appears, there another white figure, and then they disappear just as brusquely. It is this night that one sees when one looks a man in the eyes—a night that becomes *terrible;* it is the night of the world that we are confronting. *It is the power to draw images from this night, or let them fall, that constitutes the capacity to establish oneself, the interior consciousness, action, scission.*" Hegel, *Jenenser Realphilosophie* (1805-6). (Taken from K. Papaioannou's translation, *Hegel,* Paris, 1962, p. 180.)

6. From the perspective of capitalism's "logic," it would make more sense to have a

calendar with a ten-day week and thirty-six or thirty-seven days of rest instead of the seven-day week with fifty-two Sundays.

7. For the sake of brevity and convenience, let us stick to a rather banal example — that of the goddess of "the earth," the earth-goddess, Demeter. The most probable etymology (though others have been proposed — see Liddell-Scott, *Greek-English Lexicon*, Oxford, 1940) is Gé-meter, Gaia-Meter, earth mother. Gaia is the name of both the earth and the first goddess who, with Ouranos, is at the head of the genealogy of the gods. The earth was first seen as a goddess, and there is nothing to suggest that it was ever seen as an "object." This term, moreover, not only denotes the earth, but also connotes its "properties" or, more precisely, its essential qualities, its fertile and nourishing character. This is also the connotation of the signifier *mother*. The association, or rather identification of the two signifieds, Earth-Mother, goes without saying. And this first imaginary moment is indissociable from another whereby the Earth-Mother is not just divinized, but anthropomorphized — after all, she is a Mother. The imaginary dimension of this particular symbol is, if the expression can be used, of the same substance as the global imaginary of this culture — what *we* call the anthropomorphic divinization of the forces of nature.

8. ". . . That Law which leaps the sky, made of no mortal mould, undimmed, unsleeping, whose living godhead does not age or die." *Oedipus Rex* in *The Theban Plays* (Harmondsworth: Penguin, 1947), p. 49.

9. "There it is a definite social relation between men, that assumes, in their eyes, the fantastic form of a relation between things. In order, therefore, to find an analogy, we must have recourse to the mist-enveloped regions of the religious world. In that world the productions of the human brain appear as independent beings endowed with life, and entering into relation both with one another and the human race. So it is in the world of commodities with the product of men's hands. This I call the Fetishism which attaches itself to the products of labor, as soon as they are produced as commodities. . . ." And further: "It is value . . . that converts every product into a social hieroglyphic." *Capital*, 1 (New York: International Publishers, 1967), pp. 72 and 74.

10. This is most certainly the view expressed in his mature works: "The religious reflex of the real world can, in any case, only then finally vanish, when the practical relations of every-day life offer to man none but perfectly intelligible and reasonable relations with regard to his fellowmen and to Nature. The life-process of society, which is based on the process of material production, does not strip off its mystical veil until it is treated as production by freely associated men, and is consciously regulated by them in accordance with a settled plan. This, however, demands for society a certain material ground-work or set of conditions of existence which in their turn are the spontaneous product of a long and painful process of development." *Capital*, 1, pp. 79-80. Or again: "All mythology overcomes and dominates and shapes the forces of nature in the imagination and by the imagination; it therefore vanishes with the advent of real mastery over them." *Grundrisse* (Harmondsworth: Penguin, 1973), p. 110. If this were actually true, mythology would never disappear, not even on the day that man becomes the ballet master of several billion galaxies within the radius of thirteen billion light-years. (There would still be the irreversibility of time and a few other trifles to "overcome and dominate.") Nor would one understand why the mythology concerning nature has long since disappeared from the Western world; if Jupiter has been ridiculed by the lightning rod and Hermes by Crédit Mobilier, why have we not invented a cancer god, a god of atheroma, or an omega-minus god?

Of greater interest is what Marx had to say in the fourth of the "Theses on Feuerbach": "But that the secular basis (of the religious world) detaches itself from itself and establishes itself as an independent realm in the clouds can only be explained by the cleavages and self-contradictions within this secular basis. The latter must, therefore, in itself be both understood in its contradiction and revolutionized in practice. Thus, for instance, after the earthly family is discovered to be the secret of the holy family, the former must then itself be destroyed in theory and in practice." *Early Writings* (Harmondsworth: Penguin, 1975), p. 422. The imaginary would then be the fantastic solution to real *contradictions*. This is true of a certain type of imaginary, but only a derivative type. It is insufficient for understanding a society's central imaginary, for reasons explained later in the text. But in brief, these reasons come down to the fact that the very *constitution* of thse real contradictions is inseparable from the central imaginary.

11. See "Le mouvement révolutionnaire sous le capitalisme moderne," *Capitalisme moderne et révolution*, 2 (Paris: 10/18, 1979), pp. 172ff.

12(a). It is evident that needs in the social-historical sense (and not in the sense of biological necessities) are a product of the radical imaginary. It follows that the "imaginary" that compensates for the nonsatisfaction of these needs is only a second, derivative imaginary. This also applies to the imaginary, found in certain contemporary psychoanalytic tendencies, that "stitches up" a primordial gap or cleavage within the subject. But this cleavage exists only *by* way of the subject's radical imaginary.

13. Of course, one can always say that historical creation is just the progressive discovery of possibilities contained within an ideal, "preconstituted," absolute system. But since this absolute system of all possible forms cannot by definition be exhibited, and since it is not present in history, the objection is gratuitous and, in the end, a mere quarrel over words. No matter what the eventuality, one can always say, retrospectively, that it too was ideally possible. This is an empty tautology, and does not teach anyone anything.

14. The traumatic event is real as an event and imaginary as a traumatism.

15. ". . . to say that a society functions is a truism; but to say that everything in a society functions is an absurdity." Claude Lévi-Strauss, *Structural Anthropology* (New York: Anchor, 1967), p. 13.

16. Even this statement requires qualification. We have already noted the existence of dysfunctional institutions, especially in modern societies, as well as the absence of institutions necessary for certain functions.

17. As Claude Lévi-Strauss seems to be increasingly inclined to try to do. See his *Totemism* (Boston: Beacon Press, 1963), and the discussion with Paul Ricoeur in *Esprit*, November 1963, and in particular, p. 636: "You say . . . that *The Savage Mind* chooses syntax over semantics; for me there is no choice . . . meaning always results from combinations of elements that are not in themselves meaningful . . . meaning is always reducible . . . behind every meaning there is non-meaning, but the opposite is not true . . . signification is always phenomenal." Also *The Raw and the Cooked* (New York: Harper Torchbooks, 1970): "I therefore claim to show not how men think in myths, but how myths operate in men's minds without their being aware of the fact. And . . . it would perhaps be better to go still further and, disregarding the thinking subject completely, proceed as if the thinking process were taking place in the myths, in their reflection upon themselves and their interrelation. For what I am concerned to clarify is not so much what there is *in* myths . . . as the system of axioms and postulates defining the best possible code, capable of conferring a common significance on unconscious formulations . . ." (p. 12, underlined in the text). As for this "common significance": ". . . if it is now asked to what final meaning these mutually significative meanings are referring—since in the last resort and in their totality they must refer to something—the only reply to emerge from this study is that myths signify the mind that evolves them by making use of the world of which it is itself a part." (*Ibid.*, p. 341.) As the mind for Lévi-Strauss is equivalent to the brain, and the brain clearly belongs to the order of things, except that it has this rather bizarre capacity to symbolize other things, one comes to the conclusion that the mind's principal activity consists in symbolizing itself as something endowed with the power of symbolization. Our concern here, however, is not with the philosophical aporias coming out of such a position, but with what it misses: the essential character of the social-historical.

18. Lévi-Strauss, *Totemism*, p. 89.

19. This question has been newly posed by linguistics, the science that works, so to speak, at ground level with symbolism. See Roman Jakobson, *Essais de linguistique générale* (Paris: Les Éditions de Minuit, 1963), ch. VII ("*L'Aspect phonologique et l'aspect grammatical du langage dans leurs interrelations*"). And it has to be posed, with even greater insistence, in the other domains of historical life—domains where F. de Saussure would have never dreamed of extending the principle of "the arbitrariness of the sign."

20. See Lévi Strauss, *Structural Anthropology*, pp. 209-15.

21. Lévi-Strauss, *The Raw and the Cooked*.

22. As does Lévi-Strauss in *Esprit*, November 1963.

23. Lévi-Strauss, *The Raw and the Cooked*, p. 24.

24. Lévi-Strauss in *Esprit*, November 1963, pp. 637 and 641.

25. One can certainly claim that it is possible to use symbolism lucidly at an individual level (in language, for example) but not at the collective level (relative to institutions). But this has to be demonstrated, and any such demonstration cannot in all evidence be based on the *general nature* of symbolism as such. We are not saying that there is no difference between the two levels, or that the difference is only a matter of degree (that the social is more complex, and so on). We are simply saying that the difference is not due to symbolism, but to the much deeper character (also, much harder to educe) of imaginary significations and their "materialization." See below.

26(a). The critique of "structuralism" sketched here did not respond to an "internal necessity" of the author, but simply to the need to combat a mystification that very few escaped ten years ago. This critique could easily be extended and expanded, but now that the smoke of structuralism is dissipating, the task is no longer urgent.

27. We have explained what is meant by the relativity of the concept of reification in "Le mouvement révolutionnaire sous le capitalisme moderne," *Capitalisme moderne et révolution*, pp. 152-54, and in "Recommencer la révolution," *L'Expérience du mouvement ouvrier*, 2 (Paris: 10/18, 1973), pp. 317-18. What puts reification in question and relativizes it both as a category and as a reality is the *struggle* of the slaves or workers.

28. There is an "essence" of the centaur, defined by two definite sets of possibilities and impossibilities. This "essence" is "representable"; there is no lack of precision concerning the centaur's "generic" physical appearance.

29. Value and nonvalue, licit and illicit, are constitutive of history. In this sense, as abstract structural oppositions, they are presupposed by all history. But what at any given moment is valuable or valueless, licit or illicit, is historical and must be interpreted, as far as possible, in its specific content.

30. Even this minimal condition is not absolutely self-evident, except in the neo-Darwinian sense, where a society that completely inhibited heterosexual desires would soon become unobservable. On the possibility of a society going to the very limit of its self-extinction, see Colin Turnbull, *The Mountain People* (New York: Simon and Schuster, 1972).

31. Note that the term "automaton" is not synonymous with "robot" or "machine," but refers to something that can move by *itself*.

32. Why this is true is another question. The informational mechanism, like all the living being's mechanisms, seems to require considerable excess capacity or redundancy. We know that this excess capacity, in its various forms, is important for the survival of the individual and the species—and for its evolution (though this by no means "explains" the fact of evolution). In any case, it is quite possible that the division into relevant and irrelevant information is neither "fixed" nor "definitive"—a point that immediately suggests one of the limits in describing living beings as identitarian automatons.

33. The term "recognize" is here a violent abuse of language. For it covers as much the stereochemical mechanism by which, within the cell, a molecule is "recognized" as belonging to a certain class of molecules, as the "recognition" by a dog or horse of its master. But this is of no importance for the present discussion.

Chapter 3
Introduction to Baudrillard
Charles Levin

Writing of the achievements and the trans-formal power of structuralism, Jean-Marie Benoist, in his book *La révolution structurale*, has called ours the "Age of Leibniz."[1] By this he meant in part that through intellectual upheavals such as structuralism (and perhaps also through the discovery of the structure of DNA and the recent breakthroughs in particle physics) the idea of a Great Combinatory, or generative matrix, has begun to penetrate the cultural imagination. This theme of a combinatory matrix is a central concern of the following selections from Jean Baudrillard's *L'Échange symbolique et la mort.*[2] But it is not always obvious in these passages that Baudrillard is talking about the ethos of the structural "sciences." He is something of a structuralist heretic, and has a way of making the structuralist metalanguage ooze out of the body politic like sweat, or rattle it, like a tic. Words like "sign" and "code" seem to lose their aura of abstraction, and to become almost descriptive.

The shortest path into this hyperbolic thicket is through a synoptic treatment of the structuralist themes that Baudrillard has transmuted into social discourse. The theme of "formalization"—a term borrowed from the structuralist philosopher Michel Serres—serves well as a means of grasping the drift of the structuralist world view as Baudrillard interprets it, and as a way of explaining the sense of menace he extracts from the idea of a combinatory matrix. The issue of formalization can be related to three questions: why Baudrillard finds the roots of social form in symbolic ambivalence; why he sees the evolution of structural models of meaning as a process of social disintegration; and why, in a peculiar interpretation of Freud's death instinct, he ascribes so much meaning to the menace of violence and failure in contemporary life?

Serres has located the appeal and the force of structural analysis in its ability "to isolate a formal ensemble of elements and relations, on which it is possible to reason without appealing to the signification of a given content." In Serres's words, such an approach "engenders a new methodical spirit—a profound revolution in the question of meaning."[3] Claude Lévi-Strauss provides a good example of what he is talking about:

1. define the phenomenon under study as a relation between two or more terms, real or supposed;
2. construct a table of possible permutations between these terms;
3. take this table as the general object of analysis, which, at this level only, can yield necessary connections, the empirical phenomenon considered at the beginning being only one possible combination among others, the complete system of which must be reconstructed beforehand.[4]

Lévi-Strauss hoped, in this way, to "define objectively . . . the semantic field within which are found the phenomena commonly grouped under the name of totemism."[5] It was, of course, not the first time he had advocated this tabular, scriptural, or combinatory procedure; but what is interesting about the present instance of it is that Lévi-Strauss has overtly engaged himself in an effort at debunking. He is trying to get beyond the assumptions of a totalizing discourse (ethnography) and to disperse what he calls the "totemic illusion." His strategy is therefore not so much to constitute an object with the combinatory method as to dissolve the object back into a grid that can give rise to it *as an effect*. The "illusion" of totemism is that it appears, in ethnographic discourse, as an entity with an identity that can be made present; but the totemic phenomena, according to Lévi-Strauss, are only instances of a deeper logic and a wider expanse of relationships—those that he will describe in *La Pensée sauvage*.

It would be stretching a point to characterize Lévi-Strauss's book on totemism as a work of "deconstruction." Yet in his more or less standard rationalist maneuver of questioning the objectivity and priority of an event by appealing to a formal objectivity that precedes and constitutes it, the fundamental inward turning of the language paradigm has already begun. It is no surprise to find Lévi-Strauss pondering the deconstructionist paradox, when he warns (not so much the reader as himself) that "to accept as a theme for discussion a category that one believes to be false always entails the risk . . . of entertaining some illusions about its reality."[6]

In the literary-philosophic method of deconstruction, the analytic power of the structural grid was effectively turned against itself. This pattern of self-consumption is a common feature of metatheories; but in the deconstructionist view, the formal and critical successes of the language paradigm argued for further dissolution of its extralinguistic supports. This meant not only the deconstruction of the subject as a referee of combinatory interactions—a role that Lévi-Strauss probably did not wish to abandon—but also a remarkable hostility to the linguistic functions themselves, particularly the notion of the sign; for the sign marks an (arbitrary) localization of meaning within an ongoing process of signification. Like Lévi-Strauss's totemism, structuralism and structure appear as edifying illusions arising from a dynamic matrix which is self-regulating, and which generates a certain range of possibilities.

For Jean Baudrillard, this range of permutations governing structuralist thought is bounded by the *limits of formalization* as such. Formalization has always been the historical project of structuralist analysis, and this has largely remained the case in the era of its apparent repudiation; at the extreme, most forms of "post-structuralism" can still be viewed as reflective explorations of the ultimate constraints on this process. A careful reading of Baudrillard reveals the dynamic of the structuralist movement in the tension between more or less achieved harmonies (Lévi-Strauss's formalizations of cultural "logic") and the will to press the limits of this formalizing power still further back—where the latter is an effort that tends to dissolve the successes in its wake.

In the writings presented here, Baudrillard confronts the achievements of structuralist formalization with the ambiguities of earlier reflections on the process of civilization, social structure, and language—particularly those of Marx, Saussure, Freud, and Marcel Mauss. This is a selection of antecedents that has obviously been determined by a concern with the implications of structuralism as a movement and with the ideological cross-referencing that established the primacy of the language paradigm in writers like Lévi-Strauss, Roland Barthes, Michel Foucault, and Jacques Derrida.

The theme of formalization has been present in Baudrillard's work since the beginning. While analyzing the structure of the commodity and the social logic of consumption, Baudrillard discovered in his structural methods the very pattern of social reification. This work developed the Western Marxist critique of industrial civilization with unusual concreteness; perhaps more importantly, it established the various projects of formalization, including structuralism, as social dramas of the deepest significance.

It is in this unusual, critical commotion that Baudrillard's thought, while it remains allied in key respects to the deconstructionist program, begins to diverge from it. As will become clear in the selections that follow, Baudrillard refuses to forego discussion of the social and historical references of the various models and metaphors of meaning —whether they consist of the symbolic constellations repudiated by the formalizing process, or of the deconstructions of meaning that have recently challenged this process. This refusal is carried out in spite of the problem of indeterminacy that has emerged from the failure of the language paradigm, and of structuralism in particular, to guarantee the coherence of the social sciences.

For Baudrillard, meaning is incorrigibly outward-looking; there is a meaning of meaning, and one cannot talk about language at all if one denies *external* relationships between different entities and between irreducible levels of experience. The structuralist and deconstructionist touchstone of signification has always been "difference." But in order to have any difference at all, something must be different from language. The alternative—and this, it seems, is the moral tenor of Baudrillard's critical style—would be an assertion of identity so complete that it would have severely shocked even Hegel.

According to Michel Serres, formalization is an attempt to "complete a process by which one passes from a concrete mode of thought to an abstract form (or forms); it is, in other words, to eliminate noise in the optimum manner."[7] In social terms, Serres views this as a cooperative pact between communicators against a third, who is seen as hindering or undermining the information process—a "demon," as Serres describes him, but presumably not Maxwell's Demon. "To engage in dialogue is to posit a third and to find a way of excluding him; successful communication is this third excluded." Serres is explicit in making communication depend on the frustration of dialectical relationships, and compares this situation with the intellectual process of abstraction by which underlying isomorphisms are grasped. The same seeks a compatible other with which he can combine against the third "to fight together for the emergence of a truth in which the goal is to place themselves in agreement." The "kingdom of the excluded third" is the social embodiment of formal, logical principles. For Serres, "the subject of abstract mathematics is the 'we' of an ideal republic, a city of communication maximally purged of noise —a fact which demonstrates, incidentally, why Plato and Leibniz were not idealists."[8]

The peculiar thing about Serres's view is that it so deliberately links the interests of repression and exclusion with those of civilization (progress and the growth of knowledge). The family resemblance to Freudian speculation is obvious, and indeed Freud's reflections on the civilizing process are very interesting in this context. Freud's main question about civilization was why it gave rise to such expressions of uneasiness (*Unbehagen*). It seemed paradoxical to him that the very means of assuring fulfillment of the erotic drive should lead to its frustration. Yet the very conditions of assurance were also repressive demands. Sexuality must play a double part in the creation and maintenance of human culture: it would bind people together in ever larger collectives, but it would also frustrate the individual expression of erotic aims—a centrifugal tendency that counteracts the first.

This dual quality of the etiology of human culture means that in some sense culture itself is precisely what gives expression to what is suppressed by it. Social life, in this respect, is like a dream: a manifest text which, in articulating the latent contents (by devious means), represses them at the same time. Jacques Derrida has even suggested that such may in fact be the dynamic structure of all communication. That such a mechanism of internal splitting or fission should be considered foundational is not required by the Freudian point of view, but it is an intelligible derivation from it. Derrida accordingly treats *every* manifestation as a kind of positive sign of absence, of otherness, or nether process.

But there is a critical difference here that has often gone unremarked, and Baudrillard's work helps us to grasp it. The Freudian picture seems to tell us that there is no symbolization without repression, but in saying this, it accepts and even asserts the irreducibility of both the symbol and the repressed. Freud's work had nothing to do with formalization, which seems, on the contrary, to call for the suppression of the symbolic process as such. Even the critical concepts of doubling, sliding, and difference, which appeared to decentralize the structural matrix, have in fact only been withdrawn into it, and serve to justify its continuous (though indeterminate) extension. In this version of the language paradigm, reason is no longer antagonistically opposed to the otherness of a passionate or a mechanical nature; instead, the formal code and combinatory rules of the Logos are *rhetorically* opposed to what they "produce," which is by definition *immanent*: the excluded third or middle, or a postulated system of delusions about meaning, continuity, and experience. In this respect, even the deconstructionists seem to have reinforced rather than undermined the "logocentric tradition." If reason no longer appears transcendent, this is because, having been reduced to its code, its rules of distinction and recombination, it is now simply the only game in town—there is nothing left for it to transcend. Lévi-Strauss already foresaw this when he heralded the generalization of information theory "to phenomena not intrinsically possessing the character of messages, notably that of biology . . . "; and when he proclaimed that "the entire process of human knowledge thus assumes the character of a closed system."[9]

For Baudrillard, the appeal of the death instinct does not concern Freud's desire to achieve at least a theoretical equilibrium. In his interpretation, the death instinct is Freud's unconscious idea of a destructive principle that is inevitably brought into play when the trend of formalization, implicit in all culture, is "autonomized," and set apart from the ambivalent symbolic process from which it derives. The structural yearning for the pure simplicity of the discrete, the arbitrary and the insulated play of the code may reflect either the desired convenience of an inert medium (Serres), or of an infinitely plastic one. In both cases, the social-symbolic dimension is conceived as noise, as inessential effect, or illusion. Baudrillard's response is a flamboyant inversion in which the death instinct appears as the *return of the symbolic*, threatening the internalized perfection of self-contained systems. Logical levels, which are held apart, become once again interacting levels, which are socially dynamic. Thus, the structuralist versions of Freud's thought, of Mauss's gift exchange, of Saussure's linguistics, and of Marx's principle of production, all represent ways in which the formalizing imperative will periodically effect an instrumental reduction. Such efforts must rebound, sometimes with disastrous consequences, because they are based on the suppression of a repression—that is, on a suppression of their foundation in social forms. The structuralist formalizations of these sciences (of civilization, culture, the psyche, and language) all seem to lose sight of the conflict, movement, and real social difficulty of the terms in which these processes are symbolically framed. They lose sight, in other words, of the original objects of the sciences in question.

According to Michel Serres, a structural analysis

generates families of models with distinct (*distingué*) significative content which have in common a structural analagon of form; the latter is the operational invariant, abstracted from all content, which organizes them. This process of abstraction is so complete that, once the structure is isolated as such (i.e., the abstract elements and relations) it is possible to discover (*retrouver*) all the imaginable models it generates; in other words, it is possible to construct a living cultural being by filling a form with meaning (*sens*). . . .

Serres continues:

To liberate oneself from meaning and to dominate it . . . to generate a being from a formal analagon, to deploy the chain of pure consequences of a given structure and to designate at leisure to which stage of this chain a model corresponds—all this defines with precision what structuralist analysis is.[10]

What is revealed, in Baudrillard's estimation, by this kind of overt declaration of war on the symbolic is a powerful impulse toward the possibility of absolute manipulation. What is latent in the Derridean style of discourse about a kind of disembodied "play" is fully manifest in talk of being able to "construct a living cultural being" from the variations of an intellectual model. This is the methodology of "*simulation*," and for Baudrillard it is the "analagon" of the random play of precoded meanings—in the fashion industry, the mass media, political discourse—that suffuses our "molecular" society (the term "molecular" is sometimes used by Michel Foucault and Gilles Deleuze to describe the dispersion of "power" in social systems). If, with Baudrillard, we view the symbolic as deeply embedded in social forms, it will be less difficult to grasp how the means whole societies devise for communicating with themselves (to paraphrase Lévi-Strauss) have undergone a process of adjustment to the increasingly random patterns of social life since the Renaissance. Baudrillard's "three orders of simulation," which echo Foucault's periodization of *epistèmes* in *Les Mots et les choses*, are a rough sketch of this semantic evolution which has encountered increases in social mobility, the expansion of markets, industrialization, and cybernetization.

NOTES

1. Jean-Marie Benoist, *La Révolution structurale* (Paris: Denoël/Gonthier, 1975).
2. Jean Baudrillard, *L'Échange symbolique et la mort* (Paris: Éditions Gallimard, 1976).
3. Michel Serres, *Hermes 1: La Communication* (Paris: Les Éditions de Minuit, 1968), p. 32 (my translation).
4. Claude Lévi-Strauss, *Totemism*, trans. Rodney Needham (Boston: Beacon Press, 1963), p. 16.
5. *Ibid.*, p. 16.
6. *Ibid.*, p. 15.

7. Serres, *Hermes 1: La Communication*, p. 43.

8. *Ibid.*, pp. 41, 42, 43.

9. Claude Lévi-Strauss, *The Savage Mind* (London: Weidenfeld and Nicolson, 1966), pp. 268, 269.

10. Serres, *Hermes 1: La Communication*, pp. 32-3.

Chapter 4
The Structural Law of Value
and the Order of Simulacra
Jean Baudrillard

Introduction

Symbolic exchange is no longer an organizing principle; it no longer functions at the level of modern social institutions. Of course, the symbolic still haunts them as the prospect of their own demise. But this is only an obsessive memory, a demand ceaselessly repressed by the law of value. And if a certain conception of the Revolution since Marx has tried cutting a path through this law of value, it has in the end remained a Revolution according to the Law. As for psychoanalysis, although it acknowledges the ghostly presence of the symbolic, it averts its power by circumscribing it in the individual unconscious, reducing it, under the Law of the Father, to the threat of Castration and the subversiveness of the Signifier. Always the Law.

Nevertheless, beyond the topographical and economic schemas of psychoanalysis and politics, which always revolve around some kind of production (whether material or desiring) on the scene of value, we can still perceive the outline of a social relation based on the extermination of value. For us, the model for this derives from primitive formations, but its radical utopian version is beginning to explode

Translation by Charles Levin. The text is drawn from *L'Échange symbolique et la mort* (Paris: Éditions Gallimard, 1976), pp. 7-19; 77-79; 85-87; 89-90; 92; 93-94; 96-97; 98; 107-8; 110-12; 114; 116-17.

STRUCTURAL LAW OF VALUE □ 55

slowly at all levels of our society, in the vertigo of a revolt which has nothing to do with the revolution or the laws of history, nor even with the "liberation" of a "desire"—though this latter truth will take longer to appear obvious, since the value problematic of desire has emerged only recently and will take time to dissipate.

In this perspective, other theoretical developments take on a central meaning: Saussure's anagrams and Marcel Mauss's gift-exchange will appear, in the long term, as more radical hypotheses than those of Freud and Marx. In fact, it is precisely the imperialism of Marxist and Freudian interpretations that has censured these new points of view. The anagram and the gift are not just curiosities of linguistics and anthropology; they cannot be viewed as secondary issues with respect to the great machines of the unconscious and the revolution. On the contrary, we may discover in them an outline of a single form from which psychoanalysis and Marxism are derived only by virtue of a misunderstanding—a form that relates political economy and libidinal economy intimately, so that we can glimpse, in the present, a beyond of value, of the law, of repression, and of the unconscious. In fact, a supersession such as this is inevitable.

For this writer, there is only one comparable theoretical event: Freud's death instinct. At least, this is the case, so long as we radicalize Freud against himself. In all three instances, in fact, it is a question of counterreference: Mauss must be turned against Mauss, Saussure against Saussure, Freud against Freud. We must line up the principle of reversion (the countergift) against all the economistic, psychological, or structuralist interpretations to which Mauss's work has led. We must oppose the Saussure of the *Anagrams* against that of linguistics, and even against his own restrictive hypothesis about the anagrams. The Freud of the death instinct must be played off against the whole previous edifice of psychoanalysis, and even against Freud's own version of the death instinct.

At this paradoxical price—that of theoretical violence—we see the three hypotheses traced within their respective fields; but their discreteness is dissolved in the general form of the symbolic, a functioning principle that is sovereignly external and antagonistic to our economic "reality principle."

The reversibility of the gift in the countergift, of exchange in the sacrifice, of time in the cycle, of production in destruction, of life in death, and of each linguistic value term in the anagram: in all domains, reversibility—cyclical reversal, annulment—is the one encompassing form. It puts an end to the linearity of time, language, economic exchange and accumulation, and power. For us, it takes on the form of extermination and death. It is the form of the symbolic, neither mystical nor structural, but ineluctable.

The reality principle coincided with a determinate phase of the law of value. Today, the entire system is fluctuating in indeterminacy, all of reality absorbed by the hyperreality of the code and of simulation. It is now a principle of simulation, and not of reality, that regulates social life. The finalities have disappeared; we are now engendered by models. There is no longer such a thing as ideology; there are only simulacra. To grasp the hegemony and the spectacle of the present system, we have to retrace an entire genealogy of the law of value and of successive simulacra—the structural revolution of value. Political economy has to be resituated within this genealogy: it thus appears as a simulacrum of the second order, in which only the so-called "real" is ever put into play—the real of production, of signification, in consciousness, or in the unconscious.

Capital no longer corresponds to the order of political economy; it uses political economy as a simulation model. The whole apparatus of the commodity law of value is absorbed and recycled in the larger machinery of the structural law of value, and thus connects with the third order of simulation (see below). Hence, in a way, political economy is assured a kind of second life, in the framework of an apparatus where it loses all self-determination, but where it retains its efficacy as a referential of simulation. The same goes for the previous apparatus of the natural law of value, which had been taken up as an imaginary referential ("Nature") by the system of political economy and the law of the commodity. This was use value, which led a kind of phantom existence at the heart of exchange value. But in the subsequent twist of the spiral, the latter was in turn seized as an alibi in the dominant order of the code. Each configuration of value is resumed by the following in a higher order of simulation. And each phase of value integrates into its own apparatus the anterior apparatus as a phantom reference, a puppet or simulation reference.

A revolution separates each order from the next one: these are the true revolutions. We are in the third order, no longer the order of the real, but of the hyperreal, and it is only in the third order that theory and practice, themselves floating and indeterminate, can catch up with the hyperreal and strike it dead.

The current revolutions index themselves on the immediately prior phase of the system. They arm themselves with a nostalgic resurrection of the real in all its forms—in other words, with simulacra of the second order: dialectics, use value, the transparency and finality of production, the "liberation" of the unconscious, or of repressed meaning (of the signifier, or of the signified called desire), and so on. All of these liberations offer, as ideal content, the phantoms which the system has devoured in successive revolutions and which it subtly resuscitates as revolutionary fantasies. All these liberations are just transitions toward a generalized manipulation. The revolution itself is meaningless at the present level of random processes of control.

To the industrial machine corresponds the rational, referential, functional, historical consciousness. But it is the unconscious—non-referential, transferential, indeterminate, floating—that corresponds to the aleatory machin(ations) of the code. Yet even the unconscious has been reinserted into the game: it long ago relinquished its own reality principle in order to become an operational simulacrum. At the exact point where its psychic principle of reality is confused with its psychoanalytic reality principle, the unconscious becomes, like political economy, another simulation model.

The entire strategy of the system lies in this hyperreality of floating values. It is the same for money and theory as for the unconscious. Value rules according to an ungraspable order—the generation of models, the indefinite chaining of simulation.

Cybernetic operationality, the genetic code, the random order of mutations, the principle of uncertainty, and so on: all of this replaces a determinist and objectivist science, a dialectical vision of history and consciousness. Even critical theory and the revolution belong to the second-order simulations, as do all determinate processes. The installation of third-order simulacra upsets all of this, and it is useless to resurrect the dialectic, "objective" contradictions and the like, against them; that is a hopeless political regression. You cannot beat randomness with finality, you cannot beat programmed dispersion with *prises de conscience* or dialectical transcendence, you cannot defend against the code with political economy or "revolution." All these old weapons (including those of the first order, the ethics and metaphysics of man and nature, use value, and other liberatory referentials) have been progressively neutralized by the general system, which is of a higher order. Everything that gets inserted into the definalized space-time of the code, or tries to interfere with it, is disconnected from its own finalities, disintegrated and absorbed—this is the well-known effect of recuperation, or manipulation: cycling and recycling at each level. "All dissent must be of a higher logical type than that to which it is opposed."[1]

Is it thus necessary to play a game of at least equal complexity, in order to be in opposition to third-order simulations? Is there a subversive theory or practice more random than the system itself?

An undetermined subversion, which would be to the order of the code what revolution was to political economy? Can we fight DNA? Certainly not with blows of class struggle. Can we invent simulacra of an even higher logical (or illogical) order, beyond the current third order, beyond determination and indetermination? If so, would they still be simulations? Perhaps only death, the reversibility of death, is of a higher order than the code. Only symbolic disorder can breach the code.

Any system approaching perfect operationality is approaching its own death. When the system declares: "A is A" or "two and two make four," it simultaneously arrives at the point of complete power and total ridicule—in other words, of probable immediate subversion. At this point, it takes only a straw to collapse the whole system. We know the power of tautology when it redoubles this systemic pretension in perfect sphericity: the belly of Ubu Roi.

Identity is untenable: it is death, since it fails to inscribe its own death. Such is the case with closed, or metastable, or functional, or cybernetic systems, which are all eventually waylaid by laughter, instantaneous subversion (and not by a long dialectical labor), because all the inertia of these systems works against them. Ambivalence lies in wait for the most accomplished systems, those that have succeeded in construing their own functional principles, like the binary God of Leibniz. The fascination that they exercise because they are constructed on such profound denials, as in the case of fetishism, can be reversed in an instant. Their fragility arises from this, and grows in proportion to their ideal coherence. These systems, even when they are based on a radical indeterminism (the loss of meaning), become once more the prey of meaning. They fall under the weight of their own monstrosity, like the dinosaurs, and decompose immediately.

Such is the fatality of every system devoted through its own logic to total perfection, and thus total defectiveness, to absolute infallibility and thus incorrigible extinction: all bound energies aim for their own demise. This is why the only strategy is *catastrophic*, and not in the least bit dialectical. Things have to be pushed to the limit, where everything is naturally inverted and collapses. At the peak of value, ambivalence intensifies; and at the height of their coherence, the redoubled signs of the code are haunted by the abyss of reversal. The play of simulation must therefore be taken further than the system permits. Death must be played against death—a radical tautology. The system's own logic turns into the best weapon against it. The only strategy of opposition to a hyperrealist system is pataphysical, a "science of imaginary solutions," in other words, a science fiction about the system returning to destroy itself, at the extreme limit of simulation, a reversible simulation in a hyperlogic of destruction and death.

A thoroughgoing reversibility: such is the symbolic obligation. That each *term* should be ex-*term*inated, that value should be abolished in this revolution of the term against itself—this is the only symbolic violence worthy of the structural violence of the code.

A dialectic of revolution counterposed the value law of the commodity and equivalence. To the indeterminism of the code and the structural law of value, only the fastidious (*minutieuse*) reversion of death can respond.

In truth, there is nothing left to ground ourselves on. All that is left is theoretical violence. Speculation to the death, whose only method is the radicalization of all hypotheses. Even the code and the symbolic are terms of simulation—it must be possible somehow to retire them, one by one, from discourse.

The Structural Revolution of Value

Saussure offered two perspectives on the exchange of language terms when he compared them to money: a piece of money can be placed in relationship to all the other terms of the monetary system; and it can be exchanged against a real good of some value. It was for the former dimension that Saussure increasingly reserved the term "value": the relativity of all the terms among themselves, which is internal to the general system and composed of distinctive oppositions —as opposed to the other possible definition of value: the relation of each term to what it designates, of each signifier to its signified, as each monetary unit has something against which it can be exchanged. The first type of relationship corresponds to the structural dimension of language, the second to its functional aspect. The two dimensions are distinct, but articulated, which is to say, they work together and cohere—a view that characterizes the "classical" configuration of the linguistic sign, which can be placed with the commodity law of value, where the function of designation always appears as the goal or finality of the structural operation of language. At this "classical" stage of signification, there is a complete parallel with the mechanism of value in material production as Marx described it. Use value functions as the horizon and finality of the system of exchange value: the former qualifies the concrete operation of the commodity in (the act of) consumption (a moment of the process that is parallel to the sign's moment of designation); while exchange value refers to the interchangeability of all commodities under the law of equivalence (a moment parallel to the structural organization of the sign). Use value and exchange value are organized together dialectically throughout Marx's analyses and define a rational configuration of production regulated by political economy.

A revolution has put an end to this "classical" economy of value, a revolution which, beyond the commodity form, stretches value to its most radical form.

In this revolution, the two aspects of value, which sometimes used to be thought of as coherent and eternally linked, as if by natural law, are disarticulated; *referential value is nullified, giving the advantage to the structural play of value.* The structural dimension, in other words, gains autonomy, to the exclusion of the referential dimension, establishing itself on the death of the latter. Gone are the referentials of production, signification, affect, substance, history, and the whole equation of "real" contents that gave the sign weight by anchoring it with a kind of burden of utility—in short, its form as representative equivalent. All this is surpassed by the other stage of value, that of total relativity, generalized commutative, combinatory simulation. This means simulation in the sense that from now on signs will exchange among themselves exclusively, without interacting with the real (and this becomes the condition for their smooth operation). The emancipation of the sign: released from any "archaic" obligation it might have had to designate something, the sign is at last free for a structural or combinatory play that succeeds the previous role of determinate equivalence.

The same operation occurs at the level of labor power and the process of production: the elimination of all finalities of content allows production to function as a code, and permits the monetary sign, for example, to escape in indefinite speculation, beyond any reference to the real, or even to a gold standard. We are really witnessing a type of absolute liberty: disaffection, disobligation, disenchantment. It must indeed have been a sort of magic, a magical obligation, that kept the sign chained to the real; but capital has liberated the sign from this "naiveté" to deliver it over to pure circulation.

The floating suspension of money and signs, of needs and productive goals, and the flotation of labor itself—Marx and Saussure never foresaw this indeterminacy, this commutability of every kind of term, which accompanies such unlimited speculation and inflation. But they were writing in the golden age of the dialectic of signs and reality, the classical period of capital and value. Their dialectic has since disintegrated, and the real is dead from the blow of this fantastic autonomization of value. Determination is dead, indeterminism reigns. We have witnessed the ex-termination (in the literal sense of the word) of the reality of production, and of the real of the sign.

The Three Orders of Simulation

Three orders of simulation, parallel to mutations in the law of value, have succeeded one another since the Renaissance:

The *counterfeit* is the dominant scheme of the "classical" epoch, from the Renaissance to the industrial revolution.

Production is the dominant scheme of the industrial era.

Simulation is the dominant scheme of the present phase of history, governed by the code.

Simulacra of the first order play on the natural law of value, those of the second order play on the commodity law of value, and those of the third order play on the structural law of value.

The Stucco Angel

The problem of the counterfeit (and of fashion) was born with the Renaissance, with the destructuration of the feudal order and the emergence of open competition at the level of distinctive signs. There is no fashion in societies of caste and rank, where social assignation is total, social mobility nil. In these societies, signs are shielded by a prohibition that assures their absolute clarity: each sign refers unequivocally to a (particular) situation and a level of status. Ceremony and counterfeit do not mix—unless we intend black magic and sacrilege; but it is precisely these categories that brand the crime of mingling signs as a breach of the order of things. If we start yearning nostalgically, especially these days, for a revitalized "symbolic order," we should have no illusions. Such an order once existed, but it was composed of ferocious hierarchies; the transparency of signs goes hand in hand with their cruelty.

Caste societies, feudal or archaic, were *cruel* societies, where signs were limited in number and restricted in scope. Each possessed its full interdictory value, and each was a reciprocal obligation between castes, or persons; hence they were not arbitrary. The arbitrary nature of the sign arises when, instead of linking two people in unbreachable reciprocity, the sign begins, in signifying, to refer to the disenchanted universe of the signified—the common denominator of the real world, to which nobody really has any further obligation.

With the end of the *bound* sign, the reign of the emancipated sign begins, in which all classes eventually acquire the power to participate. Competitive democracy succeeds the endogamy of the sign proper to orders of status. With the transition of the sign-values of prestige from one class to another, we enter the world of the counterfeit in a stroke, passing from a limited order of signs, where taboos inhibit "free" production, to a proliferation of signs according to demand. But this multiplication of signs no longer bears any connection with the bound sign of restricted circulation. It is the counterfeit of it, not by virtue of having denatured some "original," but through the extension of a material whose clarity depended on the restrictions that stamped it. No longer discriminating (but only competitive), relieved of all barriers, universally available, the modern sign nevertheless simulates necessity by offering itself as a determinate link to the world. The modern sign dreams of the sign anterior to it and fervently desires, in its reference to the real, to rediscover some binding obligation. But it finds only a *reason*: a referential reason, the real—the "natural" on which it will feed. This lifeline of designation, however, is no more than a simulacrum of symbolic obligation. It produces only neutral values, those that exchange among each other in an objective world. Here, the sign undergoes the same destiny as work. The "free" laborer is only free to produce equivalences; the "free and emancipated" sign is only free to produce equivalent signifieds.

It is thus in a kind of simulacrum of a "nature" that the modern sign discovers its value. The problematic of the "natural," the metaphysics of appearance and reality, become the characteristic themes of the bourgeoisie since the Renaissance, the mirror of the bourgeois sign, the mirror of the classical sign. Even today, nostalgia for natural reference survives, in spite of numerous revolutions aimed at smashing this configuration, such as the revolution of production, in which signs ceased to refer to nature, but only to the law of exchange, under the commodity law of value. (We will return to these, for they are simulations of the second order.)

It was thus with the Renaissance that the false was born with the natural. . . .

The Industrial Simulacrum

The industrial revolution gave rise to a whole new generation of signs and objects. These were signs with no caste tradition, which had never known the restrictions of status, and which would not have to be *counterfeited* because they were being *produced* on such a gigantic scale. The problem of the singularity and the origin of these signs no longer arises; technique is their origin. They have no meaning beyond the dimensions of the industrial simulacrum.

This is the phenomenon of the series—or, in other words, the very possibility of two or of *n* identical objects. The relation between them is not that of the original to its counterfeit, or its analogue, or its reflection; it is a relationship of equivalence, of indifference. In the series, objects are transformed indefinitely into simulacra of one another and, with objects, so are the people who produce them. Only the extinction of original reference permits the generalized law of equivalence, which is to say, the *very possibility of production*.

But the analysis of production is beginning to falter because it is no longer able to read production as an original process, a process that lies at the origin of all the others. In fact, it discovers the reverse: a process of resorption of every original being and its introduction to identical series of beings. Hitherto, production and labor have been viewed as potential and force, as historical process and as a generic activity. This is the modern energo-economic myth. But it is worth asking whether production does not intervene, *in the order of signs*, as a *particular phase*—whether it is not at bottom only one episode in the lineage of simulacra? It would be that which, thanks to technique, produces potentially identical beings (sign-objects) in indefinite series.

The fabulous energies released in the play of technique, industry, and economy should not obscure the fact that the ultimate point was to establish this condition of indefinite reproducibility. Although it certainly amounts to a major challenge to the "natural" order, it remains a "second order" simulacrum and a rather poor imaginary solution to the problem of mastering the world. Relative to the era of the counterfeit, the double, the mirror, of theater and the play of masks and appearances, the serial and technical age of reproduction commands, in the end, less scope (but the following era of simulation models, the third order, is of considerably greater dimensions).

It was Walter Benjamin who first separated out the implications of this principle of reproduction. He showed that reproduction absorbs the process of production and alters its goals, the status of the product, and the producer. He established this on the terrain of art, cinema, and photography. . . . But we know now that today all production returns to this sphere. It is at the level of reproduction —fashion, media, advertising, information and communication networks—the level that Marx described as the *faux frais* of capital (you can almost measure the irony of history), it is, in other words, within the sphere of simulacra and the code, that the unity of the whole process of capital is tied together. Benjamin (and later McLuhan) grasped technique not as "productive force" (where Marxist analysis remains trapped) but as medium, as the form and principle of a whole new generation of meaning. The mere fact that any object can be reproduced, as such, in an exemplary double, is already a revolution. . . . That two products are *equivalent* by virtue of socially necessary labor is less interesting in the long run than the serial repetition of the same object (which is the same for individuals considered as labor power). Technique as medium quashes not only the "message" of the product (its use value), but also labor power itself, which Marx wanted to make the revolutionary message of production. But Benjamin and McLuhan saw that the real message, *the real ultimatum*, lay in reproduction itself, and that production, as such, has no meaning: its social finality gets lost in seriality. Simulacra surpass history.

Moreover, the phase of serial production is ephemeral. Ever since dead labor began to predominate over living labor, in other words, since the end of primitive accumulation, serial production has been ceding precedence to generation by models. This is a matter of reversing origins and finalities, since all forms change from the moment they are no longer mechanically reproduced, but conceived instead in light of their reproducibility, as a diffraction from a generating nucleus called a model. With this, we find ourselves in the midst of third-order simulacra. Both the counterfeit of the original in the first order and the pure series of the second order disappear in favor of models from which all forms proceed according to the modulation of differences. Only an affiliation to the model generates meaning and makes sense (*fait sens*). Nothing functions according to an end, but proceeds from the model, the "signifier of reference," which acts like an anterior finality, supplying the only credible outcome (*la seule vraisemblance*). This is simulation in the modern sense of the term, where industrialization is only the primary form. In the end, serial reproducibility is less fundamental than modulation, quantitative equivalence less important than distinctive oppositions. The potential for commutation of terms takes precedence over the law of equivalence; the structural law of value replaces the commodity law of value. Not only does it make little sense to search for the secrets of the code in technique or the economy; the very possibility of industrial production has to be traced to the genesis of the code and of simulacra. As the order of the counterfeit was seized by serial production (viz., how art succumbed entirely to a kind of "machinality"), so the order of production is in the process of being undermined by operational simulation. . . .

The Metaphysics of the Code

*The mathematical Leibniz saw in the mystic elegance of
the binary system of zero and one the image of Creation.
The unity of the Supreme Being operating in the void
by binary function would, he felt, suffice to make
all beings from the void.*[2]

The great simulacra constructed by man evolve from a universe of natural laws to one of forces and tensions, and finally, today, to a universe of structures and binary oppositions. After the metaphysics of
being and appearance, after that of energy and determination, we have
the metaphysics of indeterminacy and the code. Cybernetic control,
generation by models, differential modulation, feedback, question-
naires (*question/réponse*?): such is the new *operational* configuration
(industrial simulacra were only *operative*). Digitality is its metaphysical principle (Leibniz's God) and DNA its prophet. In fact, it is in the
genetic code that the "genesis of simulacra" finds its most developed
form. At the limit of an always increasing elimination of references and
finalities, an ever-increasing loss of resemblances and designations, we
find the digital and programmatic sign, whose "value" is purely *tactical*, at the intersection of other signals ("bits" of information/tests)
whose structure is that of a micromolecular code of command and
control.

At this level, the question of signs and their rational destination,
their "*real*" and their "*imaginary*," their repression, their reversal, the
illusions they sketch, what they hush up or their parallel significations
—all of this is swept from the table. We have already touched on first-
order signs, complex and rich with illusions, and how they have been
transformed, together with machines, into brute, flat, industrial, re-
petitive signs—echoless, efficient, operative. Yet much more radical is
the evolution of the coded signal, which is in a sense unreadable,
without possible interpretation, like a programmatic matrix buried
for light-years at the foundation of the "biological" body: little black
boxes where all the commands are fomented with all the responses.

Surely this must mean the end of the theater of representation—
the space of signs, their conflict and their silence. All this is replaced
by the black box of the code, the molecular signal emitter with which
we are irradiated. Our bodies are crisscrossed by question/answer
formulas and tests, like programs inscribed in our cells. Bodily cells,

electronic cells, party cells, microbiological cells: we are always on the lookout for the tiniest, indivisible element, whose organic synthesis arises from the givens of the code. But the code itself is only a genetic, generative cell where myriad intersections produce all the questions and all the possible solutions. The questions (the stimuli of data processing and information systems) have no finality beyond the programmed reply, which is genetically immutable, or inflected by infinitesimal and aleatory differences. This is the space of an unprecedented linearity and one-dimensionality: a cellular space for the indefinite generation of the same signals, like the tics of a prisoner driven mad by loneliness and repetition. This is the genetic code, an unchanging, radiating disk of which we are no more than interpretive cells. The aura of the sign and of signification itself is resolved along with the possibility of determination; everything is resolved in inscription and decoding.

This is the current strategic model. It takes up where the old ideological model, political economy, left off, and reappears under the rigorous sign of science in Jacques Monod's *Chance and Necessity*. Dialectical evolution is over. Now it is the discontinuous indeterminism of the genetic code that regulates life—the *teleonomic* principle. Finality is no longer located at the conclusion; indeed, there is no end, and determination is out. The finalities are established in advance, inscribed in the code. In a way, things have not really changed. The system of ends has only ceded to the play of molecules, as has the order of signifieds to the play of infinitesimal signifers reduced to aleatory commutation. It is as if the transcendental ends have been revised into an instrument panel. However, what is always involved is a recourse to nature, to an inscription in a "biological" nature. In effect, this is a fantasized nature, as nature has always been. It is a metaphysical sanctuary no longer for the origin or for substances, but this time for the code. The code has to have an "objective" seat —what better throne than the molecule and genetics? Monod is the severe theologian of this molecular transcendence; Edgar Morin is his ecstatic acolyte (ADN=Adonaï)! In each, the phantasm of the code, which is equivalent to the reality of power, is combined with an idealism of the molecule.

In other words, we encounter once more the delirious dream of reunifying the world under a unitary principle. There was the homogeneous substance of the Jesuits during the Counter-Reformation; now there is the genetic code, whose precursor is Leibniz's binary Divinity. For the current program has nothing to do with genetics; it is a social and historical program. What biochemistry hypostatizes is the ideal of a social order regulated by a kind of genetic code or micromolecular calculus of PPBS (Planning Programming Budgeting System) that irradiates the social body with its operational circuits. Technocybernetics here unveils its "natural philosophy," as Monod calls it. . . .

In its reproduction, the system puts an end to its own myth of origin and the referential values it has secreted during its process of development. By extinguishing its own foundational myth, the system also eliminates its internal contradictions (no more "reality" and no referent with which to challenge it). But it does away, in the same stroke, with its teleological myths, with the revolution itself. What the revolution always held out for was the triumph of the generic human reference, the original potential of man. If capital scratches generic man himself from the map (in favor of genetic man?), what then? The golden age of revolution was also the era of capital, when myths of origin and end were still in circulation. The irony is that the major historical threat to capital lay in the *mythic* imperative of rationality that characterized it from the beginning. But once it has short-circuited these myths in a factual operationalism, undermined rational discourse, and become its own myth, or more precisely, the indeterminate, random machine that it is today—something comparable to a genetic social code—then capital eliminates the opportunity for a determinate reversal. This is the essential violence of capital today. It remains to be seen whether this operationality is not also a myth—if, indeed, DNA itself is not a myth. . . .

Regulation on the model of the genetic code is not confined to laboratory effects and the exalted visions of biological theoreticians. The most banal aspects of ordinary life are invested with these models. Digitality is among us; it preys on the messages and signs of modern societies. Its most concrete form is the test: question/answer, stimulus/response. Content is steadily neutralized in a continual procedure of controlled interrogation, of verdicts and ultimatums to be decoded, none of which, this time, originates in the genetic code, but partakes nevertheless of the same tactical indetermination. The cycle of meaning is infinitesimally abridged into minute quantities of energy/information, bits, questions/answers, returning to their points of departure, describing only the perpetual reactualization of the same models. This is the equivalent of the code's neutralization of signifieds, the instantaneous verdicts of fashion, advertising, media messages. It dwells everywhere that supply engulfs demand, or the question devours the answer, or absorbs and regurgitates it in decodable form, or simply invents and then anticipates it. Everywhere, we find the same "scenario": the "trial and error" scenario (of guinea pigs in laboratory tests), the scenario that gives you a "range of choices," the multiple-choice testing offered everywhere ("test your personality"). The test appears as a fundamental social form of control, infinitely dividing practices and responses.

We live in the mode of the *referendum*, and this is precisely because there are no more referentials. All signs and messages (which include "functional" objects as well as fashion features, televised information, polls or electoral consultations) present themselves to us in the question/answer format. The social system of communication has evolved from a complex syntactic structure of language to the probing of a binary signaling system: a perpetual test. Yet, as we know, tests and referenda are perfect forms of simulation. The reply is induced by the question; it is, so to speak, design-ated in advance. Hence, the referendum is really just an ultimatum. The question, being unilateral, is therefore no longer properly interrogative, but rather the immediate imposition of a meaning whose cycle is instantly completed. Each message is a verdict, like the statistical ones announced in polls. The simulation of distance (that is, of contradiction) between the two poles of the communication process is, like the reality effect in the sign, just a tactical hallucination. . . ." "Reality" has been analyzed into simple elements and recomposed into scenarios of regulated opposition. . . .

It may seem that the historical movement of capital has carried it from the open competition of the oligopoly to outright monopoly, that democracy has moved from the multiparty system to bipartisanism and finally to the single-party state. But this is not what is going on. The oligopoly, or contemporary diapoly, results from the monopoly's tactical division in two. In all domains, diapoly is the highest stage of monopoly. It is not political will that breaks the monopoly of the market (state intervention, antitrust laws, etc.); it is the fact that every unitary system, if it wants to survive, has to evolve a *binary* system of *regulation*. This changes nothing in the essence of monopoly; on the contrary, power is only absolute if it knows how to diffract itself in equivalent variations—that is, if it knows how to redouble itself through doubling. This goes for brands of detergent as much as for "peaceful coexistence." You need two superpowers to maintain a universe under control; a single empire collapses under its own weight. The equilibrium of terror is what permits a strategy of regulated oppositions to be established, since the strategy is really structural rather than atomic. This regulated opposition can be ramified into more complex scenarios, but the matrix remains binary. It looks as if, from now on, we shall be dealing not with duality or open competitive war, but with couples of simultaneous opposition.

From the tiniest disjunctive unities (the question/answer particle) to the macroscopic level of systems of alternance that preside over the economy, politics, and global coexistence, the matrix does not vary: it is always 0/1, the binary scansion that affirms itself as the metastable or homeostatic form of contemporary systems. It is the processual node of the simulations that dominate us. They can be organized as an unstable play of variation, or in polyvalent or tauto-logical modes, without endangering this central principle of bipolari-ty: digitality is, indeed, the divine form of simulation. . . .

Why does the World Trade Center in New York have *two* towers? . . .

The Hyperrealism of Simulation

What I have been describing so far defines a digital space, a magnetic field of the code, with polarizations, diffractions, gravitating models and always—*always*—the flux of tiniest disjunctive unities (the ques-tion/answer cell, which is a kind of cybernetic atom of signification). It is important now to gauge the difference between this field of con-trol and the traditional space of repression—the police space—which still corresponded to a significative violence. . . .

Totalitarian, bureaucratic concentration is an arrangement that dates from the era of the commodity law of value. That system of equivalences in effect imposed a form of general equivalence, and hence, the centralization of a global process. Its archaic rationality contrasts starkly with the meaning of simulation. The latter does not secrete a single, general equivalent, but rather a diffraction of models playing a supervisory role. General equivalence is replaced by distinc-tive opposition. The code's disjunction supplants the centralist in-junction. Solicitation is substituted for the ultimatum. Mandatory passivity evolves into models constructed directly from the "active responses" of the subject, his implication, his "ludic" participation, etc., and finally toward a total, environmental model made up of in-cessant, spontaneous responses, joyful feedback, and irradiated contact.

This is (according to Nicholas Schöffer) "the concretization of the general ambience"—the great Festival of Participation, composed of myriad stimuli, miniaturized tests, infinitely divisible nodes of query and reply, magnetized by a few overarching models illuminated by the code. The culture of tactile communication is in fact burgeoning in the techno-lumino-kinetic space provided by this total, spatio-dynamic theater. It brings with it a kind of contact Imaginary, a sensorial mimeticism, a tactile mysticism that grafts onto the universe of operational simulation, multistimulation, and multiresponse like an entire system of ecological concepts. Indeed, the rationality of adaptive testing awaits naturalization through assimilation with animal mimeticism: "Animal adaptation to the forms and colors of their milieu is a phenomenon valid also for man" (Schöffer). And even for Indians, with their "innate sense of ecology"!

Tropisms, mimeticism, empathy—the whole ecological Gospel of open systems, with feedback, negative or positive, is on the verge of being swallowed up in this breach, as an ideology of regulation through information, which is surely just the modern-day avatar, dressed in a more flexible rationality, of Pavlovian reflex (psychology). Thus, we have evolved from electroshock therapy to bodily expression as mental health conditioning. The apparatuses of force and of "forcing" (*forçage*) have given way to those of ambience, which include the operationalization of the concepts of need, perception, desire, and so on. This is a generalized ecology, mystique of the (ecological) "niche," of context, and of simulations of milieu. . . . The spectacle itself is engulfed in this total, fusional, tactile, esthesic (no more esthetics) environmentalism. . . .

Reality itself founders in hyperrealism, the meticulous reduplication of the real, preferably through another, reproductive medium, such as photography. From medium to medium, the real is volatilized, becoming an allegory of death. But it is also, in a sense, reinforced through its own destruction. It becomes *reality for its own sake*, the fetishism of the lost object—no longer the object of representation, but the ecstasy of denial and of its own ritual extermination: the hyperreal.

Realism had already inaugurated this process. The rhetoric of the real signaled its gravely altered status (its golden age was characterized by an innocence of language in which it was not obliged to redouble what it said with a reality effect). Surrealism remained within the purview of the realism it contested—but also redoubled—through its rupture with the Imaginary. The hyperreal represents a much more advanced stage insofar as it manages to efface even this contradiction between the real and the imaginary. Unreality no longer resides in the dream or fantasy, or in the beyond, but in the *real's hallucinatory resemblance to itself*. To escape the crisis of representation, reality loops around itself in pure repetition, a tendency that was already apparent, before the days of pop art and pictorial neorealism, in the *nouveau roman*. There, the project was already to enclose the real in a vacuum, to extirpate all psychology and subjectivity in order to render a pristine objectivity. In fact, this objectivity was only that of the pure gaze—an objectivity at last liberated from the object, which is no more than the blind relay of the look that scans it. It attempts a kind of circular seduction in which one can easily mark the unconscious undertaking to become invisible.

This is certainly the impression created by the neonovel: the rage for eliding meaning in a blind and meticulous reality. Both syntax and semantics have disappeared. There is no longer an apparition, but an arraignment of the object, the eager examination of its scattered fragments: neither metaphor nor metonymy, but a successive immanence beneath the police agency of the look. This objective microscopics makes reality swim vertiginously, arousing the dizziness of death within the confines of representation for its own sake. The old illusions of relief, perspective, and spatial and psychological depth linked to the perception of the object give way to an optics functioning on the surface of things, as if the gaze had become the molecular code of the object. . . .

A possible definition of the real is: *that for which it is possible to provide an equivalent representation.* This definition is contemporary with science, which postulates a universal system of equivalences (classical representation was not so much a matter of equivalence as of transcription, interpretation, commentary). At the conclusion of this process of reproduction, the real becomes not only that which can be reproduced, but that which is always already reproduced— the hyperreal. But this does not mean that reality and art are in some sense extinguished through total absorption in one another. Hyperrealism is something like their mutual fulfillment and overflowing into one another through an exchange at the level of simulation of their respective foundational privileges and prejudices. Hyperrealism is only beyond representation because it functions entirely within the realm of simulation. There, the whirligig of representation goes mad, but with an implosive insanity which, far from being ex-centric, casts longing eyes at the center, toward its own repetition *en abîme.* Like the distancing effect within a dream, which tells one that one is dreaming, but only in behalf of the censor, in order that we continue dreaming, hyperrealism is an integral part of a coded reality, which it perpetuates without modifying.

In fact, we must interpret hyperrealism inversely: today, *reality itself is hyperrealistic.* The secret of surrealism was that the most banal reality could become surreal, but only at privileged moments, which still derived from art and the imaginary. Now the whole of everyday, political, social, historical, economic reality is incorporated into the simulative dimension of hyperrealism; we already live out the "esthetic" hallucination of reality. The old saying, "reality is stranger than fiction," which belonged to the surrealist phase of the estheticization of life, has been surpassed. There is no longer a fiction that life can confront, even in order to surpass it; reality has passed over into the play of reality, radically disenchanted, the "cool" cybernetic phase supplanting the "hot" and phantasmatic. . . .

There once existed a specific class of objects that were allegorical, and even a bit diabolical, such as mirrors, images, works of art (and concepts?)—of course, these too were simulacra, but they were transparent and manifest . . . they had their own style and characteristic savoir-faire. In these objects, pleasure consisted more in discovering something "natural" in what was artificial and counterfeit. Today, the real and the imaginary are confounded in the same operational totality, and esthetic fascination is simply everywhere. It involves a kind of subliminal perception, a kind of sixth sense for fakery, montage, scenarios, and the overexposition of reality in the lighting of models. This is no longer a productive space, but a kind of ciphering strip, a coding and decoding tape, a tape recording magnetized with signs. It is an esthetic reality, to be sure, but no longer by virtue of art's premeditation and distance, but through a kind of elevation to the second power, via the anticipation and the immanence of the code. An air of nondeliberate parody clings to everything—a tactical simulation—like an undecidable game to which is attached a specifically esthetic pleasure, the pleasure in reading (*lecture*) and in the rules of the game. . . .

For a long time now art has prefigured this transformation of everyday life. Very quickly, the work of art redoubled itself as a manipulation of the signs of art: this oversignification, or as Lévi-Strauss would call it, this "academicism of the signifier," introduced art to the sign-form. Thus art entered the phase of its own indefinite *reproduction*; everything that redoubles in itself, even ordinary, everyday reality, falls in the same stroke under the sign of art, and becomes esthetic. The same goes for production, of which one can say that today it is commencing this esthetic doubling, at the point where, having expelled all content and finality, it becomes, in a way, abstract and nonfigurative. It begins to express the pure form of production; it takes itself, like art, as its own teleological value.

Art and industry can thus exchange signs: art, in order to become a reproductive machine (Andy Warhol), without ceasing to be art, since this machine is only a sign; and production, in order to lose all social purpose and thus to verify and exalt itself at last in the hyperbolic and esthetic signs of prestige that are the great industrial combines, the 400-meter-high business blocks and the statistical mysteries of the GNP. . . . In this vertigo of serial signs—shadowless, impossible to sublimate, immanent in their repetition—who can say where the reality of what they simulate resides? Apparently, these signs repress nothing . . . even the primary process is abolished. The cool universe of digitality absorbs the worlds of metaphor and of metonymy, and the principle of simulation thus triumphs over both the reality principle and the pleasure principle.

NOTES

1. Anthony Wilden, *System and Structure: Essays in Communication and Exchange* (London: Tavistock, 1977), p. xxvii.

2. Marshall McLuhan, *Understanding Media: the Extensions of Man* (New York; Mentor, 1964), p. 111.

Chapter 5
Modern Power in Reverse Image: The Paradigm Shift of Michel Foucault and Talcott Parsons
Arthur Kroker

> *At the deepest level of Western knowledge, Marxism introduced no real discontinuity; it found its place without difficulty, as a full, comfortable and, goodness knows, satisfying form for a time (its own), within an epistemological arrangement that welcomed it gladly (since it was this arrangement that in fact was making room for it) and that it, in return, had no intention of disturbing and, above all, no power to modify even one jot, since it rested entirely upon it.*
>
> Michel Foucault, *The Order of Things*

The Splitting of the Atom

In *Madness and Civilization,* Foucault writes that "Marxism exists in nineteenth-century thought like a fish in water,"[1] precisely because both bourgeois and revolutionary theories of economics, while displaying a surface opposition, share a common condition of possibility in the appearance of a "new arrangement of power." Now, however, on the question of power as opposed to capital, and in the midst of the radical anxiety of twentieth-century experience, it might fairly be said that Foucault's meditation on power, a meditation which by his own account ranges through the entire corpus of his work, takes its place quietly and without a fundamental note of discordance in the *episteme* of bourgeois sociology. I would say further, and this without criticism, that Foucault's understanding of the surface play of power, what Jean Baudrillard has described elsewhere as a "mythic discourse" on the filiation *en abîme* of power,[2] is perhaps nothing more than the completion, and certainly not less than the mirror image, of another disembodied discourse on power, presented by that most grimly realistic of bourgeois sociologists, Talcott Parsons.

The event that, taking place at the beginning of the twentieth-century, clearly and decisively divides the modern bourgeois sociology of power from its nineteenth-century counterparts, and from which Parsons' theorizations and Foucault's thought follow, is nothing less than the movement from classical physics to modern biology, and particularly to the "new" genetic biology. For in the change from physics to biology as the mode of theoretical knowledge that constitutes power, there swiftly emerged a bourgeois discourse on power, its origins and methods of operation, which claimed, for the first time, that power was not after all to be reduced to an innocent (and why should we not say, in nostalgic remembrance, sentimental) struggle between entities (interests, classes, groups) separated at a distance and causally interconnected, but was, in fact beyond all specific contents (phenomenal existence), the form, or transparent medium, through which the life of the social species was to be prolonged and, to further that "natural purpose," improved.

Bourgeois sociology has by now completed the great shift to the biological conception of power, which announces a grand reversal of the "order" or "structure" of control, between culture and economy, between the categories of power and capital. Even when presented in the crudest of Darwinian terms by Herbert Spencer, this conception already contained the essential bourgeois discovery that political economy would now take its place within a "regulatory" order of dominations and powers. Who could have suspected that of the two thinkers, Marx and Spencer, it would have been Marx's fate to bring the classical discourse to a close (in the release of a dynamic vision of human freedom), and Spencer's fate to initiate a modern, structuralist discourse on power? And, ironically, in the same tired way in which new cultural forms are often energized by the content of preceding historical periods, Marxism is now a main content of the Spencerian age. That this is a Spencerian age is attested to in the articulation, at first by Parsons and then by Foucault, of the principles of the new structuralist discourse. This discourse is the outcome of three strategic lines of thought, all of which meet in the creation of a radically new, and thus radically structuralist, conception of power, truth, and life. The new genetic biology of combinants and recombinants contributes (analogically, it is true, but in the specific sense of structural similitude) to an interpretation of power as a "site of battle" between genetic heritage (the categorical imperative?) and the empirical "range of variations" (the phenomenal world).[3] Cybernetic theory undermines, with one contemptuous blow, the theoretical justifications of the old materialism by establishing the new epistemological premise that information is *regulatory* of energy in much the same way that culture is *constitutive* of economy. And linguistic theory (which is only the most visible "sign" of a modern discourse that also involves molecular biology and cybernetics) displaces the "commodity conception" of power by emphasizing that power, understood as a specialized language, is a "medium" of exchange precisely in the sense that the grammar of power (the "code" of authority and its political significations) is the discursive form (the "silent language") within which the adaptation, or shall we be honest and say the "disciplining," of the social species takes place.[4]

With a proper, and perhaps even prim, sense of Victorian innocence, the contemporary tradition of political economy insists on its right to be the last defender of Newtonian politics. With all the theoretical naiveté of a tradition that has managed (and this against a political history that declares its falsity) to miss not only the point but also the century, the political economy of power rushes past the actual ways by which the power apparatus now constitutes itself to take on in battle the representational "spooks" of the past: class struggle, capitalist hegemony, power as possession—the works! But Foucault is not a political economist, nor does he aspire to energize the radical structuralism of the modern century with the ideological content of the Newtonian regime. Whatever the origin of Foucault's turn to biology, it is within the deep logic of the trajectory of thought traced out by the modern political biologists, ranging from Spencer to Parsons, that his thought is to be located. This is not to say, of course, that Foucault's thought is party to "evolutionism," nor is it to maintain that his project is the advocacy of a simple organic metaphor. But then, need it be said, Parsons' political biology always claims that there is an order of difference between natural and social management of the species and that, in justifying itself (by way of analogy to natural evolution), power, understood as a social strategy, finds in the need to work on behalf of the *life* of the human species a discursive validation for the extension of its order of normalizing practices.

It is, perhaps, of only the least importance that Parsons and Foucault do not participate in a common political practice or that they reach different conclusions with regard to the political practices that follow from the constitution of power in the image of the biological metaphor. Was it not, in fact, precisely because these other curious intellectual pairings—Augustine and Faustus, Marx and Smith—did *not* repeat one another but, in their grand reversal of categories, opposed one another, that each represented the completion of the trajectory of thought initiated by his opponent? Foucault is entangled with the Parsonian discourse. For between Parsons and Foucault, there is not the emptiness of nonidentity, but, might it be said, the comforting similitude of the identity of opposites. With the happy sigh of one who has finally come home, Parsons confessed that he had ended up as a Kantian. And Foucault is, perhaps, the primal scream of a theory that, having renounced the possibility of knowledge of the *Ding an sich* (all in the name of the critique of ontology), is forced into a nominalism that is bleak with despair. Both theorizations of "bio-power" rush to a common fate: that of Parsons, the revelation of the totalitarianism that is at the center of the metaphysics of Western knowledge; and that of Foucault, to be the truth-sayer of the political practices that follow when, in his blank expression, "history has no meaning."[5]

"Bad Infinity"

Discourse is not life: its time is not your time; in it, you will not be reconciled to death; you may have killed God beneath the weight of all that you have said; but don't imagine that, with all that you are saying, you will make a man that will live longer than he.

Michel Foucault, *The Archaeology of Knowledge*

Why, after all, be unfair to Foucault? From "The Discourse on Language" to *The History of Sexuality*, he never tires of trying to free himself from being named a structuralist—from, that is, developing a thematic on power that makes reference ". . . to the great model of signs and language," or from the invocation of a theory of language which is situated only within the sociology of signs and symbols.

And yet, for all of his protestations, and precisely because of the fact that Foucault does not trade in the semiology of power, I consider his meditation on power a classical example of hyperstructuralism. What has been called structuralism, at least in its literary representations from Bataille to Barthes and Derrida, is but the surface sign at the level of sociolinguistics (or, perhaps, psycholinguistics) of the symbol of a more pervasive "deep structuralism" that is now the horizon, the limit and possibility, of the production of Western knowledge. It is not to the barren world of semiology nor to the sociology of signifiers and significations that Foucault's thematic on power makes reference. Foucault is a structuralist, not in the linguistic, but in the profoundly philosophical sense that his discourse on power reflects a radical transformation of the form and, need it be said, content of Western experience in the direction of structuralist principles. Thus, Foucault's thought is structuralist in a mimetic sense: its categories—discursive knowledge, not intuition; relation, not sense; conditions of possibility, not ontology—reflect a social reality which, at the level of categorical knowledge and categorical politics, has been transformed in a structuralist direction.

It is to the philosopher of Königsberg that Foucault's structuralism may be traced. For is it not Kant who, in his radical scission of sensuous experience from the categories of understanding and in his intimations of a world invested and controlled by a power that would be radically relational, was the precursor of "deep structuralism"? And is it not really Kant's "relational" understanding, his silencing of the "maundering fanaticism"[6] of the sensible world in favor of a "pure consciousness of form," which is the siren that calls forth the new world-hypothesis of structuralism? The thesis of bio-power is profoundly structuralist because it is radically Kantian; and it is Kantian to the extent that the new genetics, language theory, and cybernetics are strategies—yes, nothing but political mechanisms— for suppressing the "maundering fanaticism" of sensuous experience. It is at this more intensive philosophical level, and *not* at the conventional, narrow empirical site of semiology, that Foucault's thought is, almost constitutively, structuralist. And it is in this unnoticed region of metaphysical assumptions, a domain that is far from the surface conflicts of the sciences of signs and symbols, that Parsons and Foucault reach agreement really on nothing less than what Karl Jaspers has said of Kant. This is, simply, that understanding in the modern age (and, hence, the relation of truth and power) is discursive ". . . because it produces objects in respect to its form, not in respect to its existence."[7]

The "Kantian subordination" is not only the vital principle but the actual epistemological context within which Foucault's reflections on power, and also Parsons', take shape. Parsons' famous dualism —phenomenal "exigencies" and noumenal "normativity"—represent in the language of sociology what Kant has previously termed the struggle of existence and the "understanding." And, for Foucault, the connection is all the more transparent. He says, and this without recrimination, that in every society ". . . the production of discourse is at once controlled, selected, organized and redistributed according to a certain number of procedures, whose role is to avert its powers and its dangers, to cope with chance events, to evade its ponderous, awesome materiality."[8] And later, in speaking of the investiture of sex by the will to knowledge, Foucault writes of himself: "You, on the other hand, are in a symmetrical and inverse position: for you, there remain only groundless effects, ramifications without roots, a sexuality without a sex. What is this if not castration once again?"[9] What does Foucault mean by his "analytics of power"; what could he have been speaking of in his meditation on the "will to truth," other than the implications of the Kantian investiture, or should we say *siege*, of sensuous experience by the categories of "discourse"? Foucault is not incorrect, or in bad faith, in claiming against conventional formalisms, whether linguistic, sociological, or psychological, that he should not be victimized by a misplaced nominalism: one that places his writing in the camp of the new monism of language. No, Foucault is after something more fundamental, something that escapes the vision of the linguistic monad: his project is to discover, after Parsons, the discursive implications of Kant's will to knowledge. And, to this end, Parsons and Foucault stand now as positive and negative polarities, really the environment and antienvironment, of the spread of the will to truth across twentieth-century experience. The conjunction of truth, life and power as the axes of the discourse of "bio-power" makes the modern age the century of Kant.

All of this is to say simply that the discourse of political biology is the "mother lode" of structuralism. In the meeting of Kant and Spencer, the will to truth finds its embodiment in the (admittedly rarified) claim that knowledge now will combine with "governance" for the perpetuation of the "cultural heritage" of the society. Thus, what quickly appear in the writings of Parsons and Foucault are monochromatic images of a power that is made inevitable by its presuppositions, and that operates by transforming its conditions of possibility (a "normalized" society) into a methodology of political practice (rules of inclusion, exclusion, and prohibition). The discourse of political biology claims not only that power speaks for life, but insists also that the management of the life-functions of society (the regulation of health, intelligence, affect, body, and population) is "limitless." As Hegel foresaw, the formalism of modern power would only lead to "bad infinity"; that is, to a dynamic of instrumental activism in which everything is reduced to the nihilism of "means in search of means."[10] Durkheim was the first to seize on the significance of a regime of bio-power that was driven forward by the principle of the "bad infinity." He said, in the fateful language of *normativity*, that suicide now becomes a deviation from the norm specifically because the struggle of contemporary politics is carried on at the fundamental threshold of life and death.[11] Death was less a private tragedy than a public threat to the order of permissions and prohibitions represented by the normative (life-managing) order. And is it not almost unremarked, because it is so unremarkable in its self-transparency, that within the apparatus of death rituals there has been imposed a normalization of death? The mourning ritual is thus to death as psychiatry is to madness and art criticism to artistic creation: a normalization, and thus incarceration, of an absence that is made less menacing by being confined to the silent region of non-reason.

The "bad infinity" wagers its struggle on the methodological possibility of substituting social life for biological death, and this on behalf of a power apparatus which to the extent that it manages to substitute *its* survival for my death finally overcomes the tragedy of finality. Jean Baudrillard has, of course, sensed something of this awesome truth in noting that the power that is in play in the form of the "bad infinity" is fascist in character. It presents itself in the "aesthetic ritual of death" as a power that is not the signification of a sovereignty, a people's will, a trust. And power can do this because it has *no* representational function: the secret of power's existence is, quite simply, that "power does not exist."[12] Limitlessness means that power is the name given to a certain coherency of relations: the terms to the relation (existence, ontology, corporeality) disappear and the "radical relationalism" that is the language, the medium, of power transcends sensuous experience. But then, in a reversal too bitter for acknowledgment, it returns to the source of its energy—sensuous existence—but in the form of that which is most positive and benign: it returns, that is, under the guise of the "ideolect" of life management and in the garb of truth. Is this so surprising? Kant, who sensed the terrorism (he insisted that this was freedom) of truth, spoke of the "transcendental deduction"; and Spencer thought of power in terms of the regulation of life. Yes, Spencer embodies Kant, and what is put in play by both is a power that is a matter of "ground-less effects" and "ramifications without roots."[13] A limitless power is also a fascist power; but could it be that fascism is only a little pro-legomenon to the play of power to come?

Foucault's theorization of power, such as it is, delivers us now only to the ascending spiral of the "bad infinity." A procedural image of power appears which, in being groundless—a matter, that is, of re-lations rather than representations—reproduces itself in an endless spiral of exchanges: a spiral of exchanges which, at once, plays the finite against the abstract, desire against order, as in a house of mir-rors. Parsons, of course, never promised more than unhappy con-sciousness. His is the easy consciousness of the bourgeois personality who finds in the "relational" conception of power nothing more stir-ring than the search for a permanent and immutable basis for politics. But Foucault is the limit of the critical attitude; for he finally delivers on the relentless determinism which is at the center of Nietzsche's "will to power" and of Goya's "sleep of reason." Perhaps, just as Foucault saw clearly that Marx, because of his radical affirmation of history, was destined to be the last citizen of the nineteenth century, so too Foucault, because of his radical assent to a power that "does not exist," is the first theorist of power of the modern century. And, to the extent that Marx could finally complete the truth of Capital, so, equally, Foucault is only able to bring to the surface of language, without the hope of an easy exit, the strategies of this new mode of power: the "disciplinary society," "technologies of power," and an endless play of interventions upon the population and within the body.

Beyond the "Marxian Subordination"

At the heart of power is a war-like relation and not that of an appropriation.

Michel Foucault, *Power and Norm*

We consider a generalized medium (like power) to be contentless.

Talcott Parsons, *Action Theory and the Human Condition*

In the fateful convergence of Parsons' and Foucault's images of a "relational power" there is to be found a truth-saying about the actual operations and circumlocutions of the modern "power apparatus" that is so transformative in its logic, so comprehensive in its critical implications, that its very statement threatens to jeopardize the way in which power is "thought" within the Western tradition. In an almost clumsy fashion, with arguments that reveal traces of their deep embeddedness in the classical economy of power, Parsons, and then Foucault, have stumbled upon a new terrain or, dare we say, a new, constitutive dimension, of twentieth-century politics. Martin Heidegger once said that the fate of the modern age was coeval with the transformation of Nietzsche's will to power into the more symbolic relationship of the "will to will."[14] What is at stake in a politics mediated by the "will to will" is the possibility that the *noumenal forms* of the life-order (which might be called, in their various symbolic representations, "discourse," "structural logic," "scientific-technical rationality," "the family of the generalized symbolic media") may have broken free of their anchorage in sensuous existence, moved now by the dynamic impulse of an autonomous life-will. The "mirror" of politics is the apellation given to a political discourse in which nothing "in-itself" is at stake, only the symbolic play of a "power" that can never be appropriated, or for that matter, grounded, once and for all, in any of the *terms* to the power relation.

The silent, theoretical compact, the new Magna Carta of power, struck by Foucault and Parsons on the "relational" character of modern power, is as explicit, and terrifying, a political description as could be provided of the truth that is carried forward by the eruption of the will to will. Parsons continues to think in the mental framework of the old world of Newtonian politics when he insists that the category of "freedom" still has some representational bearing on a "power" that recedes now like the shadow form of abstract realism into the invisible grammar of social discipline.[15] But Foucault, perhaps not even yet aware of the magnitude of the "discovery" of relational power, nonetheless has the sense to be alert to the opening of a new continent of the will, as we can see when he reflects, almost naively like a thinker pushed ahead by events, on the existence now of a "diabolical" will.

Now, I know that the threshold conflict, this golden egg, in Foucault's discourse on power has to do with the struggle that he has provoked against the "Marxian subordination" of power to some final, reassuring originary: class, commodity-form, instrumental state, historical dialectics. But, to be honest, what is less noticed, but undoubtedly of greater theoretical, and hence practical, significance, is that Foucault's famous refusal of the Marxian subordination must take its place in a queue that forms behind Parsons' quiet refusal of the "liberal subordination" of power. Like Foucault, Parsons also renounces the task of searching for a monistic ground (a class, a state, an individual's magical "capacities") to which power may be referred for its explanation. Thus, we have not one but two "famous post-Marxists," who declare against Marxism for precisely the same reasons that they were motivated, perhaps even compelled, to declare against the liberal regime of power.

Parsons and Foucault are conspirators of a common kind: whether their thought moves against classical Marxism (the search for the "headquarters"[16] that presides over rationality) or against classical liberalism (the nostalgia for the "individual"[17] who is the exerter of his capacities), an entirely common, and specific, series of theoretical renunciations appears. It is as if, although entering the discourse on power against radically different manifestations of the classical *episteme* (as different, I imagine, as that curious dissimilitude, but also filiation of identity, between Hobbes's "possessive" conception of power and Marx's "appropriation" of the power-relation on behalf of Capital), Parsons and Foucault turn out to be mining the very same historical vein. Consequently, I might conclude that the ultimate similarity of these two grand "refusals," originating as they do in quite opposite, incompatible, and oh! so independent, lines of theoretical analysis, is like a laboratory experiment which, in its independent duplication of findings, verifies an emergent truth. And that truth is simply that the "relational" power of which Foucault and Parsons speak undermines the *whole* foundation, both liberal and Marxist, of the classical representation of power. This, at least, is the implication of the "four refusals" of the Marxian, and I now add, liberal, subordinations of power.[18] To these I now turn, *seriatim.*

The Refusal of a "Representational" Power: The theorizations of Parsons and Foucault converge, at first, in a common refusal to grant "regulatory" priority (and here I do not mention *critical* or *ontological* priority because these have also been refused as the categories of the classical discourse on power) to the mode of economic production in the relationship of power and capital. Foucault has said of the Marxian conception of power that it is premised on an "economic functionality of power." This economic functionality presents as the condition of possibility of power that it serve simultaneously to maintain "relations of production and . . . class domination which the development and precise forms of the forces of production have rendered possible."[19] Or, as Foucault says in "Power and Norm: Notes," power is to be freed "from the notion of subordination . . . from the idea that power is a definite type of

maintenance, continuation or reproduction of a mode of production
. . . which is always prior, if not historically, then analytically."[20]
Parsons, of course, long precedes Foucault in the refusal to make
power representational of an economic mode of production and, behind that, of an originary class or of a founding act of individual self-
interest. For Parsons, power is to be liberated from its dependency
on an economic *logique* precisely because the constitution of modern
society around a silent "order of cybernetic control" (relations govern content, information regulates energy) situates the "power system," not as a subordinate of economy, but as *constitutive* of labor
and capital.[21]

    The Refusal of a "Distributive" Power: Foucault severs his per-
spective from the traditional viewpoint that power is a finite commodity—an "appropriation" or a "possession"—that can be taken
out of circulation with the intention of reducing the total amount of
power available to be distributed. Power is to be freed from the prison
house of the commodity form, that is, from ". . . the theoretical
scheme of appropriation . . . the idea that power is something that
is possessed—something that definite people possess—something that
others do not possess."[22] Against the "commodity conception" of
power, Foucault insists that power is the name (we will return to his
nominalism) that one ". . . attributes to a complex strategical situation in a particular society."[23] And against the viewpoint that power is something that is "acquired, seized, or shared, something that
one holds on to or allows to slip away,"[24] Foucault speaks of power
as a multiplicity of force relations and of their struggles and confrontations which, sometimes forming a "chain or a system," find embodiment in the "state apparatus, in the formulation of the law, in
the various social hegemonies."[25]

    In much the same way as Foucault, but with a theoretical rigor
that is "technical and positive," Parsons also refuses to ground the
play of power in a discourse that insists that power be envisaged as
something hierarchical, fixed, and determinate in its quantity, an object finally of appropriation and possession. To Foucault's image of
the "complex strategical situation" of power, we might counterpose
Parsons' refusal of a "zero-sum conception of power."[26] Over and
against the classical liberal conception of power as the "capacities of
a man," Parsons insists that the condition of possibility of power is
that it be de-individuated (having a "collective," not "individual"
reference) and that it produce "bindingness" (he sometimes says
"diffuse social solidarities") across the "social community." In what
catastrophe theorists would describe as a perspectival drama, Parsons

refuses a distributive conception of power (". . . who has power and what sectoral interests he is serving with his power")[27] in order to speak of power as a "generalized, symbolic medium of exchange": in short, to say of power that it is a *language* and not a possession.[28] In his reflections on the secret that was to be disclosed by the disciplinary power of Bentham's *Panopticon*, Foucault mused, in "The Eye of Power," that the ascendant quality of power today is that "it is a machinery which no one owns."

The Refusal of a "Sovereign" Power: Parsons and Foucault have not transgressed the limits of representation and distribution, these nodal points of the classical discourse on power, only to fall back into the comforting explanandum of the juridical model of power. The fateful "chopping off of the head of the king" also meant that power was freed of its exclusive relation to law, to the juridical discourse, in order to enter society (to act, in fact, as a condition of possibility in the creation of the "disciplinary society") under the mythic, and almost benign, form of the "normalizing discourse" of the human sciences. This negation of the classical association of power and sovereignty is really the decisive line of demarcation between a "relational" and "combinatorial" conception of power (the "threshold of modernity") and the now obsolete interpretation in which power could finally be localized in a fixed, almost reassuring, model of stratification and hierarchies.[29] Sovereignty, the actual person of the monarch or, now, of the State, was taken to be the limit, even at the elemental level of life and death, of power-relations: sovereignty was thus considered to be constitutive of, rather than constituted *by*, the relations of power. For Foucault, the juridical model of a sovereign power is relative to the classical age of the West: a history in which power was exercised "mainly as a means of deduction, a subtraction mechanism, a right to appropriate a portion of the wealth, a tax of products, goods and services, labor and blood, levied on the subjects."[30] And what follows, of course, is that the juridical existence of sovereignty puts into play as its condition of possibility power as a fundamental "right of seizure." The great model of sovereignty does not place in question the "biological existence of a population"; it insists only on the right of the state to appropriate life as a way of "suppressing" it.[31]

And for Parsons equally, the juridical limitation on power is refused because it does not reflect the transformation of the basis of power away from its prior "localization" and "externalization" in the State apparatus, and toward its new presentation as a transparent "symbolic medium of exchange." In an awful, but fully faithful, *technical* language, Parsons speaks of power as the "circulatory process" of any "collective system"; and he means by the collective system, not a fixed institution or structure, but really a mobile, disciplinary coherency—an imposed normativity—that is given to any of the relations of society.[32] Foucault says that power has escaped its localization in the institutions of the state, and is put into play now as a fluctuating series of discursive procedures in the regions of sexuality, the family, asylum, prison, hospital, and school. Parsons is probably the more radical in insisting that power does not now only take on the disguise of the norm, but conceals itself in the form of the *normativity* of health, knowledge, public morality, and even eroticism. Perhaps it is for this reason that Parsons claims that "theoretical knowledge" is the storm center of the contemporary age; and that theoretical knowledge is exercised now within a domain of clinical practices: medicine, penology, the "helping professions." But, ironically, the sequel to this conjunction of truth and power is that when the glorious day finally comes that Marxism manages to overcome its cranky bias against the "relative autonomy" of the State and liberalism succeeds in transcending a constitutional interpretation of power, the locus of power will have already taken flight from its juridical basis; and from the sites of the languages of sexuality, of health, of technology, it will glance back, laughing, at nostalgic mentalities which insist that that which is itself constituted by power (the state) be mistaken as a site for the constitution of power.

The Refusal of Power as an Order of Prohibitions and Transgressions: Following in the tragic sense of Nietzsche, rather than in the *laicisme* of Marx, Foucault has reflected that power is tolerable "only on the condition that it mask a considerable part of itself."[33] For Foucault, and for Parsons, the paradox of the way in which power comes into play is simply that the great order of prohibitions and transgressions, the eternal "no" that stands in front of and outside of human discourse, represents, not the essence, but the necessary failure of power. Parsons states this new "truth" of relational power most clearly when he writes that "force, rather than being the characteristic feature"[34] is, in fact, a special limiting case of the deployment of power. Coercion, this most manifest of the order of prohibitions and transgressions, represents the regression of power to a lower domain of generalization: the prohibition, backed up by even the most magisterial "show of force," is the emblematic sign of the failure of the *symbolic* currency of power. Do we need to recall that for Parsons the "freedom" that is put into play as a result of the transformation of the "nature" of power (from a bureaucratic to a cybernetic power) is not our liberty, but this strange and terrible freedom of *power to power* (or, as Heidegger said, the "will to will"). Little wonder that Parsons can say with such equanimity that the language of power appears now not only in the form of "compulsory suppressions" but also of "permissive order."

And Foucault follows this register of truth by noting, and this paradoxically, that power is "negation," as a "pure limit set on freedom" is, perhaps, the "general form of its acceptability." The existence of prohibition makes power bearable by setting a limit on the incarceration of desire. To establish the limits of transgression is also to suggest that there is a tiny space left for the play of human freedom. And, of course, Foucault with resigned melancholy and Parsons with melancholy resignation theorize that the great, and almost sacred, order of negations and compulsions operates now only as a deflection, a path around, the empirical functionings of the power apparatus. Foucault maintains that power "that counts" is typified by positivity and helpfulness; and Parsons says that the "sanctions" that matter are not those of the open "refusals" but the strategies of inducement and persuasion that are the signs of ideology, but also of a whole range of "normalized discourse." In the midnight sun of domination, power is no longer limited to the drawing of the blood of appropriated *and* exteriorized subjects. There is no elegant simplicity of "binary opposition," of the struggle between master and bondsman, which, after all, always had the easy merit of preserving *both* terms of the relation. The modern discourse of power absolves the old, comforting dualisms ("activity-passivity," "rulers-ruled," "center-margin")[35] in favor of a power experience that situates symbol and effect as mirrored images of one another. Power can appear in the disguise of seduction, because it is first a discipline; and it maintains a surface disguise of punishment because *its* freedom depended on the overcoming of its disciplinary threshold.

Yes, A Fascist Power

The classical discourse of power has been undermined by that most insidious and irreproachable of opponents: a profound, sudden, and irreversible transformation of the historical mode of constitution of power. The "analytical realism" of Parsons and the "analytics of power" of Foucault respond to a common truth: it was not, in the end, the ideological recriminations leveled against one another by socialism and liberalism, these political expressions of the classical economy of power, that brought to its conclusion the representational theory of power.[36] No, it was something more fundamental and sin- ister. And this was, simply stated, that unnoticed in the clash of per- spectives between the great, worldly "power systems" (which took up, and loudly so, as their justificatory ideologies and as their ener- gizing contents the political economy of a class that was absolutized as the "universal class" and, on the other side, the liberation of an "individual" who was constituted through a system of property rights), there was taking place the ascendancy and universalization of the *medium* of power itself. That the developing, real autonomy of power (in opposition to the historical regime of ideology—the his- torical nucleus of classical discourse) as the new capital of twentieth- century experience went relatively unnoticed may have been because its presence was first apparent, not in the surface play of warring contents, but at the level of structure; not in its empirical effects, but in the form of symbolic exchanges; and not in the struggle of ideology, but in the language of procedure and mediation. And who knows that it was not without some embarrassment that the advo- cates of the classical ideologies of the age of capital (yes, organized socialism and institutionalized liberalism) realized one fine day that beyond the false appearances of ideological discord, they were bound together in a common discourse—a discourse of a power that operated now in the life-form of relationality and symbolic exchanges? And who can say that these same gangsters, realizing that skepticism could only be hidden by the administration of universal terrorism, did not also acknowledge that by a trick of fate they were the shifting, pro- visional "content" (I would say "controllers," but who is really in control of the "mirror of politics"?) of a power that needed to have its functions, its conditions of possibility, embodied in human speech?

The language of power, transparent, mediational and contentless, stands at the end, not at the beginning, of civilization. For to the *history*, and thus to the substance, of civilization, the modern dis- course on power reveals only a void, a "dead power" (Baudrillard). And why? Perhaps because on the dark side of power, the side in which power has no existence as a representation, there remains only a power that is put into play as symbols without founding referents. Yes, a fascist power. And a fascist power specifically in the sense that Baudrillard in "Forgetting Foucault" speaks of fascism as a "simulta- neous resurrection effect" of a dead power.[37] "As the violent reac- tivation of a form of power that despairs of its rational foundations (the form of representation that was emptied of its meaning during the course of the nineteenth and twentieth centuries), as the violent reactivation of the social in a society that despairs of its own rational and contractual foundation, fascism is nevertheless the only fascinating modern form of power."[38] Fascism remains a politics that reenacts the "ritual prestige of death"; and this because it is the truthsayer (an "eternal inner simulation") of power, which is (as those who have sought to capture finally its representations have discovered) ". . . never already (*jamais déjà*) anything but the sign of what it was."[39] A fascist power, of the left and of the right, is encouraged to play itself out at the thresholds of life and death (the trajectory that moves from nuclear politics to genetic engineering) because the *void* that is Baudrillard's "dead" power is a pure instrumentality without signification. The loss forever of a founding subject, of signification, also means that fascist power must commit its fate to the amnesic language of formalism (and, quite appropriately, semiotics makes its appearance as a Gregorian Chant of a *structuralist* power).

Foucault and Parsons are explorers of the new topography of fascist power: a power that displays its symbolic effect in a discourse that ranges from the language of "macropower" (the sociology of cultural functionality) to that of the "micropowers" (the "verification" of sexuality, penology, health norms). It is not at all from the same perspective that Parsons and Foucault witness the birth of fascism as the secret of modern power. Indeed, their images of power are *reverse images* of one another; and to shift from the "macropower" of Parsons to the "micropower" of Foucault is to move, as if in a tiny catastrophe of perspective, from the background to the foreground, from white to black topography, in an Escher painting. But still in this swift, silent change of perspective, from the foreground of Foucault to the background of Parsons, there remains a continuity of vision, a common morphology, in which the play of fascist power is traced back and forth from its deep assumptions to its practical manifestations. And it might be said that the perspectival reversal of Foucault and Parsons in these reverse but mirrored images of the same continent of power intensifies the resulting description of the power apparatus.

Thus, Parsons approaches the "problem" of power from the viewpoint of "institutionalized liberalism,"[40] a new ideological formation that shifts the center of power from the "possessive individual" to the "freedom" that is to be found within "positive social organization." By contrast, but still in an almost morphological relation of similitude, Foucault addresses the play of micropowers within the dark underside of these very same "positive social organizations." And Foucault reveals that Parsons' "institutional freedom" is the unrelenting domination of a society that seeks to install a normalizing discourse across human experience. Foucault is the interlocutor of the actual strategies and tactics by which the "technical and positive" power of institutionalized liberalism is put into play as a "circulating medium": one which resists localization in the name of "generalization" and which, finally, circulates through the social body, not as an end, but as a "symbolic effector."[41]

To read Parsons and Foucault *against* one another (but also on the basis that we are in the company of *the* polarities of the same discourse on power) is to travel simultaneously down both sides, or really to oscillate from foreground to background, of a common discursive understanding of power. What, after all, could be a greater clash of perspectives, yet more entangled in a common truth, than the convergence of Parsons' image of the "societal community"[42] as the outcome of the new biology of power and Foucault's haunting description of the "disciplinary" society? Parsons always defended the societal community as the locus of "diffuse enduring solidarity,"[43] and he maintained that the societal community (a new type of collective formation that superseded class, individual, nation) was a product of an "institutionalizing" discourse that wedded politics and the biological canon. Foucault writes of the conjunction of power and truth (the truth, that is, of power's claim to speak on behalf of the social species) that it would be more accurate now to consider society, not as a penal system, but as a disciplinary system: "that is . . . a society equipped with an apparatus whose form is sequestration, whose aim is the constitution of labour-power and whose instrument is the acquisition of discipline and customs or habits."[44] Foucault's "sequestration" is the parallel, but reverse, image of Parsons' "diffuse enduring solidarity"; and to the "institutionalization" of the societal community, he provides the mirror of the "normalizing" society. ". . . (T)he apparatus of sequestration fixes individuals to the production apparatus by producing habits by means of a play of compulsions, teachings, and punishments. This apparatus must manufacture a behaviour that characterizes individuals, it must create a nexus of habits through which the social 'belongingness' of individuals to a society is defined, that is, it manufactures something like the norm."[45]

From an appreciation of the "societal community" (benign and monotonous, almost a fantasy of the managerial ethos, in its technical and positive play of power) as the foreground of the "disciplinary power," everything follows. The circulation of power which, being "contentless," poses continuously, and almost teasingly, the challenge of "simulated recoveries" can be resurrected at the level of a "macrophysics" of power (Parsons) or in the language of "micro-physics" (Foucault). The circulatory medium of power can be explored in its interiority (what is actually said about sexuality, about the medicalization of madness) or in its exteriority (Parsons was, after all, an *analytical*, not an empirical, realist). Or the mirror of power can be reflected in its production of discursive knowledge. Foucault says, with anguish, that what gives power its vitality, "what makes it accepted, is quite simply the fact that it does not simply weigh like a force which says no, but that it runs through, and it produces, yet induces, pleasure; it forms knowledge (*savoir*), it produces discourse; it must be considered as a productive network which runs through the entire body much more than a negative instrument whose function is repression."[46] And, to this, Parsons might respond that, yes, power is a "specialized language"; but it is also a language that is *regulatory* of that matrix of exchanges that takes place (everywhere) between normativity and the play of empirical variations.

The "Power System"

That Parsons and Foucault represent complementary, although opposite, phases in the "strange loop" of modern power is of more than suggestive importance. Over and beyond their shared and explicit "refusals" of the Marxian subordination, they have also "discovered" four secrets about the ways in which fascist (normalizing) power now constitutes itself. We should not be surprised to learn that the "will to will," this emblematic sign of a power that is "limitless" precisely because it no longer has the responsibility of representing real existence (ontology), presents itself now in the discursive form of the "power system." Foucault reminds us that the "power system" is not to be thought of as an institution or a structure, but rather as a complex strategical intervention by which power is set in sway across a "multiplicity of sites."[47] And Parsons notes that the power system is a "fluctuating medium" which is not only capable of inflating and deflating its extensiveness, but is also the disenchanted currency that mediates the relations of *all* parties to the human discourse.

This is, after all, a power that resembles in its operation more the model of the computer (with its programming, relays, transmissions, and encoding of language) than the classical symbol of the machine; a power, that is, that is no longer a matter of fluid mechanics but of the "field" of electronics. While the classical conception of power coincided, and perfectly so, with the birth of bureaucracy (*distributive* power being the power that could be doled out, controlled, or

92 □ ARTHUR KROKER

even saved within the great schemata of a hierarchical administrative rationality), the modern discourse of power complements the development of "technocracy." For in substituting managerialism based on professional knowledge for "line authority," and in setting in play a conception of power that has as its limit and possibility the "management of life," technocracy carries forward the modern discourse of power. But this is only to say, of course, that the "power" that circulates as the life-force (and why not be frank and simply confess, as the blood of the social body) is *not* the same power as that which was always held in bondage by the classical discourse. For the classical discourse, from Hobbes to Marx, could never escape the representational theorization of power.

The representational image of power always insisted on taking power out of play (or, perhaps, on removing the threat of power) by displacing its mediational qualities into the surface play of its effects. At work was an eternal reduction that limited the power of power to manifestations of interest, ideology, psychological "drives." This may have simply been the classical rumblings of ontology, or perhaps of history, at work; but, in any event, we know that everyone present at the feast of classicism had a strong, almost proprietary, interest in maintaining the illusion that power could be localized, perhaps in the state, but at all costs could, most certainly, be safely incarcerated. This is such an apparent characteristic of the classical discourse (a "world-hypothesis" shared by all ideologies) that we might say now that the great struggle over capital (which everyone took to be the sign of materialism) was really a last defense of history and, thus, of ontology against the coming liberation of an (ahistorical and de-ontologized) power.

If it is strange to think of Adam Smith as the last of the ontologists, then it is at least as peculiar to consider Kant, and most certainly not Marx, as the precursor of the modern discourse. This, at least, is the radical implication of the modern discourse on power summed up in the image of the "power system." There is now only the silence of non-recognition between classical and modern power. The classical interpretation of power, because it was representational, always held open the promise of freedom *in* ontology, and sometimes *against* history. But the modern presentation of power, because it *begins* with the abandonment of representationalism (which was also the space of "otherness"), speaks of a New World of power that is unrelentingly deterministic. This is a power that is *transparent and mediational* rather than representative, *normalizing* as opposed to prohibitional, and *regulatory* rather than critical. Or, to put this another way, the power system is a confluence of four secrets: power now justifies itself through appeals to a biological metaphor; it combines with theoretical knowledge in producing a normalizing discourse; the "field" of power relations is experienced as a "circulating medium" of symbolic exchanges; and power has as its political effect the creation of a technocracy that makes "authority" prescriptive.

The Discovery of Power and Life (the Biological Metaphor): The primary line of theoretical convergence between Parsons' and Foucault's images of the power system lies in their mutual recognition that power now justifies itself on the basis of an appeal to a biological ethos. Of this radically new realignment of power and biology, Parsons says: "My own present view is that the theoretical logic of social science theory should be closer to the Mendelian than to the Newtonian model."[48] Of course, for Parsons there was in the sound of this new combination of politics and biology ("with its endless reshuffling of qualitatively distinct units")[49] only the comforting sign of a final "coming home" to his first discipline, the study of biology. And while he is careful to say that the relationship between the *gene* and the *symbol* (between the "system of cultural symbolic meaning" and "genes in biological heredity") is only an *analogous* relationship (and this in the "structural" sense), he also notes that the regulative function of power is to mediate the genetic constitution of the species (yes, that gray region of "normative culture") and the "phenotypical organization of organisms" (history).[50] The appeal to the biological ethos thus makes the "management of life" both the condition of possibility of power and the categorical imperative of politics. It is, indeed, a change of profound magnitude when power invests life, for this indicates that just as nothing escapes life, without being a threat to life, so also nothing may evade power without representing a menace to the claim of power to speak on behalf of the species. The "therapeutic" investiture of medicine, education, labor, and sexuality is, consequently, central to the task of the power system in making the biological norm of a "healthy society" prescriptive.

Parsons is explicit about the theoretical impossibility of separating power from life, or of discussing the "regulatory" functions of power outside of the biological discourse. Thus, for example, he follows the geneticist Alfred Emerson in remarking on the similarities between the genetic reproduction of the species and the social "requirements" for the reproduction of the societal community. And he says with Ernst Mayr (in *Population, Species and Evolution*) that there is an explicit analogy between the properties of biological communities and those of the societal community: the "reproductive community" is like the "population" of the societal community; "territorial community" is analogous to a "politically organized society"; and the "genetic community" is structurally similar to "common culture."[51] Thus, on the basis of analogy (but then Parsons always replaced concrete action with *analytical* action), the genetic canon of the natural species is transcribed onto the level of the human species. In a theoretical rupture that is surely equal to the naming of a "possessive" power in Hobbes's *Leviathan*, Parsons equates the relationship of gene and phenotype (the biological canon) with the order of relationships between normative culture and its environment (the social canon). In both instances, it is a matter of producing a discourse that will mediate, or should we say *regulate*, the relationship between the genetic heritage of the social species and the limitless play of practical existence. And the discourse that will produce this active mediation of symbol and effect will be that of a normalized (institutionalized) society.[52]

Foucault has done nothing else really than to account, after the fact and in a tragic and elegiac prose, for the consequences that follow the alignment of power and life into a common discourse. What can Foucault have meant, after all, when he said in *The History of Sexuality*: "The mechanisms of power are addressed to the body, to life, to what causes it to proliferate, to what reinforces the species, its stamina, its ability to dominate . . ."?[53] Foucault follows the "Copernican Revolution" of Parsons by noting that when the "technologies of power" invest life, then power itself speaks to "both sides" of the discourse. For this is an age in which the strategies of "adaptation to the species" and the practice of "social eugenics" upon the "body" and the "population" replace the warring dualities (always safely externalized) of the classical discourse. For when Foucault can say that sex now becomes "a crucial target of a power organized around the management of life rather than to the menace of death,"[54] then he has also recognized that power now wagers itself on the possibility of overcoming finality.

The Discovery of Power and Normalization: The biological canon makes culture constitutive of economy by reversing the order of control between the realm of symbolization and material signification. Parsons and Foucault achieve a second ground of "consent" to a relational power when both can say that the conjunction of power/life releases in its wake a dense matrix of "micropowers"; a presentation of power not under the awesome sign of the state or of economy, but under the more banal sign of the lowly *norm*. Thus, Foucault describes the discourse "that will accompany the disciplinary power

[as] that which grounds, analyzes, and specifies the norm in order to make it prescriptive."[55] And Parsons replies, observing always from the side of the technical and positive play of the power system, that "institutionalization [Foucault's "normalization"] is like natural selection."[56]

The secret that is revealed by the association of power with the production of normalized discourse is that "truth" itself is drawn within the discourse of modern power, and that a precise and dramatic line of convergence is established, not only between power and truth, but really between the triumvirate of life/power/truth. The constitution of truth (the establishment of normativity in health, education, labor) becomes both a condition of possibility for and an object of the (biological) ethos of life-management. The epistemological region of truth/falsity is thus drawn into a fateful parallelism with health/disease, life/death, knowledge/ignorance, labor/unemployment, and realism/utopia. Who might have known that the lowly norm, this small play of micropower, would constitute itself as an epistemological division between truth and error that, in an endless *mirrored* effect, would rebound and amplify into a series of exclusions, prohibitions, and divisions at the levels of axiology, esthetics, necessity, and politics. Small wonder that the policing of the Gulag and of the "positive social organizations" of the West is done in the name of "verification." For what is verified is political loyalty itself; and thus, in a small but momentous step, the epistemological norm (truth/error) is made convergent with the political norm (loyalty/disloyalty). Foucault says of the political strategy effected by the conjunction of power and the will to truth: "Modern humanism is . . . mistaken in drawing the line between knowledge and power. Knowledge and power are integrated with one another, and there is no point in dreaming of a time when knowledge will cease to depend on power . . . it is not possible for power to be exercised without knowledge. It is impossible for knowledge not to engender power."[57] In the silent "shuffling and reshuffling" of possibilities for normativity, the truthful becomes the real, the real becomes the desired, and the desired, the manageable *for life*.

And how could it be otherwise that Parsons is not the more explicit on the significance of normalization as the procedural logic by which a line of convergence is established between the mirrored images of cultural heritage (symbol = gene) and the phenotypical (the *Ding an sich*) level of organisms? Following in the therapeutic mode, Parsons notes that "living systems" require a code or a program ". . . and another set of symbols which implant the genetically given pattern at the phenotypical levels in organisms."[58] For Parsons, power serves now as the "language" that mediates the sphere of cultural practices (the genetic code of authority) and the multiplicity of sites (exigencies) that are to be invested by the will to truth. It is surely a sign of an Orwellian "vaporization" of sensuous experience that Parsons is then to say, in words that are dull and chilling in the revelation of a fascist power, that institutions are ". . . complexes of normative rules and procedures which, either through law or mechanisms of social control, serve to regulate social action and relationships."[59] The sounds of history recede, the struggles of warring ideologies abate, and what is left is, again and again, the quiet "shuffling and reshuffling" of all contents through the regulatory procedures of institutions. In the Mendelian politics of normalization, a radical structuralism is installed in which all "events are evacuated of their contents." And is it not the radical structuralism of the normalizing discourse, this center of fascist power, that Foucault describes, wearily now, as the "apparatus of sequestration," creating only the "social *belongingness* of individuals to a society . . ."?[60]

   The Discovery of Power/Language (a Limitless "Circulating Medium"): But what is the center (the degree of ontology) of this power system which, in a mimicry of natural life, produces its disciplinary effects through a set of discursive practices that are, to be sure, always rooted in the will to truth? To the insistent demand for an ontological grounding for power, Foucault replies, almost laconically, that the secret of power is its transparency: "power in the substantive sense, *'le' pouvoir*, doesn't exist. What I mean is this. The idea that there is either located at or emanating from a given point something which is a 'power'. . . ."[61] Beyond the great binary divisions of society and beyond even the "locus of great Refusal," there exists a "network of power relations" that ends by "forming a dense web that passes through apparatuses and institutions, without being exactly localized in them. . . ."[62] It might be said that Foucault consents to the exclusively "relational" character of power relationships, and thus theorizes a power that is not exterior to other relationships ("economic processes, knowledge relationships, sexual relationships") but, rather, *immanent* in the interplay of "nonegalitarian and mobile relations." Thus, much as in the tradition of radical empiricism (one end of pragmatism), Foucault postulates a "power experience" that, in its condition of possibility and in its practice, both encircles the "subjects" who are drawn into the power network and, moreover, as a certain "field of force relations," always manages to evade localization in the terms (caste, class, group, individuals) that it mediates.

And, as might be expected, the power experience is intimately linked with the production of discourse; for it is "discourse which transmits and produces power" and it is the analysis of the specific productions of discourse that reveals the exact relationship that holds between power and knowledge (the shifting curvature of normativity). A microphysics engenders a field of micropowers; and this play of micropowers cannot be located in the search for "general unities" but is discernible only in the interstices, the fissures, of the power network. And between the actual experience of micropower (at the level of sexuality, penology, the family) and "macroscopic" institutions, there is not a relationship of causality or simple dependency, but "analogical" relationships that draw together the center of "authority" and its range of prescriptive practices.

It would not be inaccurate to state that Foucault's opaque way of circling around and around this decentered power is an almost crude description (and a nonspecific one) of what Parsons has already described as a "generalized, symbolic medium of exchange." What Foucault alludes to, sometimes under the rubric of "the rule of double conditioning" or of "the rule of the tactical polyvalence of discourses," Parsons describes as the constitution of power in the modern regime as a "circulating medium" without limit. For Parsons, the secret of the "power network" is that power circulates now (always immanent to but never localized in) through the societal community (or, inversely, the "disciplinary society") like a language, and much like those other languages that are disenchanted symbols— money, intelligence, health, influence, and value-commitments. Power has its own grammatical-syntactical structure, its own specific codes (authority), and its own "symbols of effectiveness." Thus, those who would search for the historical originary of power will be disappointed; for power operates now, not in the name of representation, but always as a *symbol of effectiveness*.[63] In a description that is remarkably convergent with Foucault's insight into the relational character of power relationships, Parsons also posits that the power network is a circulatory medium, and one that is relational and combinatorial in character. The power system is combinatorial to the extent that the magnitude of the power network can be expanded or contracted, inflated or deflated from the sites of power itself. And power is relational because it is "dead" in itself; and has now value only in exchange: the production of social "belongingness"; the "authoritative" legitimation of rules governing contractual agreements in the economy; the translation of health norms into prescriptive practices.

The Discovery of Power/Technocracy (The "Transcendental

98 □ ARTHUR KROKER

Deduction" and the New Class): There is a final moment of theoretical convergence between Parsons' and Foucault's interpretations of power as a circulating medium. And this is simply that the "regulatory" functions of the power network (the production of rules governing the use of power; that is to say, how the norm is to be made prescriptive) are embodied finally in a *professional* ethos that is carried forward by a new class—really a class that acts as the verifiers of the norm. Parsons always insisted that "professionalization was at the center of modern societies"[64]; and for the same reasons he noted that the swift emergence of "theoretical knowledge" also meant that the *cognitive complex* was becoming a central aspect of the societal community. For Parsons, power could safely pass from its ground in "individualistic liberalism" to the domain of a "circulating medium," specifically because the conversion of power into a symbolic language opened up possibilities for a full normalization of society. When power is conceived as a "specialized language," it reveals a new possibility for the social species to be "governed" within the invisible and formal "regulator" of cybernetics itself.

And this entails, of course, that in the new power system, "information controls energy" in much the same way that the "code of authority" governs the actual mode of operation of political practice. Cybernetics in conjunction with language theory discloses the real methodology by which a normalized society will be produced. Cybernetics introduces the division between "rules of use" and "empirical situations," between, that is, procedures (programs) high in information and practices (deployments) high in energy—this old division between reason and existence—as the radically new condition of possibility of the power system. And language theory (in the sense of a grammatical-syntactical structure that contains codes and symbolic effectors) provides for the "embodiment" of cybernetics in the actual play of the power network. For power to be a language that is limitless (because it is always deployed in exchange, not in use), it must first have as its condition of constitution a structure of grammatical-syntactical rules (authority) that may be wagered at the practical level in a struggle that is no less serious for being always symbolic.

It is, finally, the discourse of *professionalism* that embodies the discursive logic of the power network. In the professional ethos, there is to be found the governing idea that power should speak now, not in terms of transgressions and prohibitions, but really on behalf of life. Carrying forward into practice the biological metaphor, the professional complex serves to define, to administer, and to verify the implantation of the discursive practices of normativity. Thus, Parsons can say that after the industrial and democratic revolutions there was another, and this time less visibly turbulent, revolution; this was a "cognitive" revolution that centered on education itself.[65] And Foucault can say: "The discourse of the king can disappear and be replaced by the discourse of him who sets forth the norm, of him who engages in surveillance, who undertakes to distinguish the normal from the abnormal; that is, through the discourse of the teacher, the judge, the doctor, the psychiatrist, and finally and above all, the discourse of the psychoanalyst."[66]

The deployment of the normalizing discourse as the center of the power network is, in its practice, dull and prosaic. At work is a power that does not gambol with mythical discourse, but simply a power that expresses itself in the normalizations of the human sciences. And, of course, what is at stake in the normalizing strategies of the human sciences and, by extension, in a developing technocracy that also prides itself on being a major site for the deployment of "theoretical knowledge," is the management of the technical, procedural logic of the societal community itself. The logic of the human sciences has also become the discursive practice of the power system — because the power system ultimately needs its programmers and decoders; because it, too, requires that power take on the appearance of the norm and that the norm be presented as nothing more sinister than managerialism itself. What this indicates, perhaps, is that the new class of "technocrats" — the famous membership of the "helping professions" and of the technical intelligentsia — may be the practical embodiment of a power that finally works by abolishing the *Ding an sich* and by instituting in its place the "bad infinity" of a shifting normativity. The question that remains, however, is whether the Gulag and the disciplinary society are exceptions to the *positive* discourse of normalization or emblematic of a power system that, based on the logic of the "bad infinity," is also condemned to the bad destiny of a fascist power.

The Image of Prison and the Prison of the Image

It is likely, I would conclude, that the reverse, but parallel, visual imaginations of René Magritte ("Black Magic," "The Lovers," "Discovery," "La Clef des champs," "La Mémoire," "Ceci n'est pas un pipe") and Edward Hopper ("The Secret") provide an intense expression of the relationship of Parsons and Foucault on the question of power. To migrate from Hopper's melancholy realism to Magritte's lament on a nameless power is an almost identical movement of thought to that other migration: the shift in perspective, but not essential identity, from the positive domination of Parsons' societal community to the negative truth of Foucault's disciplinary society. In his wonderful commentary on the secret of Bentham's *Panopticon*, Foucault has remarked that the modern prison, understood as the centering point of the epistemology of discipline, has radically reversed the principle of incarceration.[67] In contrast to the traditional (or should we say *classical*) order, where transgression (in the symbolic form of the prisoner) is excluded into the darkness of the cell, the modern *Panopticon* reverses the order of imagery. The jailer, in his central citadel, watches in darkness; and what he observes across the circular courtyard of the carceral are prisoners who are brought, not fully into light, but into the light that makes of the prisoner a silhouette. The absurdity, and yet transparency, of this new form of domination (the prisoner who is reduced to the universal form of the "silhouette" and the jailer who is also incarcerated in darkness) symbolizes that nameless, relational power that has been meditated upon, in reverse but identical ways, by Parsons and Foucault. And I might wager that it is possible, just possible, that in the almost serpentine twisting of Parsons and Foucault as they confront one another across the space of a common, but reverse, image of power, they, too, are locked together like jailer and prisoner in the modern *Panopticon*.

Perhaps in the next century another poet may have the insight to say of Foucault what Octavio Paz has remarked, in our times, of Sade:[68]

> *Prisoner in your castle of crystal of rock*
> *you pass through dungeons, chambers and galleries,*
> *enormous courts whose vines twist on sunny pillars,*
> *seductive graveyards where the still black poplars dance.*
> *Walls, things, bodies, reflecting you.*
> *All is mirror!*
> *Your image persecutes you.*

NOTES

1. Michel Foucault, *Madness and Civilization* (London: Tavistock, 1967), p. 274.
2. Jean Baudrillard, "Forgetting Foucault," *Humanities in Society*, 3:1 (Winter 1980), 87. Baudrillard begins with the important insight that Foucault's discourse, representing as it does a "mirror of the powers it describes," constitutes not a discourse of truth, "but a mythic discourse in the strong sense of the word."

3. Talcott Parsons, "Some Problems of General Theory in Sociology," in *Social Systems and the Evolution of Action Theory* (New York: The Free Press, 1977), pp. 229-69.

4. Talcott Parsons, "Social Structure and the Symbolic Media of Exchange," in *Social Systems and the Evolution of Action Theory*, pp. 204-28.

5. Michel Foucault, "Truth and Power," in Colin Gordon, ed., *Power/Knowledge* (New York: Pantheon, 1980), p. 114.

6. Karl Jaspers, *Kant* (New York: Harvest, 1962), p. 96.

7. *Ibid.*, p. 98.

8. Michel Foucault, "The Discourse on Language," in *The Archaeology of Knowledge* (New York: Harper Colophon, 1972), p. 217.

9. Michel Foucault, *The History of Sexuality. Volume I: An Introduction* (New York: Pantheon, 1978). p. 151.

10. See, in particular, G. W. F. Hegel, *The Phenomenology of Mind* (New York: Harper Colophon, 1967), pp. 207-13.

11. Emile Durkheim is perhaps the first modern theoretician of "normalization" and, for this reason, Parsons and Foucault commonly locate the "regulative" conception of power in his analysis of normativity.

12. Baudrillard, "Forgetting Foucault," p. 108.

13. Foucault, *The History of Sexuality*, p. 217.

14. An excellent description of the "will to will" is to be found in Michael A. Weinstein, "Lament and Utopia: Responses to American Empire in George Grant and Leopoldo Zea," *Canadian Journal of Political and Social Theory*, 5:3 (1981), 44-55.

15. For Parsons, freedom is a correlate of "institutionalized individualism." Advanced liberalism differs from the classical doctrine of liberalism by severing the question of freedom from its basis in "individual capacities" and, in turn, transforming freedom into a matter of "choices" within positive social organizations. A "relational" power also is aligned with a freedom that is dead.

16. Foucault, *The History of Sexuality*, p. 95.

17. Talcott Parsons, "On the Concept of Political Power," in *Politics and Social Structure* (New York: The Free Press, 1969), p. 353. Parsons' theorization of a relational mode of power begins with this essay, which provides the basis for his later development of a complete theory of the "family of generalized, symbolic media" as the mediational points of advanced industrial societies.

18. An insightful, although overly sociological, collection of readings by and about Foucault's theorization of power is provided in Meaghan Morris and Paul Patton, eds., *Michel Foucault: Power, Truth, Strategy* (Sydney: Feral Publications, 1979). For an explicit discussion of Foucault's four refusals, see "Power and Norm: Notes."

19. Foucault, "Two Lectures," in *Power/Knowledge*, pp. 88-89.

20. *Michel Foucault: Power, Truth, Strategy*, p. 59.

21. Parsons, "The Relations between Biological and Socio-Cultural Theory," in *Social Systems and the Evolution of Action Theory*, p. 120.

22. Foucault, "Power and Norm: Notes," in *Michel Foucault: Power, Truth, Strategy*, p. 59.

23. Foucault, *The History of Sexuality*, p. 93.

24. *Ibid.*, p. 94.

25. Foucault writes in *The History of Sexuality*, p. 93: "The analysis, made in terms of power, must not assume that the sovereignty of the state, the fear of the law, or the over-all unity of a domination are given at the outset: rather, these are only the terminal forms power takes." Foucault's meditation on a "relational" power is strikingly similar to William James's theorization of a "relational" consciousness. At a moment far earlier than Foucault or Parsons, James anticipated the decline of the "entitative" (Newtonian) model of the social

universe and the emergence of a radical relationalism as the basis of epistemology, politics, and ontology.

26. Parsons, "On the Concept of Political Power," p. 353.

27. Ibid.

28. Parsons, Social Systems and the Evolution of Action Theory, pp. 204-28.

29. Parsons, Politics and Social Structure, pp. 356-59.

30. Foucault, The History of Sexuality, p. 137.

31. Ibid.

32. Parsons, Politics and Social Structure, pp. 387-95.

33. Foucault, The History of Sexuality, p. 86.

34. Parsons, Politics and Social Structure, pp. 365-66.

35. Michel Foucault: Power, Truth, Strategy, p. 60.

36. The "analytics" of Foucault and Parsons reflect their common deployment of a discursive rather than intuitive logic. Parsons says, in fact, that the logic of teleonomy is nomic rather than nomological. Nomic propositions imply a "putative necessity" in the domain of social relationships and are the epistemological sign of a "deductive-propositional" system of human action. Foucault also says that the power system appears in the form of a deductive-propositional system, and that we might best proceed nominalistically, by naming the concrete expressions of power. Thus, while nomological thought is the analogue of the Newtonian sciences, nomic thought is the epistemological epicenter of the biological model.

37. Baudrillard, "Forgetting Foucault," p. 110.

38. Ibid.

39. Ibid.

40. For Parsons, the central element of institutionalized liberalism is that it is typified by the public morality of "instrumental activism." The public ethic of instrumental activism makes the maximization of the generalized symbolic media of exchange—money, power, influence, value-commitments—the "regulatory idea" of advanced liberal societies. This entails, of course, that the standards by which normalization is governed and its immanent value-principles are linked together as complementary aspects of the maximization of the transparent and relational media of exchange, these conditions of possibility, of modern society. In the discourse released by the "morality" of instrumental activism, there is now only an absence, a void, that seeks to be filled by any energizing content. I do not think that Foucault is mistaken when he says of structuralism that it evacuates the concept of its content, but he might also have remarked that the turn to this empty region of sign and signification is a reminder of the death that inhabits, that pulsates from, the decentered surface of modern life.

41. Or, as Foucault states:

Now, the study of this micro-physics presupposes that the power exercised on the body is conceived not as a property, but as a strategy, that its effects of nomination are attributed not to "appropriation," but to dispositions, manoeuvres, tactics, techniques, functionings; that one should decipher in it a network of relations, constantly in tension, in activity, rather than a privilege that one might possess. Discipline and Punish: The Birth of a Prison, trans. Alan Sheridan (New York: Pantheon, 1977), p. 26.

42. Parsons, Politics and Social Structure, pp. 41-55.

43. Parsons, Social Systems and the Evolution of Action Theory, pp. 366-88.

44. Michel Foucault: Power, Truth, Strategy, p. 64. Foucault's basic essay on the unity of power/knowledge in a society of normalization is to be found in "The Carceral," in Discipline and Punish, pp. 293-308.

45. Michel Foucault: Power, Truth, Strategy, p. 65.

46. Ibid., p. 36.

47. Foucault, *The History of Sexuality*, p. 93.

48. Parsons, *Social Systems and the Evolution of Action Theory*, p. 134.

49. *Ibid.*, p. 133.

50. For a full description, see Parsons, "The Relations between Biological and Socio-Cultural Theory," pp. 118-21.

51. Parsons, *Social Systems and the Evolution of Action Theory*, pp. 110-11.

52. For Parsons' most complete statement of this process, see "A Paradigm of the Human Condition," in *Action Theory and the Human Condition* (New York: The Free Press, 1978). pp. 352-433.

53. Foucault, *The History of Sexuality*, p. 147.

54. *Ibid.*

55. *Michel Foucault: Power, Truth, Strategy*, p. 66.

56. Parsons, *Social Systems and the Evolution of Action Theory*, p. 220.

57. *Power/Knowledge*, p. 52.

58. Parsons, *Social Systems and the Evolution of Action Theory*, p. 120.

59. Parsons, "Social Structure and the Symbolic Media of Interchange," in *Social Systems and the Evolution of Action Theory*, p. 207.

60. Foucault and Parsons converge on the claim that "something like belongingness" is produced by the play of power. Parsons views belongingness as the attribute of "diffuse collective solidarities," while Foucault envisions it as the positive side, the reverse image, of the code of punishments typical of disciplinary power.

61. Foucault, "The Confession of the Flesh," in *Power/Knowledge*, p. 198.

62. Foucault, *The History of Sexuality*, p. 96.

63. Parsons' most significant, but also least noticed, theorization of a "relational" society is found in *Action Theory and the Human Condition*. In this collection of essays, Parsons traces out fully the implications of the theory of the symbolic media of interchange for such newly appropriated regions as health, disease, intelligence, and affect. Always, the movement is against a representational logic and toward a "symbolic" understanding of the play of modern power. In *Discipline and Punish*, Foucault also notes this extension of the *nomos* of a symbolic power in saying that now punishment is not of a different order from education and health.

64. Parsons, "The Professional Complex," in *Action Theory and the Human Condition*, pp. 40-45. Parsons' analysis of the "professional complex" is convergent with many of the assumptions behind Alvin Gouldner's reflections on the "new class." Parsons views the professional class as the ascendant class in advanced industrial societies. This is a new social class that is drawn together by its common foundations in theoretical knowledge, fiduciary responsibility, specialized competence, technical solidarity, and the use of symbolic capital. The development of the "professional complex" is the organizational expression of Foucault's normalizing society.

65. Parsons, "The University Bundle," in *Action Theory and the Human Condition*, p. 136.

66. *Michel Foucault: Power, Truth, Strategy*, p. 66.

67. Michel Foucault, "Panopticism," in *Discipline and Punish*, pp. 195-228; and "The Eye of Power," in *Power/Knowledge*, pp. 147-65.

68. Octavio Paz, "The Prisoner (Hommage to D. A. F. DeSade)," *Early Poems 1935-1955* (Bloomington: Indiana University Press, 1973).

Chapter 6
The Paradigm of Language:
Wittgenstein, Lévi-Strauss, Gadamer
György Márkus

It is increasingly recognized that two prominent trends have brought mid-twentieth-century academic philosophy into rather sharp contrast with its immediate and more remote predecessors: the *antisubjectivist* turn and the *linguistic* turn. The first comprises a rejection of the conceptual framework of both traditional, seventeenth- and eighteenth-century metaphysics (commerce between the given, individual subject and the world of natural objects, regulated by laws of nature "indifferent to man") and epistemological theories constructing and "constituting" the world of objects out of the isolated subject, be it empirical or transcendental. Philosophical reflection now tends to start, not from the alleged certainty of some form of individual consciousness, but from the fact of *intersubjectivity* understood as intercourse and commerce between finite and historical individuals—an intercourse that, in one or another objectified form, outgrows these individuals, determines them, and carries them along.

It is symptomatic that Descartes, the father of "modern" philosophical subjectivism, the hero of the Enlightenment, now becomes the main villain of the piece for such very divergent thinkers as Ryle

This essay has been abridged by the editor from a longer article available in German. See György Márkus, "Positivismus und Hermeneutik als Theorien der Objektivation," in Ernst Bloch, ed., *Marxismus und Anthropologie: Festschrift für Leo Kofler* (Bochum: Germinal, 1980). English translation by John Fekete and the *Telos* editorial group.

and Heidegger. And it is notable that this change occurred with a relative suddenness, on one hand, and pervasiveness, on the other. At the beginning of this century, the various "subjectivist" conceptions (neo-Kantianism, positivism, pragmatism, Husserl's early phenomenology) still completely dominated the scene of philosophy. The comprehensiveness of their rejection, meanwhile, is best illustrated by the very evolution of those among the above-mentioned trends of thought that survived at all: e.g., by the history of positivistically oriented philosophy of science as it moved from the frank subjectivism of Mach and the "fundamentalist" and constructivist approach of the early Vienna Circle to Carnap's later, pragmatistically motivated acceptance of the irreducible postulate of intersubjectivity (from "Testability and Meaning" on), and then to Popper's theory of "objective" knowledge or Kuhn's insistence on the sociohistorical character of the basic paradigm of science.

The second, the much more often emphasized *linguistic* turn, comprises the rejection of the earlier dominant (especially in empiricist epistemologies) quasipsychological ways of argumentation and genetic-psychological method of constitution, and their replacement by an argumentation from, or on the analogy of, language. The way in which language became central for the methodological self-understanding of philosophy itself is well known—one need only add that this transformation also had a more widespread character than is usually realized. This again can best be seen by reference to the evolution of philosophical tendencies that originally stood rather far from this whole problematic, e.g., the development of German existentialism from Heidegger's *Sein und Zeit* to the "philosophical hermeneutics" of some of his followers.

While these two trends had different sources and distinct intellectual genealogies, at mid-century they became interlocked into one characteristic, broad structure of thought that can be defined through the fact that in it language and linguistic communication became considered as the *universal paradigm* of all forms of human intercourse and human objectivation. Language, accordingly, is treated, not simply as the central or even the sole remaining subject matter of philosophical inquiry (as in early logical positivism and analytical philosophy), but as the starting point and orienting model whose employment makes it possible to recapture and re-embrace in a meaningful way the metaphysical, anthropological, and social concerns of traditional philosophy.

In what follows I propose to examine comparatively the place of the language paradigm in the "therapeutic philosophy" of Ludwig

Wittgenstein, the structuralism of Claude Lévi-Strauss, and the hermeneutics of Hans-Georg Gadamer. In order to provide suitable frames for that comparison, it is useful first to contextualize it by retracing certain strategic moves in the history of the philosophical discussion that concerns us here. It is clear that Hume's ideas signified a decisive break in the history of bourgeois thought. It was his unsparing critical analysis of knowledge and social life that transformed the great aspiration of the early Enlightenment into its opposite: the Enlightenment endeavor to demolish the transcendent validity of norms and values and to establish man as their sole source and creator gives rise, in Hume's philosophy, to a consciousness of the mere subjectivity of all norms and the impossibility of their rational justification. Positing goals worthy of human beings thereby ceases to be a task of reason. Reason, it is concluded, can at most determine the means through which the anthropologically given and socially modified "passions" may be adequately satisfied; it is, and ought only to be, "the slave of the passions." And reason shows itself dependent, a function of an "irrationality" not only in its practical, but also in its theoretical use: in Hume's analysis of induction, the basis of all causal-empirical knowledge is discovered in a psychological mechanism, in a "custom" that cannot be vindicated rationally.

It is worth noting here that what Karl Popper and others have seen as Hume's irrationalism—the latter's deep skepticism concerning the possibilities of reason—was actually Hume's awareness of that unavoidable *loss of value* that is involved in the reduction of reason to a mere means, in its degradation to an instrumental goal-rationality. Hume still knew that this conception of reason—which his penetrating criticism shows to be an inevitable consequence of the basic presuppositions of the Enlightenment itself—means bidding farewell to the best dreams of humanity, formulated in the great ideal of the Enlightenment about men determining their own fate by their own deeds. His was the position of a deep, resignative disillusionment, with the result that his system constitutes not only a part and parcel, but in a sense the consummation, of the philosophy of the bourgeois Enlightenment: the recognition of its limits within the ideological and conceptual framework of the Enlightenment itself. By contrast, paradoxically, it is Popper's positivist identification of human reason with goal-rationality, in his persistent effort to rehabilitate the *same* reason whose fragility and irrationality Hume had already laid bare, that makes a final break with the Enlightenment when he questions and denies not only the *realizability* of the great utopias about the man- and history-forming power of a human reason transcending the limits of instrumental rationality, but the very *value-character* of this ideal (as clearly attested in his joint criticism of Plato, Hegel, and Marx).[1]

From the very beginning, with the Kantian distinction between "technico-pragmatical" and "pure practical" reason, German classical idealism attempted, facing the challenge of Hume, to formulate a new idea of reason, based primarily on the *practical* relations between men. Fichte's conception of *Tathandlung* pointed for the first time to *human activity* as that *tertium datur* in relation to which the strict, Humean opposition of facts to norms collapses. And the Hegelian utopia of the self-realization of absolute spirit at least formulated the idea (though in a deeply contradictory fashion) that it is neither the *subjective insight* into the transcendental legitimacy of already given values, nor the *choice of optimal means* for the realization of given goals, but rather the progressive, *practical-historical creation* of a world of values, embodied in human relations, that constitutes the essence of human rationality.

It is this tradition of German idealism to which (though with a stoical awareness of crisis) the "first" hermeneutics culminating in Dilthey is linked. Of course, already in Dilthey's work, the practical problems of historical progress are replaced by questions concerning our adequate theoretical (and therefore contemplative-individual) relation to history. Nonetheless, Dilthey still sees the ultimate function of a "historical consciousness" to be the liberation of the individual from particularity and from the limitations of those goals and values that appear as "natural" under the given, historical conditions. His whole method of "understanding" is designed to make other historical worlds intelligible to the individual, to let him experience the infinite, value-creating energy of life, and thus to form in him through this process of cultivation (*Bildung*) a free and humanistic moral attitude.

The "second" hermeneutics, found in the later philosophy of Heidegger and, especially, in H. G. Gadamer, starts from a compelling critique of the naive presuppositions of this "historical enlightenment"—above all, from criticism of the belief that it is possible to transcend the perspectival character (*Standortgebundheit*) of thought through purely theoretical acts and thereby to find an "adequate," neutral standpoint over and beyond history. At the same time, already in this criticism and also in the whole model of thought underlying it, this narrowly conceived new hermeneutics shows some essential structural similarities with certain other tendencies of contemporary thought, which appear at first to be quite alien to its problematic.

K. O. Apel and Jurgen Habermas have already brought to light this structural link between the philosophies of Heidegger and Gadamer, on one hand, and the later Wittgenstein, on the other. I want to draw out another parallel concerning the structuralism of Lévi-Strauss.

I do not mean to suggest that there is an "essential" identity between these modes of thought. The focal point of Gadamer's hermeneutics is the historicality of *Dasein* conceived as temporality. This whole problematic of historicality lies beyond Wittgenstein's conceptual framework. Lévi-Strauss's structuralism, on the other hand, is precisely an attempt to transcend this historicality by finding invariable, structural interconnections that would constitute the constant and "natural" basis and presupposition of all historical change. The link between these disparate views is to be found in a single, but crucial, relation: in all of them, *language as language* (and not, as in Popper's "three worlds" theory, for example, linguistically formulated *logical content*) appears as the *paradigm and model of social objectivation.*

The differences in the approaches work themselves out in terms of differences in the ways these thinkers understand language itself. At the center of Wittgenstein's analysis are the irreducible differences between linguistic functions, the various pragmatic models of the use of language. For Lévi-Strauss, who in this regard follows Saussure, language in general means only that homogeneous system of relations conceived as a unified structure that lies behind the particular speech acts understood as purely individual, psychological phenomena. Finally, for Gadamer, language is the continuous "occurrence" (*Geschehen*) of dialogue, i.e., of interpersonal understanding and transmission of tradition, which makes up our *Dasein* and our history. But, in spite of these drastically different interpretations, there is a common starting point: the relation of man to his world is understood as analogous to the model of language. This common starting point accounts for crucially important theoretical and ideological agreements among these philosophies.

The traditional argument of hermeneutics against positivism was based on a sharp distinction drawn between natural and sociohistorical phenomena. Natural events and processes are indifferent to the goals and intentions of men. This implies that even the conceptualization offered by the cognitive subject is only externally related to the object known. Of the practically infinite number of true (and general) descriptions applicable to a complex state of nature or to a natural event, the most valuable to science are those that can be incorporated into the most comprehensive and prognostically most fruitful network of nomic relations. The correctness of an interpretative description, an answer to the "what?" question, therefore depends on the value of the causal-functional explanation, on the answer to the "why?" question. However, in the case of historical phenomena—as Dilthey explicitly states, referring to Vico's famous dictum—the subject and object of knowledge are essentially of the same character. History is the result of goal-setting human activities which, as such, carry with them an inherent *meaning*. Causal explanations of human activities and their results have a cognitive significance only insofar as they concern this effective meaning of the explicandum rather than its "accidental" determinations. "Explanation" is here a function of interpretative understanding.

It is characteristic of the entire "first" hermeneutic from Schleiermacher to Dilthey that this inherent "meaning" of social activities and their products is identified with the *subjective, psychological intentions* of the acting subjects. The methodological problem of the hermeneutic "understanding" *vis-à-vis* "explanation" in the natural sciences becomes therefore transformed for these thinkers into the question of how it is possible to elevate the reenactment of alien mental states to the level of a universally valid scientific method. Toward the end of his life, Dilthey realized the problematical character of this psychologistic way of posing the question. However, his attempts to proceed in other (sometimes even contradictory) directions, though undoubtedly insightful, did not lead to a coherent answer.

The significance of Wittgenstein's later works from the standpoint of hermeneutics is to be found above all else in the fact that, through an analysis of language use, he mercilessly destroyed this psychologistic theory of meaning (together with its complementary, the platonistic conception of meaning that played a large role in neo-Kantian conceptualization of the *Kulturwissenschaften*). The critique of these two views constitutes the starting point of Wittgenstein's later philosophy. His own solution—the tentative identification of "meaning" with "use"—may at first suggest some kind of naturalistic pragmatism. This impression disappears as soon as one realizes that he does not identify use with any act of behavior describable as a natural event. Rather, he sees it as something that is inherently either right or wrong. The concept of "use" presupposes the concept of a rule and, therefore, with respect to use, "every prescription can be understood as a description, every description as a prescription."[2]

The meaning of a word within a language is constituted and determined by the "grammatical" rules of this language; something can be a word or a sentence only if it is a component of that rule-directed activity called language. The notion of a rule presupposes the possibility of *mistake* and, consequently, criticizability by others; the observance of a rule is only possible as *public* behavior, a *practice* (put differently, a custom or an institution). The rejection of the possibility of a "private language" means not only a critique of the fundamental presuppositions of subjectivistic theories of knowledge; it also implies a definite interpretation of social reality and of human life. Rules are possible only in regard to repeatable, "external"-social activities that are carried out in identifiable situations. However, the reverse is also true: the tremendously complicated and incessantly changing constellations of external conditions that arise in the course of human life, and the concrete acts of behavior within them, *become* identifiable and recurring "states of affairs," definite "situations," and kinds of social activities only through, and in respect to, definite rules—because only the rule contains the criterion of their identity. "The use of the word 'rule' and the use of the word 'same' are interwoven."[3] Language is social activity in the world; at the same time, it is also the form of objectivation through which both "world" and "human activity" became first constituted. This insoluble unity of linguistic rules, objective situations, and social modes of action, Wittgenstein calls a "language game." Language games are the primary data, "Ur-phenomena" of human, social life: the *normativity* of concrete linguistic rules, "existing in the world," is a final irreducible *fact* of human life.

A language game is a form of life, or as formulated elsewhere by Wittgenstein, "an entire culture,"[4] a definite form or fragment of practical-social reality that constitutes a unity from the viewpoint of the pragmatic function of language use. Wittgenstein stresses the principle of the plurality of language games: every one participates in several and can acquire in principle any of them. This acquisition of language games is, however, an eminently *practical* process ("the mastering of a technique"), guaranteed only by *participation* in the appropriate form of life. *Understanding* the meaning of some social action (including that of an act of language use) does not involve a reenactment of the intentions of the agent; generally it designates neither a mental state nor a purely theoretical performance; it is essentially a practical activity. It means the establishment of a practical-communicative relation with the actor, the adoption of his "form of life," a participation in his culture (completed perhaps only in fantasy).

By disclosing the social-practical character of human understanding,

Wittgenstein attempts to indicate the inherent limits of understanding as well as those of conscious social praxis. Rules of a language game *eo ipso* contain the criteria for their application. They make possible the judgment as to whether the verbal and nonverbal performances within the given "form of life" are correct or incorrect, true or false, good or bad. However, criticism must always remain relative to the context of a given language game. Only the *intersubjective* rules of a language create the possibility of developing *subjective* beliefs and opinions, critical or uncritical. Of course, reform of a language (in terms of some restricted practical end, e.g., improvement of terminology to avoid misunderstandings) is always possible. What is not possible, however, at all, is a critique of a language game (i.e., a form of life) as a *totality*. Either one plays a game or one does not; either one participates in a "culture" or one does not, and this according to the conditions of one's life and one's needs. In the course of life and history needs change, and so does culture: ". . . new types of language, new language-games, as we may say, come into existence, and others become obsolete and get forgotten."[5] However, one can never have as a meaningful goal the conscious, rational creation of a form of life in its totality. This possibility is excluded because there are no absolute evaluative criteria independent of the context of *some* language game; to "criticize" a language game means only that we participate in an alternative one and therefore simply do not understand the first "language."

This "lack" of absolute criteria is not an empirical fact but a consequence of the "grammar" of the concept of "criterion." Since it is completely senseless to seek such criteria, it is also senseless to assert their nonexistence. The rules and "paradigmata" of a language game are not only noncriticizable; they never can be made completely conscious—explicit in pure theory. Every linguistic articulation of the rules smashes against the limits of the language itself. *Either* the linguistic formulation expresses what is a norm as an empirical state of affairs *or* it expresses what is a fact of life as a conventional prescription; the *rule as a fact of life* can be adequately grasped and expressed only in the *practice of participation*. "Nonsense arises in the attempt to express through the use of language that which should be embodied in the grammar."[6] Forms of life as totalities understood as "language"—and, simultaneously, the totality of these forms of life—are radically impenetrable to conscious reflection. In interpreting practical, human relations paradigmatically as linguistic interactions, practice is conceived as *participation*, and as such establishes an insuperable barrier to theory.

For Wittgenstein, real rationality, as distinct from instrumental expediency, means therefore the self-criticism of reason, the recognition of its finitude. Philosophy as opposed to metaphysics has the task of cultivating the attitude of awakened spirit; through its practice, which constantly makes us remember the limits of language and understanding, it evokes a reverence for all manifestations of human life. "Here one can only *describe* and say: so is human life. . . . One would like to say: This and this event has taken place: laugh, if you can!"[7] The paradoxical conception of philosophy in the *Tractatus*— the saying of the unsayable—essentially returns in the *Investigations*, too, in changed form: this time philosophy becomes a pure and incessant activity which, however, "leaves everything as it is." Rationality becomes the self-prophylaxis of reason, a curb on its own senseless arrogance. "The philosopher is the man who has to cure himself of many sicknesses of the understanding before he can arrive at the notions of the sound human understanding. If in the midst of life we are in death, so in sanity we are surrounded by madness."[8]

The major unstated (and unstatable) premise of Wittgenstein's philosophy—the universality of the paradigm of language—becomes the explicit starting point of Lévi-Strauss's structuralism. The model of language provides, however, for Lévi-Strauss the answer to a question which, from the viewpoint of Wittgenstein, runs against the untranscendable limits of language itself. As an ethnographer Lévi-Strauss starts out from a problem-situation (and a concrete mode of experience) in which the task is to understand alien "cultures," foreign forms of life, *as alien*. It is the function of the ethnographer, who, in his very science, represents "Western," "industrial" civilization, to understand "primitive" societies and render them intelligible. To perform this task, he has to distance himself from the particular value judgments and patterns of thought that his own society spontaneously impresses upon him. The ethos of structuralism as represented by Lévi-Strauss is directed against the latent ethnocentrism of earlier ethnography.

However, this problem of the ethnographer is not solved by a reference to the fact that another form of life (another "language game") can, in principle, be appropriated through practical participation in it. The task of the ethnographer is not simply to step out of one society and enter another, so that he personally attains an internal experience of another culture. Rather, he must make this culture intelligible with a *universal validity*; and he must do this with the conceptual and methodological instruments of *his own* science. To accomplish this, he must stand simultaneously both *inside* and *outside* both the foreign culture and his own. This goal, moreover, has a peculiar touch of the tragic that makes it of practical (or at least moral) consequence. For the two cultures in question are not only different, they are also *inimical*. In his science, the ethnographer represents a society that in its practical effects undermines and destroys those very societies the understanding of which it posits as a theoretical goal.

One can actually understand "the dilemma of the ethnographer" as an implicit critique of Wittgensteinian "linguistic philosophy." The very formulation of the question shows that the attempt to transcend the limits of particular language games, to reflect on that which is "common" to all of them, is not merely a metaphysical claim, signifying an "idling" of language; it can also be a task connected with practical life situations. And if Lévi-Strauss believes that he can solve this problem by postulating a "structural analogy between different arrays of social facts and the language . . . which represents the social fact *par excellence*,"[9] in doing so he unwittingly illuminates the complex, multisided character of "language." Because this much is clear from the beginning: the conception of language that provides the solution to *this* problem must stand in sharp opposition to the Wittgensteinian conceptualization of "language as a social fact." The real interest, however, lies in the fact that despite these great differences in the starting point of the interpretation, the use of language as a kind of universal paradigm leads in both authors to similar conclusions.

One can conceive anthropological structuralism (especially in the early work of Lévi-Strauss) as an extension of Saussurean linguistic structuralism (with its binary pairings: signifier/signified, *langue/parole*, synchrony/diachrony) to the entirety of social life and social science. Since all social actions and their products carry with them an (objective) *meaning*, being meaningful and understandable at least to the members of the given community, it has to be possible, on this account, to comprehend all the forms, institutions, and objectivations of social life as "languages," as complex systems of signs. This means, however, that one can discover behind every cultural formation some abstract, universal, nonconscious structures, constituted by systematic relations among definite variables. The formation in question represents only an individual instance of these relations. As human, cultural universals, as invariants of social life, these systems of relations are products and projections of the nonconscious activity of "spirit," and in the last instance Lévi-Strauss relates them in a naturalistic manner to the universal structural characteristics of the human brain. This conception provides him with a positive answer to the problem of anthropological understanding. The nonconscious activity of spirit and the laws of this activity define that "third" which at the same time stands inside and outside both the foreign culture and one's own. From this vantage point a simultaneous distancing from and an inner reflection on both cultures becomes possible.

But the very fact that Lévi-Strauss extends the structuralist notion of language to the whole of social life introduces essential theoretical changes into the original (linguistic) conception. The first of these transformations concerns the opposition of synchrony and diachrony, of systematic states and merely factual history. Their methodological separation was originally explained by Saussure in terms of the peculiar nature of language. Its justification in the last instance rested with him on the fact that the history of the language is not given to, and does not exist for, the speaker. However, as soon as one stretches this dichotomy to the entirety of social life, it unavoidably takes on the character of a universal theory of history. If every "culture" is in its self-reproduction a "linguistic system" in the sense that it is one of the permissible combinations from an inventory of identical formal elements, then historical change is in principle nothing more than a new equilibrial arrangement of the same material constituted by a finite number of variables. The kaleidoscope metaphor of *La Pensée sauvage*, according to which the cultural "arrangements" are determined through the concurrence of some accidental events (the shaking of the kaleidoscope) and a law (the structure of the kaleidoscope), therefore illustrates not only the structure of the "savage" mind, but also the nature of history.

From this standpoint, the belief in historical progress appears as an expression of a presumptuous and aggressive ethnocentrism, and actual history becomes an "eternal return." "For millennia, man has been able to do nothing else but repeat himself," and "one must recognize that all societies represent a choice from among the possibilities open to human societies, and that these choices are incomparable since they are equivalent."[10] In this radical rejection of the idea of progress, Lévi-Strauss is in complete agreement with Wittgenstein (see the latter's polemic against Frazer's "evolutionism"). But the historical relativism of Wittgenstein follows from his insistence on the irreducible differences in principle among forms of life conceived as language games, differences that make any comparisons between them impossible. For Lévi-Strauss, the same result flows from exactly *opposite* premises, from the structural invariance that guarantees for him the theoretical comparability of cultures.

Even more essential is the transformation that the dichotomy of *langue-parole* undergoes in the theory of anthropological structuralism. Saussure interpreted this distinction in such a way that the *meaning* of a sign (as opposed to its formal linguistic value) was the result of interaction between these two levels of analysis. In principle, Lévi-Strauss attempts to generalize the same solution. So he emphasizes that the meaning of a linguistic or nonlinguistic structure is "on one hand, a function of history and the cultural context, and on the other, a function of the structure of the system in which it is located."[11] However, the claim of the structuralist method to universality precludes the implementation of this principle. Simply put, the method provides no way to comprehend "history" and "cultural context" except, again, as a "function" of the structure of the same "system," as one of its possible instantiations. Thus, the "real" meaning at the end becomes identified with the structural "position" occupied at the deepest, i.e., purely formal, plane. The initial concept of *langue* is thereby transformed: from now on it no longer delimits and articulates (in the sense of the laws of symbolic function) that which is in principle expressable, but it also contains all that is actually expressed. "Linguistics confronts us with a dialectical and totalizing being standing outside (or below) consciousness and will. As a nonreflexive totalization, language is human reason (*raison*), which has its own reasons (*raisons*) and which man does not know."[12]

From this perspective, Lévi-Strauss is fully consistent and justified in calling the unconscious (in its capacity as the common basis of language and culture and as the storehouse of the constraints that permeate the totality of social life) *spirit* (*esprit*). In spite of all its tendencies toward naturalism, the logic of the theory points to the inseparability of the expression and the expressed, to "a plane on which the objective and the subjective meet," to an insoluble and *unmediated subject-object identity*.[13] But since this identical subject-object of social life is seen as "nonconscious" and a "nonreflexive totalization," "spirit" appears to be the real subject of history, completely transcendent to the consciously acting individuals. This becomes immediately clear if one looks at the relationship of the conscious to the "unconscious" in the system of structuralism.

For Lévi-Strauss, the only adequate relation between "spirit" (the ahistorical, structuring principles of society) and the concrete individual is a purely "contemplative," theoretical one: ". . . the laws of unconscious activity are actually always outside subjective apprehension (we can of course be aware of them, *but only as object*)."[14] Since the notion of sociality is conceived already in the initial conceptualization of language as external *constraint* limiting individual activities, the subject-object unity can be grasped by the individual merely as (a theoretical) object. Every practical relation, in which the individual himself appears as subject, is inherently and necessarily distorted and inadequate. Practice means that the individual strives for the realization of a goal that acquires, therefore, an absolute meaning for him. But the *real* meaning of any goal is merely positional and relative—as determined through its position in the nexus of all the given goals in the given society. Thus, acting prevents the individual from reaching that universal human foundation through which he could understand himself and his society. The *actor* is always a prisoner of his own society, a mere instrument of external determinants unintelligible to him; when we conceive of ourselves as acting subjects, we are mere objects. When we produce change, "it is not dependent on our wishing or lack of wishing what we are compelled to realize by our situation."[15] The agent is in chains; only the spectator can be free.

Only insofar as we gradually transform *ourselves* into objects through acts of theoretical self-understanding do we become actual "subjects," conscious participants in the unconscious activity of spirit as the ultimate bearer of subjectivity. And, since understanding is possible only through the mediation of the unconscious, interaction and communication among individuals can be actual and authentic similarly only insofar as the ego becomes an object for itself. Accordingly, a communicative relation can exist only between "an objective *ego* and a subjective other."[16] Consequently, we find in Lévi-Strauss's critique of the present a rejection of both the "cult of action" in "modern" societies and the unequal and instrumental relations of domination that destroy all personal bonds among human beings. The two elements in this critique are inseparably intertwined, just as the privileged position of "primitive" societies is explained through the authenticity of reciprocal "communicative" relations and through the alleged fact that members of these societies experience and interpret their own actions as *occurrences* in a cosmic natural order. The peculiar ambiguity of structuralism—at least of the type represented by Lévi-Strauss—lies in what he wants to set as the *goal* of a new humanism: the attempt to find a "third," "which thinks in me and which lets me doubt whether I am it who thinks."[17] This goal, however, lends itself (contrary to Lévi-Strauss's intentions) much more to a *description* of an alienated consciousness, which has lost even the feeling of self-identity under the pressure of anonymous social relations, than to a program of its overcoming.

For Wittgenstein, it is through *practical* participation in a given, *particular* form of life as a "language game" that human rationality, the ability to judge actions and thoughts critically, becomes possible. This ability is always relativized to a given cultural system of rules as facts of life. Thus the possibility of theoretical reflection on individual language games as totalities as well as reflection on them in their entirety is necessarily excluded. In contrast, for Lévi-Strauss, real rationality is that *universal* that makes all societies and cultures instances of one and the same nonconscious structure. This universal is given by nature "unconsciously" in each individual. But individuals can participate in it adequately and consciously only by taking a radically theoretical and objectifying stance toward it. This necessarily excludes the possibility that any active practice, bound as it always is to the particular presuppositions of a given society, could in the deepest sense be rational. The opposing initial interpretations of language as a universal paradigm also have opposite theoretical results in Wittgenstein and Lévi-Strauss, but with one and the same practical-ideological effect: the negation of the possibility of a *practical critical* attitude toward a society as a *totality* and of a *rational* stance toward the entirety of social life. The ethos of the two philosophies —Wittgenstein's "reverence" (*Verehrung*) and Lévi-Strauss's "*pitié*" —exhibit a thoroughgoing affinity. This is by no means accidental: both thinkers conceive the relation of theory and practice, of society and individual, on the basis of the same abstract schema, the same "model," only with reversed value-signs.

These connections become still more evident if one compares Gadamer's hermeneutics. Gadamer interprets language as the universal paradigm of all forms of social interaction and objectivation just as clearly and explicitly as Lévi-Strauss. "All forms of human community of life are forms of linguistic community: even more, they constitute language."[18] But Gadamer objects to those (among them structuralist) views that see historicity as accidental to the essence and functioning of language and that identify the latter with a synchronous system of formal, structural relations. Such views neglect the "world-constituting" (one could say "objectifying") character of language; since they see the signifier-signified relation as arbitrary, they transform language into an instrumental, artificial system of signs: "the means of expression, which appear in a language in order to say certain things, are not accidental. . . . On the contrary, it is in this way that a definite articulation of the world is constructed."[19] Consequently, one cannot separate the linguistic form and the transmitted content from each other. The "original" meaning might seem to be superseded. However, each particular instance of the use of language is marked by a specific historicity that cannot be ignored without losing the real meaning of the expression. This moment of historicity, the self-constituting and developing life of language in dialogue—where "language has its true being . . . in the exercise of understanding between people"[20] —is the central interest of Gadamer's hermeneutics. It enables him to transcend the rigid and mutually exclusive opposition of particularity and universality present in both Wittgenstein and Lévi-Strauss.

Gadamer's characterization of understanding as agreement (*Verständigung*) with the other about the thing itself is in a sense analogous to the Wittgensteinian concept of the language game as the presupposition for the objectivity of meaning. But precisely because "the game of language is a performance of life" (in Wittgensteinian terminology, a form of life), Gadamer finds it impossible for the understanding to establish a "playful" (gamelike) suspension of belief concerning the *truth* of the presuppositions of either one's own or the other's standpoint. Understanding the other does not mean that one gives up one's own language game, by suspending the question about the truth of its presuppositions (regarded as in principle meaningless), and assumes that of the other. Rather, it means that in an actual or supposed dialogue one attains an interpretation of the truth of the other language in the language of one's own.

A linguistic relativism that sees the differences between particular languages, be they natural languages or their pragmatic units, i.e., "language games," as untranscendable limits, ignores the universality of human linguistic competence (*Sprachlichkeit*), even while this relativism itself presupposes that universality. The latter implies the *boundlessness of each particular* language, i.e., that "each one contains potentially within it every other one, i.e., everyone is able to be extended into every other one. . . . [T]he connection with language which belongs to our experience of the world does not involve an exclusiveness of perspectives. If, by entering into foreign linguistic worlds, we overcome the prejudices and limitations of our previous experience of the world, this does not mean that we leave and negate our own world. . . . The linguistic nature of our experience of the world is able to embrace the most varied relationships of life."[21] The reintegration of currently isolated forms of life into the unity and continuity of a linguistic, historical constitution of the world is just as much a central concern of Gadamer as is the demonstration of their nonreducible differences for Wittgenstein.

Hence, for Gadamer, just as for Lévi-Strauss, understanding presupposes something "common" between the I and the You. For him, as well, this common factor is to be found in a nonconscious sphere, in *"prejudices"* as relived traditions that dominate us and that constitute the prior orientation of our ability to experience and understand. But since the place of "nonconscious laws of spirit" is taken by prejudices, Gadamer goes beyond Lévi-Strauss's conception of a quasi-natural universal situated beyond history. Prejudices are not only alterable, they comprise the actual, historical character of our being. They give concrete expression both to our being thrown into a nexus of traditions that addresses us and to the perspectival casting of a horizon of our future possibilities on which this tradition is projected and which contains its meaning. The understanding of another or of a past culture is therefore not the result of an act of reflection that lifts us outside history but rather the result of actively positing ourselves within the workings of history.

This also means that the rigid opposition between theoretical and practical relations disappears. Understanding as a human relation to the world does not signify a purely theoretical activity — as in Lévi-Strauss, transforming the ego as far as possible into an object — in which the unconscious structural relations merely reveal themselves. The merging of the horizons that comprises the essence of understanding arises only when one relates to an "other" as to a "you," when one sets one's own prejudices to work, tests them against the truth of the tradition and, in doing so, changes them and oneself: "agreement concerning the object, which it is the purpose of the conversation to bring about, necessarily means that a common language must first be worked out in the conversation. . . . To reach an understanding with one's partner in a dialogue is not merely a matter of total self-expression and the successful assertion of one's own point of view, but a transformation into a communion, in which we do not remain what we were."[22]

In the end, however, Gadamer dissolves in a generalizing synthesis, rather than really solves and transcends, the one-sided positions found in Wittgenstein and Lévi-Strauss. The reason for this is to be sought in his conception of historicity itself as the uninterruptable continuity of temporality, "the actual duration of a constant present."[23] And this interpretation of historicity is clearly linked by Gadamer himself to the universalization of the model of language, to what he designates the "language event."

For Gadamer, the "common," i.e., that which makes understanding as the universal form of human interaction possible, is not participation in an effective nexus achieved through active and reflexive life relations. This nexus, that is, language itself existing in a continuous dialogue between the past and the present, is itself an *event* that the individual subjects do not complete; it completes itself in them. For language is not a conscious creation of self-reflecting individuals: "It is not just that the use and development of language is a process which has no single knowing and choosing consciousness standing over against it. (Thus it is literally more correct to say that language speaks us, rather than we speak it. . . .) A more important point is . . . that language constitutes the hermeneutical event proper not as language, whether as grammar or as lexicon, but in the coming into language of that which has been said in the tradition: an event that is at once assimilation and interpretation. Thus here it really is true to say that this event is not our action upon the thing, but the act of the thing itself."[24]

The methodological procedure of Gadamer's hermeneutics is very consistent. In his argument against contemporary "subjectivism," he unconvers the intersubjective relations hidden behind all relations of individual subjects to objects. He then represents these relations as dialogue, i.e., radically de-objectifies them (whereby all life-relations to the "traditions" of the past preserved in objectified forms become stylized as kinds of communicative contact with a You, necessarily acquiring moral overtones). At the same time, this subject-subject relation is represented as the "thing itself," the object, a fated event for the "encompassed" individuals. What arises in this way is not so much a subject-object identity as an ambivalent subject-object indifference that dissolves every objectivation only to appear itself as an object, except that "this object is not a factum brutum, not something that is merely at hand . . . but it is itself ultimately of the essence of There-being."[25] The hermeneutical program is therefore properly formulated as the inversion of the procedure of Hegelian *Phenomenology*: "we discover in all subjectivity the substantiality that determines it."[26]

Thus, in the end, there remains a basic similarity between Gadamer and Lévi-Strauss as far as the relationship between consciously acting individuals and the social relations limiting their possibilities (and comprising the substance of their lives) is concerned. They work with the same model, except that Gadamer interprets "social substance" not as a nonreflexive and naturally present, "given" totality, but as a continuous flow of life. What appears in Lévi-Strauss as the fixed, natural presupposition of human existence (in the historical as well as the logical sense) is for Gadamer an uninterrupted, self-reproducing result. Where Lévi-Strauss writes in the introduction to *Mythologiques*: "We do not pretend to demonstrate how men think in myths, but how myths think in men, behind their backs,"[27] Gadamer concludes

Truth and Method in the same way: "it is, rather, the game itself that plays, in that it draws the players into itself and thus itself becomes the actual subjectum of the playing. What corresponds to this in the present case is [not] play with language . . . but the play of language itself, which addresses us, proposes and withdraws, asks and fulfills itself in the answer."[28]

"In fact history does not belong to us, but we belong to it."[29] This view appears in Gadamer as an ontological consequence of human historicity and finitude. It is clear that on this basis it is not possible to separate objectivation and alienation from one another conceptually. To be more exact: from this viewpoint it is precisely the idea of "making" and "planning" history that appears as the negative utopia of transforming the whole human world into a thing, as the ultimate symptom of the "oblivion of being," of the alienation of contemporary human beings. If the understanding as the mode of being of human *Dasein* can be realized only in, and is produced by, the uninterrupted process of transmitting tradition, then every attempt radically to break the continuity of this process appears as both a utopian illusion and a grave danger to our human existence.

The historicity of our *Dasein* is concretized in the "prejudicial" structure of all understanding, and this historicity itself becomes an untranscendable limitation on historical consciousness. "Reason exists for us only in concrete, historical terms, i.e., it is not its own master, but remains constantly dependent on the given circumstances in which it operates."[30]

Of course, Gadamer does not deny the possibility and the historical function of a rational, conscious critique. In spite of his decidedly conservative stance and his efforts to rehabilitate tradition and authority, critique of former authorities is just as much a valid component of the process of tradition-transmission for him as the spontaneous appropriation and acceptance of that tradition. But critique can only be a mere moment in this process, "only a flickering in the closed circuits of historical life."[31] A critique of the totality of the tradition, a critique that attempts to give meaning and direction to this continuous, never repeating and, therefore, unplannable process of becoming, negates the presuppositions of our being human, of our historicity conceived as finitude. *Participation* in the uninterrupted span of dialogue (as the basis of human existence) makes it impossible to know the totality of its presuppositions or to change that totality consciously, just as participation in a language game makes it impossible for Wittgenstein. Contemporary metaphysics conceived as theoretical science becomes for Gadamer (and Heidegger) a mere form of appearance of the practical, historical danger involved in the "oblivion of being," in whose concept the rejection of capitalism (with its reifying "rationalism") and of socialism (conceptualized as an "anarchistic utopia") are merged in an inextricable unity.

This "romantic anti-capitalism," which appears in different ways in all of the three thinkers considered, represents at one and the same time a *continuation* of the great tradition of German classical idealism (the fight against the identification of human reason with pure goal-rationality), and a *rejection* of the animating ideal of this tradition (the idea of a community of free and conscious individuals who themselves determine their life through their own common and rational decisions and actions). This ambivalent attitude actually is extended to the entire tradition of philosophy. It is not by accident that one meets in all of these systems of thought with the slogan of the "end" of philosophy, of metaphysics, of humanism, and so on. The great task of all philosophy—to constitute a relation between Is and Ought, between facts and norms, a task seen by positivism as in principle insoluble and, consequently, as a pseudo-question—also appears as a pseudo-question from the standpoint of the "hermeneutical" views, but in an inverted way: not because it is insoluble, but because it does not require a solution at all—it is not a problem, but a facticity, an ultimate fact of our life.

On this account, the indissoluble unity of "facts" and "norms" comprises the fundamental character of the social, historical world, of our *Dasein*. This unity is "spirit" existing in reality as language, which for Gadamer is "the language of reason." Reason is actual (*wirklich*) and it is therefore impossible to counterpose reason to reality. The actual "natural" language of social intercourse, embodied in the given forms of life, in cultures, or in the moving horizon of the historical present, is the "language" in which the individuals can and do "express" themselves—and there is no such thing as an "ideal language" through which the adequacy of these expressions could be judged. Radical, social, or historical, self-awareness can only be a *description* and not a *critique*.

This self-characterization of their own philosophy, which we find in all the three thinkers concerned, stands, however, in collision with their critical stance (sometimes explicitly articulated, sometimes merely implied) toward the realities of contemporary social life. The ambiguous relation to philosophy conceals a critique of the present which—devoid of all perspective—tries to mask its own critical character as pure description; the "overcoming of metaphysics" is actually a helpless resignation. All these theories come up, therefore, against insuperable difficulties as soon as they are confronted with the task of self-reflection, of justifying their own claims to truth. In Wittgenstein, the description of language games itself presupposes a language game, but the possibility of such a comprehensive metalanguage as a separate language game is definitely excluded by the very conception of language implied. Hence, we find a self-characterization of his philosophy not as theory, but as activity, an activity however of mere "description," which therefore does not activate anything. In Lévi-Strauss this takes the aporic form of a declaration that every practical human relation is in principle inadequate, but at the same time the theory claims to constitute the foundation of a "new humanism" (paradoxically based on the thoroughgoing self-reification of man). Finally, the same difficulty is found in Gadamer's philosophy, which regards self-understanding as the mode of being of human *Dasein* and simultaneously hopes to overcome the horizon of this understanding by making it thematic.

I have attempted to point out certain essential, common characteristics of three views that share only one explicit theoretical premise: each sees linguistic competence (*Sprachlichkeit*) (although in decidedly different and partly even contradictory ways) as the real foundation of existence, and each finds in language the universal paradigm of all forms of social interaction and objectivation. And these three views seem representative and significant because their common conclusions do not spring from a misunderstanding of language but from an understanding of its nature. Three interrelated aspects of language are especially significant from this point of view.

The first concerns the problem of the "development of language." If "knowledge" (and especially knowledge conceived in the form of the natural sciences) is the most striking and at least intuitively most obvious example of *cumulative* historical progress (no matter how complicated it may be to account for this notion of "scientific progress" in the terms of a philosophy of science) and, for that reason, functions as the basic model for all positivist theories of social "evolution," then language, by contrast, constitutes a system of objectivation whose historical modifications do not exhibit any sign of cumulation. In its development we find no progression, merely change. In the history of any particular natural language one can occasionally find long-term tendencies, but it is impossible to demonstrate the existence of any general trend whose presence would characterize all languages or satisfactorily describe and explain the history of even one language. Consequently, there are no general evaluative criteria with the help of which one could order languages or their historical states in some "series of development," and it is not clear whether the supposition of such criteria makes any sense at all. All languages seem to be "equivalent" or equally "perfect," i.e., in all of them everything that the members of a given linguistic community wish to communicate under the given life-relations can be expressed. (At the same time, every natural language appears equally "problematical" and "inadequate" in this or that respect as soon as certain higher forms of cultural objectivation—poetry, philosophy, science— come into being.)

This property of language is undoubtedly connected with a second: linguistic changes are usually not the result of conscious activity designed to bring about these changes. They arise in the course of the productive application of given linguistic rules in spontaneous, unreflected ways. Encroaching on linguistic rules is not (even potentially) an expression of a critical attitude toward them; it results only in nonsense. There is no such thing as a critical relation to the system of rules of a given language. A language can appear "illogical" or unduly "complicated" only to one who has not mastered it. For the native speaker it is *transparent*. This transparency means not only that the language is "uncriticizable," but, also, that the system of linguistic rules is unexplicated in the everyday use of language. To acquire a language is nothing else than to acquire a competence for the creative application of rules (and since it is a question of rules, this involves also a competence to distinguish between correct and incorrect usage: the normal use of language naturally presupposes the possibility of critical reflection about the concrete linguistic performances of individuals). This in no way includes, however, an ability to explicate the rules in question. Not only is the average speaker generally not capable of this, but it constitutes a scientific task entirely outside the sphere of everyday life and commerce. ". . . A person is not generally aware of the rules that govern sentence-interpretation in the language he knows; nor, in fact, is there any reason to suppose that the rules can be brought to consciousness. Furthermore there is no reason to expect him to be fully aware even of the empirical consequences of these internalised rules."[32] Of course, the rules of a natural language can always be formulated within that language itself, but the "perfect" use and understanding of this language does not presuppose an awareness of the rules so formulated. The appropriation of language as the universal premise and foundation of all "theoretical" knowledge (knowing that) is itself the most typical example of "practical" knowledge (knowing how).

Transparency so conceived is also connected with a third aspect in the peculiar relation between the individuals who speak and understand the language and the system of linguistic rules. As a system of rules, language does not generally exist outside the concrete speech acts of concrete persons; independently of these acts, language has no objective, separate form (leaving aside here its existence in fixed "texts" first made possible through the historical development of writing as a secondary system of linguistic objectivation), although no practically specifiable series of speech acts would exhaust a language. In this sense language, as Humboldt says, is *energeia* (activity) rather than *ergon* (work). Its system exists primarily as the competence of the individuals to produce creatively and to understand meaningful sentences appropriate to their situation. In principle, and ideally, this competence is *equally* present in *all* members of a linguistic community. It is the virtual identity of the generative rules in the speaker and the listener that makes communication possible between them. "Communication is never comparable to the transmission of some material. . . . In the person who understands, just as much as in the one who speaks, the same thing must be developed out of his own, inner power. . . . In this way language is to be found in its entirety in every man. . . ."[33] The relation of an individual to the language is *participatory*, and the relations of individuals to each other are (from the viewpoint of linguistic communication) *symmetrical* and *integrating* relations based on common participation. Social relations understood as a system of communication necessarily appear therefore as an integrating totality, equally embracing all individuals and completely internalized by them all. Or, if the reflection is primarily directed at the factual multiplicity of languages (or linguistic situations), then the relations understood in this way appear as a finite but theoretically nonreducible series of totalities, independent of one another and "equivalent" (because incommensurable), simply existing next to one another.

In consequence, we need to raise a basic question: how far can one treat language as the paradigm of social objectivations, or linguistic communication as the paradigm of the relations of social interaction in general? This question is not satisfactorily answered by simply pointing to types of social objectivation that clearly exhibit structural and developmental characteristics essentially different from those of language, because the actual question concerns the meaning and significance these different kinds of objectivation have for human history. If, for example, we counterpose the views discussed to the Marxian understanding of *objectivation as production*, we find that the contrast involves not only a different "understanding" and "explanation" of history but also a difference in what is intended and meant when we speak of making history intelligible. It is not simply a question of which view better satisfies certain common criteria, but of *which criteria* ought to be satisfied by the general "philosophical" conceptualizations of human society and history.

All of these philosophies are *theories of objectivation*, i.e., attempts to give an immanent explanation for human life, to interpret exhaustively the variety and multiplicity of historical forms of life through human, social activities and the uninterrupted social appropriation of their results. This is precisely why all these views present philosophical "subjectivism" as the arch-enemy, which hypostatizes isolated, individual consciousness and its content as the ultimate source of certainty. The implication is that all these theories, in strictly epistemological matters, are "anti-idealistic." But the opposition between materialism and idealism can easily lead one astray—and especially in basic historico-social, nonepistemological aspects. Language, objectified knowledge, and work are nonreducible constituents and necessary elements of all forms of social life. No one of these can be taken as "primary" with respect to the others in terms of temporal precedence or logical derivability. Thus it is of necessity that the Marxian analysis of production explicitly and emphatically starts out from the *conscious* character of labor-activity and, consequently, implicitly presupposes also the existence of *language* as "practical consciousness, as it exists for other men, and for that reason is really beginning to exist for me personally as well."[34]

It might seem that one could speak of the question of "priority" to the extent that these different constituents of social life have distinct logical and theoretical importance for the explanation and/or understanding of society and history, i.e., with respect to the comparative "explicative power" of this or that "paradigm." For instance, one could thus say (using a rather common type of argumentation) that the "paradigm of language" offers no possibility for uncovering the causal mechanisms of historical change. That is to say, changes in a linguistic usage surely cannot be conceived in either a narrow or a broad sense as the basic determinants of social change. Rather, the opposite seems to be true: they are consequences and results of the most diverse and heterogeneous social changes, whose course is completely independent of them. The "paradigm" therefore gains its apparent plausibility from a dubious method of analogy that understands every social relation *ab ovo* as a form of language and by this very transposition in principle excludes the possibility of raising questions about the "causal" mechanisms of change, at least in a general form.

This argument, formulated here in the roughest manner, is valid in a certain sense but, at the same time, its role is rather to show up the shortcomings of using the notion of "priority" for formulating the basic elements of an intended critique. After all, it is only under certain practical presuppositions that the "theoretical inadequacy" posited and supposedly demonstrated by this argument turns out to be a deficiency at all. The general principle of linguistic-historical explanation, according to which the very application of a rule in ever new situations necessarily brings about, in the long run, a change in that rule, proves itself fully adequate and needs no theoretical supplement as long as one sees history merely as becoming, as pure *change*. This kind of "explanation" will prove inadequate only if we conceive of history as a *development*. Only then would it be meaningful to ask questions about the "causal" mechanisms that ensure this development or make it possible. However, the question of whether history is mere "change" or "development" is not simply a question about facts. Just as it is factually beyond doubt that there are societies whose history can in *certain respects* be described as a "development," so is it also beyond doubt that they exhibit other structural characteristics as well whose modification cannot be interpreted in terms of progress *vis-à-vis* prior periods or societies. And even this restricted notion of progress cannot be, in all probability, applied to every society in history. An interpretation of history based on the alternative of "change" or "development" depends on our *practical relation to the future*, and on the way in which we judge *our* "inherent" possibilities and their place in human history.

Even more generally: the epistemological analysis of the concept of "cause" reveals that this concept is related to the idea of *action*. The causal nexus as a nomic, necessary connection, different in principle from "accidental" universal concomitance, is bound to the idea that there are things that we can *do* directly, thereby giving rise to other things.[35] If we understand the connection between certain events as a causal nexus, we understand it in terms of possible (or at least conceivable) action. The apparently purely theoretical objection raised by the Marxist perspective against the language paradigm—that within its framework the question about the "causal mechanisms" of historical change cannot even be formulated—actually includes a practical demand for the kind of relationship to history in which man is not merely an observer or a suffering participant of historical process as fateful occurrence, but is, rather, the active and conscious co-creator of his own history.

The "practical materialism" of the Marxist viewpoint proposes that it is *now* possible for human beings, through their own conscious activity and according to their own ends, to change the entirety of their life conditions (whose basis is to be found in the sphere of production) in such a way that the history of humanity thereby *gains* the meaning of *human* development for the first time. The Marxian "paradigm of production" is beset, of course, by various difficulties of its own, as has been rather convincingly argued by a number of contemporary radical thinkers, from Habermas to Baudrillard. In this context, the contrast between the production paradigm and the variants of the language paradigm may perhaps help to clarify what is both practically and theoretically at stake in, and what should be accomplished by, attempts aiming at paradigm reexamination or revision.

NOTES

1. See Karl Popper's lifelong writings, especially the recent *Objective Knowledge: An Evolutionary Approach* (Oxford: Clarendon Press, 1972).

2. Ludwig Wittgenstein, *Philosophische Bemerkungen* (1930), ed. Rush Rees (Oxford: Basil Blackwell, 1965), II, 14. English trans. R. Hargreaves and R. White (Oxford: Basil Blackwell, 1975), II, 14. (The English translation from the German has been modified by the present author.)

3. Wittgenstein, *Philosophical Investigations* (Part I, 1945; Part II, 1947-49), ed. G. E. M. Anscombe and Rush Rees, trans. G. E. M. Anscombe (Oxford: Basil Blackwell, 1st ed., 1953; 2nd ed., 1958; 3rd ed., 1967), I, 225.

4. Wittgenstein, *Lectures and Conversations on Aesthetics, Psychology and Religious Belief* (1938), comp. from notes taken by R. Rhees, Y. Smythies, and J. Taylor, ed. Cyril Barrett (Oxford: Basil Blackwell, 1966), p. 8.

5. *Philosophical Investigations*, I, 23.

6. G. E. Moore, "Wittgenstein's Lectures in 1930-33," *Mind* (1954), 312.

7. Wittgenstein, "Bemerkungen über Frazers *The Golden Bough*" (1931 and later), ed. Rush Rees, *Synthèse* (1967), 236.

8. Wittgenstein, *Remarks on the Foundations of Mathematics* (1937-44), ed. G. H. von Wright, R. Rhees, and G. E. M. Anscombe, trans. G. E. M. Anscombe (Oxford: Basil Blackwell, 1956), IV, 53.

9. Claude Lévi-Strauss, "Religions comparées des peuples sans écriture," in *Problèmes et méthodes d'histoire des religions* (Paris: P. U. F., 1968), p. 6. This and all subsequent citations from the French are in the present author's translation.

10. Lévi-Strauss, *Tristes tropiques* (Paris: Plon, 1955), pp. 424, 416.

11. Lévi-Strauss, *La Pensée sauvage* (Paris: Plon, 1962), p. 74.

12. *Ibid.*, p. 334.

13. Lévi-Strauss, "Introduction à l'oeuvre de Marcel Mauss," in M. Mauss, *Sociologie et anthropologie* (Paris: P. U. F., 1950), p. xxx.

14. *Ibid.*, italics added.

15. *Tristes tropiques*, p. 415.

16. "Introduction à l'oeuvre de Marcel Mauss," p. xxxi.

17. Lévi-Strauss, "J. J. Rousseau, fondateur des sciences de l'homme," in *J. J. Rousseau* (Neuchatel: La Baconnière, 1962), p. 240.

18. Hans-Georg Gadamer, *Wahrheit und Methode. Grundzüge einer philosophischen Hermeneutik*, 2nd ed. (Tübingen: Mohr, 1965), p. 422. Hereafter cited as *WM*. In English, *Truth and Method*, 2nd ed. (New York: Seabury, 1975), p. 404.

19. Gadamer, *Kleine Schriften*, I (Tübingen: Mohr, 1967), p. 109. All translations from this text are the present author's.

20. *Truth and Method*, p. 404; *WM*, p. 422.

21. *Ibid.*, pp. 406-7; *WM*, pp. 424-25.

22. *Ibid.*, p. 341; *WM*, p. 360.

23. *Kleine Schriften*, I, p. 10.

24. *Truth and Method*, p. 421; *WM*, p. 439.

25. *Ibid.*, p. 232; *WM*, p. 247.

26. *Ibid.*, p. 269; *WM*, p. 286.

27. *Le Cru et le Cuit* (Paris: Plon, 1964), p. 22.

28. *Truth and Method*, p. 446; *WM*, p. 464.

29. *Ibid.*, p. 245; *WM*, p. 261.

30. *Ibid.*; *WM*, p. 260.

31. *Ibid.*; *WM*, p. 262.

32. Noam Chomsky, *Topics in the Theory of Generative Grammars* (Hague: Mouton, 1966), p. 10.

33. W. V. Humboldt, *Über die verschiedenheit des menschlichen Sprachbaues* (Bonn: Dummlers, 1960), pp. 64-65. Present author's translation.

34. Karl Marx, *The German Ideology* (New York: International Publishers, 1947), p. 19.

35. See, for example, G. M. von Wright, *Explanation and Understanding* (Ithaca: Cornell University Press, 1971).

Chapter 7
Structuralism and the Dislocation of the French Rationalist Project
Andrew Wernick

*There are no gospels which are immortal, but neither is
there any reason for believing that humanity is incapable
of inventing new ones.*

Durkheim, *Elementary Forms*

What is the meaning of enlightenment?
Have you finished your rice?
Yes.
Then wash your bowl.

Zen Koan

Lévi-Strauss's dismissal of dialectical reason as mythology, Althusser's repudiation of lived experience and subjectivity, Foucault's proclamation that Man (epistemologically speaking) is dead, and Derrida's deconstruction of ontotheology and logocentrism continue to challenge the capacity of any progressivist humanism to provide an adequate account of itself before the bar of the contemporary theoretical imagination. However, the very real difficulty of formulating a counterresponse at the substantive level has been complicated by what I would argue is a fundamental paradigmatic confusion that haunts the entire intellectual context in which the drama of the "structuralism controversy" has had to unfold.

Briefly put, it is a fateful contingency that the predominating categories of transformist thought have derived since left Hegelianism and by way of Marx from a characteristically German categorial mesh that originated from the fusion of an immanentized Protestantism with a historicized and scientifically updated neo-Aristotelianism and has been presided over for two centuries by the ghosts of Kant and Hegel. "Subject," "consciousness," "alienation," and "transcendence" are the trademarks of its discourse, and indeed circumscribe the outer limits of intelligibility for those who choose to communicate in it. French structuralism emerged against the background of a quite different tradition, and the polemic of the 1960s was itself directed as much against the most general metatheoretical features of the alien "German" *episteme* as against any particular humanist or emancipatory notions expressed in its terms.[1]

Under the circumstances, it is vital to disentangle structuralism's philosophical challenge to the particular idiosyncracies of the "German" *episteme* from its more substantive challenge to the reasonableness of a transformist perspective as such. Not to do so is to risk misidentifying the direction and character of the attack. Moreover, once we abandon the neo-Hegelian map and seek instead to understand French structuralism against the background of the metatheoretical formation from which it sprang, we are led to reflect that even more is at stake than the credibility of time-honored emancipatory categories.

The historical paradox of structuralism is that the reflections set in motion by Durkheim's and Saussure's turn to structure, synchronicity, and language have culminated in the past few decades not in the hypersystematized scientism critics of its reifying formalism might have expected but, rather, with the rise of post-structuralism, in a spiral of self-criticisms and decenterings in which the knowledge project that most proximately animated the original turn has itself been radically called into question. Derrida has attributed this vertiginous development to the dissolvent logic of "structurality," which became apparent from the moment when "language invaded the universal problematic . . . in which everything became discourse . . . a system where the central signified, the original or transcendental signified is never absolutely present outside a system of differences. The absence of the transcendental signified," he adds, "extends the domain and interplay of signification *ad infinitum*."[2]

But the relativist implosion Derrida describes (and endorses) is not attributable exclusively to the "invasion" of linguistics. Taken in conjunction with the modern French reception of psychoanalysis and the earlier offensive of classical positivism against subjectivism and teleology, it is, rather, part of a larger dynamic in which French thought has been led by degrees over the past century from a missionary scientism so confident of its cognitive grounds that it thought itself able to provide the spiritual as well as practical impetus for civilizational renewal, to the very brink of irrationalism. With each round of scientifically inspired demystification, the will-to-know has been forced to shed more and more of its claims to positivity—to the point now where all that threatens or promises to remain is the pure negativity and circularity of a will to demystify, standing playfully and demonically on its own.

Not only has the Cartesian ego been undermined, and behind that the scholastic optimism in *intellectum*, but also the dream, which classical positivists inherited from the Encyclopedists, of articulating science with humanism in the formation of a rational praxis. It is not too much to say therefore that, in the detotalizing passage from Durkheimian sociology to Derridean deconstruction, an entire epistemic formation and the rationalist project that has guided its development for a millennium have come unstuck. An effort to clarify structuralism's first-order significance thus uncovers a second: as the expression of a crisis that has rocked an "alternative" (i.e., non-"German") intellectual tradition to its foundations. In the first instance, it is precisely this tradition that structuralism and its post-structuralist outgrowth have placed in question—and sustained attention to it as a tradition is long overdue.[3]

In the current context, critical reflection on the imminent dissolution of French rationalism offers above all an ecumenical opportunity. If emancipatory thought is to go beyond the fragments of the Western mind, the mutually incoherent "national" epistemic formations that make it up need to be disentangled from one another, mined for the insights they contain, and brought together in an intersubjectively sensitive metadiscourse in which their various truths can be rendered intelligible to one another.[4] From this perspective, the sympathetic interrogation of French rationalism, from its medieval origins to its postmodern aporias, is both part of a broader project of critical recovery and a propaedeutic which, in combination with a parallel willingness to problematize the quasiprivileged categories of "German" thought, might also be expected to contribute toward an unblocking of the interepistemic rivalries and mutual misunderstandings with which contemporary theoretical discussion is beset.

The fundamental epistemic paradigms of rationalism, phenomeno-logical historicism, and empiricism which, in a complex cross-fertili-zation, have come to center the respective intellectual traditions of modern France, Germany, and England, express differentiated meta-theoretical responses to the medieval Christian formation from which they all derive.

The sense of historical continuity between theological origin and secular outcome is particularly marked in the French case, both be-cause of the vital role within its medieval ensemble played by Paris and the ecclesiastically sponsored schools of Northern France and because of the relatively uneven way in which the process of France's theoretical and ideological modernization subsequently occurred. The survival of Gallic Catholicism for two centuries beyond Luther prolonged the influence of the scholasticism that the Counter-Refor-mation had revived and left an imprint on the reconstructive attempts of the secular intelligentsia to fill the theoretical and ideological vacuum that was suddenly left when clerical Christianity was con-sumed in the fires of Enlightenment and Revolution.

Thus, from Anselm and Abelard to Althusser and Derrida the dis-tinctive problematic underlying the development of French rational-ism has been the dilemma prototypically represented in theology itself: the attempts of a redemptive mystery-religion driven by the promptings of a derivatively Greek philosophical conscience to dem-onstrate the intellectual coherence and cogency of its *credo*. In medi-eval thought it was as if two contradictory override programs were seeking to co-regulate the same conceptual terrain: an aprioristic commitment to the truths vouchsafed by Revelation, as mediated authoritatively by the Church, and an ultimately just as irreducible commitment to the revelatory capacities of human reason. For the guardians of theological totalization, rationalism represented the ever-present danger that reason would abjure its purely supplemental function and, motivated by skepticism or in search of a self-grounded retotalization, strike out rebelliously along the path of secular inde-pendence.

To preempt this possibility, two contrasting metatheoretical strat-egies were deployed: the neo-Augustinian response of negative theol-ogy, according to which the penetrating power of the human intellect was too puny to comprehend the mysteries of faith, and the Boethian path of reconciliation, summarized in his pregnant phrase *fidem si poteris rationemque conjunge*.[5] Whereas negative theology effectively renounced the whole attempt from the Patristic Fathers onward to provide Christianity with a philosophical rationale, and insisted on rigidly separating the realms to which the principles of *fides* and *intellectum* properly applied, the Boethian *conjunctio* was committed to the view that not only could faith usefully adduce the support of reason, but their combination might provide a privileged point of intellectual access.

In the culminating phase of scholasticism, from the reception of Aristotle to the *Summae* of Albertus and Aquinas, the guiding Anselmian slogan of *credo ut intelligam* expressed the reconciliationist program in its strongest form as the adoption of a master override, which directed intelligence to grasp both ends of the faith/reason contradiction and synthesize them in the conceptual unity of a single discourse. The same imperative was likewise built into Comte's later formative attempt to reconstitute scholasticism, *mutatis mutandis*, on a secular basis in the guise of Positive Philosophy.

Thus, in the most expanded metatheoretical sense, the architectonics of French thought derive not merely from the process in which the rationalist principle did in fact establish its autonomy from within and finally against the whole scholastic ensemble, but also from the privileging of the rational at the second-order level at which that ensemble was itself originally constituted as an ultra-Boethian response to the inherent contradictoriness of the theological enterprise as such.

The pivot on which both the reinvigorated synthetic ambition and the incipient rationalist dissolution of high medieval scholasticism turned was the displacement of neo-Platonism by Aristotelianism within its theoretical matrix. The analytic logic, rationalist metaphysic, and monist ontology that were derived from Aristotle's rediscovered writings strengthened and in a certain measure scientifically reformed the *fides rationis* in the very process of seeking its final Christian consummation. However, the impact of Aristotelianism on the incorporation of the scientific spirit into the *ratio* of reconciliationism was ambiguous, and in a sense more ideological than actual; and the speculative, substantialist metaphysics into which Aristotelian science rapidly congealed provoked an empiricist reaction that dovetailed with the conservative post-Thomist *revanche* of negative theology to split the late medieval intellectual field into two antipodal clusters: a monist, realist rationalism on the one side and a dualist/eclectic, nominalist empiricism on the other. In turn, these clusters formed the complementary but mutually inconsistent starting points for a fresh thematization of the rival claims of faith and reason—but this time between a faith in process of attenuation and interiorization and a reason increasingly dominated not by the consistency requirements of theological demonstration but by the incipiently mathematical and instrumental ethos of what positivists later thought of as science with a capital "S."

The anti-Aristotelian and empiricist program of Occam and the Oxford nominalists, which entered deeply into the formation of the modern English *episteme* and which, by virtue of both its agnosticism and instrumentalism, has provided the development of science and its industrial application with their principal metatheoretical supports, rejected the need for any further project of reconciliation out of hand.[6] In the rise of an efficiency and market-oriented utilitarianism that took axiology for granted in the givens of actual preference, in the evacuation of philosophical ontology from the applied sciences and in the rise of conventionalist philosophies that refused to leave the pages of common sense and "ordinary language," the negatively theological dictum of Wittgenstein has been replicated in every dimension: "what we cannot speak of we must pass over in silence."[7]

By contrast, with secularism and the development of empirically based science, the reconciliationist project, in any case marginalized by the reduced importance for the self-reproductive processes of postfeudal society of any overarching ideological institution or sense of mission, was forced to rethink its medieval matrix entirely. The first move was to immanentize and reconceptualize the axiological core of Christianity as faith in and commitment to the good that inheres in the human species, and then to seek the reconciliation of that faith with a scientifically corrected principle of rationality. But within this new pairing, the sense of religious certitude that had anchored Christian scholasticism was missing, so that, in effect, reason was now forced to construct out of its own ratiocinations the very faith with which it aimed to be reconciled. Furthermore, even if this new circle could be squared, the *ratio* of Aristotelianism needed to be refashioned, if not jettisoned altogether, so as to bring it into line with the manifestly effective principles of cognition that the scientific revolution had disengaged, and for which the Newtonian conjunction of mathematical systematicity and observationally verified laws provided the pregiven and authoritative practical paradigm.[8]

It was in fact precisely here—in deriving the epistemological and ontological implications of Newtonianism for the Aristotelian dimension of reconcilationism's medieval formation—that the modern French and German attempts to retotalize that project both crystallized and diverged. In the French Enlightenment, where Newtonian science was conceptualized in the medium of a heady Baconian and Cartesian optimism as objective knowledge guaranteed by the correct application of method to facts, Aristotelian logic was scientifically refined and the substantialism to which it was attached was refigured (at first reductively) as a materialism, and on that modified ontological terrain campaigned against totalistically as the shadow of prescientific metaphysics. In the German case, deflected from this path under conditions of political and technological backwardness by a heavily interiorized Protestantism, objective scientificity was grasped "from the side of the subject"[9] as a mode of consciousness. As such, it was supplemental to but not coextensive with human understanding, to which in a wider sense the teleological evolutionism of Aristotle itself both provided a necessary complement and, with Hegel, the master key to a higher logic and a trans-Newtonian cosmology.

But if the German incorporation of Newtonianism thereby preserved and even built on reconciliationism's Aristotelian frame, the price of subjectivizing scientific epistemology in this way was to raise to a higher power the Humean specter of skepticism that had already surfaced within the empiricist tradition itself. Kant's "Copernican Revolution" was intended to ace the problem by demonstrating the necessity within the very conception of a rational mind of the cognitive categories by which science—and indeed universalist ethics— organized the *plenum* of experienced reality. But that very move denied the identity of concept and referent, indeed the possibility of ever being able absolutely to bridge that gap; and therewith, once the hypermentalist essentialism with which Hegelian and Comtean identity theory reunited subject and object was itself judged scientifically unsupportable, its ultimate effect was to undermine that naive (as it now seems to us) "faith in the power of [scientific] reason"[10] which Kant took for granted and which Durkheim—through whom the Humean problematic entered classical positivism in its Germanically reworked Kantian form[11] —was himself perhaps the last great French thinker to espouse.

However, it is not possible to understand the wider ramifications of these attempts to conjugate the Newtonian and Aristotelian modes without taking account of the way in which the reconciliationist metaframework within which the encounter took place was itself expanded by the entry of one further dominant of modernity into its matrix: politics, and the sociohistorical analytic that was its reflexive shadow.

Within a medieval Christian framework, the whole dimension of praxis had been effectively displaced and reduced to the otherworldly problematics of salvation. Around that fixed point, heavily reinforced by ecclesiastical censorship, public discussions about this-worldly issues of social organization (recoded in terms of church-state relations) were forced to revolve. By releasing the reflection on praxis from so exclusively mystical a focus, the contrapuntal rise of the centralized state and civic republicanism engendered a secularized preoccupation with the constitution and direction of the polity, which opened a space for the efflorescence of a revived ethical and political philosophy—and later, with the social upheavals of capitalist industrialization, for the rise of social science. In effect, a bipolar architectonic—faith/reason: theology/philosophy—was replaced by a triangular one consisting, in secular terms, of ideology, science, and politics. Within this schema, praxis was, from a reconciliationist standpoint, privileged as the locus for the conceptual grounding and actualization of the humanized transcendental that fixed its reconstructed humanist faith. In the ideological world at large, however, the opening out of thought onto the pragmatics of social life was a two-way street: it removed a shield protecting thought from its subsumption as *techne* as well as creating the opportunity to theorize a helpful historical intervention on behalf of a humanly rooted, substantive rationality (for the French Enlightenment, Reason *tout court*[12]).

The acquisition by thought of practical interests also brought the domain of the human into focus as a new and culminating target for an objectivizing scientific cognition. And in fact it was on the terrain of that reflexive project that the gravitational tension between modern reason's sacred and profane commitments was most acutely felt and also that the problem inherent in any attempt to Newtonize the Aristotelian *ratio* was most sharply posed. Of the available ontologies, only Aristotelianism made conceptual space, through the category of natural entelechy, for the mediation of the Enlightenment's materialist problematization of determinacy and freedom, facticity and value.

The biological metaphor, given renewed credibility and impetus by the eighteenth-century development of the life sciences, provided a way in which, by grasping the sociohistorical itself as a kind of lifeform, both the German and the French streams of reconstructed reconciliationist thought were able to synthesize a scientific with a teleological view of the species in a perspective that made thinkable deliberate facilitative interventions into the determinate complexity of its evolving self-institution. In Germany, thought hovered between the Kantian option of a dualist ontology and the Hegelian solution of a hyperorganicized Nature. Either way, the *Geisteswissenschaften* effectively split themselves off from the methods of the natural sciences,[13] and sought to grasp empathetically the underlying patterns and process of consciousness whose unfolding construct the social world was presumed to be. In France, by contrast, the biological character attributed to the sociohistorical was approached in a severely natural scientific way as the empty conceptual frame for the inscription of objective laws yet to be empirically discovered.

At first sight (and so post-Hegelian transformism has traditionally regarded it), the French path was the more politically capitulationist.[14] Certainly the formative totalizations of St. Simon and Comte were thematized in close relation with the bourgeois need to reinstitute order after the rupture of 1789. But if so, and leaving to one side the evident capacity of St. Simonianism to generate a radical variant, the more whole-hearted French embrace of Newtonianism was not per se a movement of technicist closure. It was, rather, a historically determined option, no less one-sided in its theoretical effects than the less forthrightly scientific and phenomenologically formulated German reappropriation of Aristotle, within an essentially theological game. And on that level—as the expression of a commitment to reconcile the scientific, humanist, and political dominants of modernity from all three sides of its triangle—the positivist campaign to erase the last traces of Aristotelian metaphysics, even from the scientifically reinstituted metaphor of biology, was paradoxically in stricter fidelity to the Boethian imperative that had led the medieval scholastics to endorse Aristotelianism so enthusiastically in the first place.

In its fully reconstructed articulation, modern reconciliationism crystallized in the same historical moment at which the progressivist teleology of national-democratic politics also announced its passionate arrival. Fashioned in that incandescent late eighteenth-century context, the founding constructs of positivism and Idealism reflected an experiential core of historically reinforced insights and commitments whose interconnection must have seemed for an instant blindingly clear. The cognitive unity in both cases derived from the way in which a rationally penetrated sociohistorical reflexivity was simultaneously grasped as the highest stage of human understanding, the summit of the historical process, the coming to self-consciousness of the transcendent human subject (as Society or *Geist*) and the privileged cognitive medium within which the necessity of this whole process could be grasped.[15] The history of Western philosophy's attempts to reconceptualize the gyroscope of substantive rationality within the logocentric parameters of this matrix has been the story of that project's evermore elaborate collapse.

On the German side, the new sources of conflict and barbarism that a further round of historical development revealed undermined the Hegelian faith in a reason that had already arrived, and either transmuted that faith into a tragic or activist romanticism, or else provoked an absolute existential and phenomenological relativization of the value-question as such. On the French side, where it continued to be linked to the project of industrial society's theoretical-ideological reconstitution, the route to detotalization was more circuitous and followed less the logic of a directly experienced disillusionment than the logic of positivism's internal self-destruction. The central motif in this process was positivism's self-corrective ambition to positivize the problematic of a humanized, political theology by placing it on a fully social scientific basis. Four times in that context—with St. Simon, Comte, Durkheim and, most recently, Althusser—the attempt was made to launch the sociological project by means of some new and definitive *coupure epistémologique*;[16] but, each time, the sociological organon thereby constructed was distended by the central role it was preassigned within the whole system of positive philosophy, religion, and politics, and so fell back into an ideological closure. Of these, Durkheim's neo-Kantian mutation of Comte was historically the most important, both because it came closest to effecting the actual positivization of sociology and because in so doing it strained the positivist totalization to the breaking point. The culmination of the positivist project-matrix in Durkheim was in fact the beginning of its crisis, the point at which not only the Comtean framework, but the Boethian impulse underlying it began to disintegrate altogether.

Durkheim's critical point of departure[17] was to revoke the tautology according to which St. Simon's and Comte's sociological diagnosis of the reproductive (for Durkheim, "moral") crisis was given in advance by the arguments on which social science's methodological *raison d'être* depended.

If sociology was to provide the categorical imperative with a reality-principle, it first had to disengage cognitive from ideological interests and assume a posture of radical Cartesian doubt before the object-world it aimed to know. This note of scientific agnosticism provisionalized the status of Durkheim's own urgent recommendations[18] and opened the positivist totality to an uncoupling of its scientific from its practico-ideological projects.

However, the *épochè* in which Durkheim sought to redefine sociological reason as a rigorous, empirically based comparativism was itself incomplete, for its methodologically self-confident treatment of "social facts" as indices of "social states" still rested on a fixed metaphysic of the social as God and organism.[19] Accordingly, the epistemological and ontological reflections with which he tried to establish the scientific surety of this starting point only led to further difficulties.

The epistemological issue Durkheim was not able to circumvent was the one posed by Kant: the noetic prestructuring of even scientifically penetrated experience. Durkheim's solution—that the fundamental categories of pure (and, by a parallel argument, practical) reason represent the authoritative imprint within the individual consciousness of the mode in which society demarcates the dimensions of its own being—only pushed the Kantian dilemma to a higher level. At the limit, in which the social derivation of reason's irreducible conceptual frame was to be regarded positivistically as its essence, the sociologization of Kant[20] could only lead to the dead end of a social solipsism in which the "real" referent of sociological (indeed all scientific) discourse disappeared impenetrably behind the social process of its signification and the knowledge project was brought to a halt before the deep and autonomously determined cultural patterning of the mind that sought to know.

Durkheim's attempt to secure sociology's ontological grounding— by both demonstrating the irreducibly transindividual specificity of the social and also purging this knowledge-object of its protoideological character—similarly foundered. The dilemma was that he both needed the biological metaphor as a term, and was scientifically suspicious of any ascription to society of a natural entelechy. First, therefore, he tried to decompose Comte's evolutionist and functionalist logic into the more Newtonian logic of efficient causality.[21] Then, after he had flirted with a determinist environmentalism which deprived society of any causal dimension *pour-soi*, he transposed the problem to the plane of cultural formation, where the social protoplasm could be said to emerge from the interfusion of individual consciousness. On that hypermentalist level, Durkheim finally sought nonreductively to dissipate the teleological illusion by reframing the principles of social causality in terms of the anti-intentional metaphor of contemporary associational psychology. In the objectivist image of this latest life science, Durkheim was led to redirect the sociological enterprise toward an analysis of the ideational objectivations of collective mind which, in parallel fashion, abandoned the model of an integral consciousness and aimed rather to comprehend the configurational logic according to which those objectivations were permuted and combined.[22]

But once the society-object was redefined in this way, the society-subject in which positivism's secularized Aristotelian Christianity had reinvested its sense of deity was effectively vaporized behind the laws that impersonally regulated the combinative play of the collectivity's conjoint mental representations. We must bear in mind, moreover, that the transcendental signified of society was also positivism's reality-pole, as the mediating term between nature, experience, belief, and praxis. It is easy to see, then, how Durkheim's switch from the body metaphor of the social group to the mental-spiritual metaphor of the social *conscience*, combined with his attempt to grasp this latter through a decentering, quasimathematical associationism, effectively generated a rogue ontology that undermined the rational supports for both the humanism and the scientism that inspired it.

The end came swiftly. Once structuralism had, with Lévi-Strauss, dismissed the society-subject as a metaphysic and simultaneously reduced the organismic image of its evolutionary progress to the status of a myth,[23] the cultural complex Durkheim had identified as society's only scientifically cognizable element was cut adrift from all sociohistorical referentiality and reconceptualized as one vast, internally self-structured language game. In that same post-Durkheimian moment, the Saussurean paradigm of *langue* (developed in close theoretical and chronological parallel with Durkheimian sociology itself) provided cultural associationism with a superior, because more positively based, logic of configuration—and at the same time focused the deracinating realization that thought itself was inescapably captive to that logic. It remained only to relate that reflection to the epistemological aporia generated by tracking the Kantian categories down to their sociocultural originary for the hyperrelativistic circle to be complete.

Durkheim himself, anxiously determined to prevent reason's collapse, was held back from pursuing the corrosive implications of his incipiently structuralist move, and preferred instead to track back and forth between the inconsistent ontologies of mechanism, organicism, and structuralism in order to rethink Comte's paradigmatic anti-thesis of individual and group in terms that made it more subtle as a tool of analysis. By relocating discursive rationality at the level of the individual, exploring the relation of individuation and social differentiation, and postulating a model for the reproduction of industrial society that drastically reduced the role for mechanically solidary elements, Durkheim was able to adduce a programmatic formula for reconstruction that was far more plausible and historically congenial than those of St. Simon and Comte. The centralist elements were jettisoned, the program for theoretical-ideological reconstruction was subordinated to institutional change and refocused as a curriculum reform within the state education system, and society-worship, though retained,[24] was refigured as cooperative solidarism, buttressed by the cult of the moral-rational individual. But by instantiating society as culture, occluding power as morality, relegating interest to the nether world of individual contingency, and mystifying the forced ideological unity of a contradictory ensemble as the solidarity of community —in short, by retaining an organismic and deificatory ontology of the social as Society, Durkheim drastically underestimated the transformist gap between industrial capitalism and the cooperative human "we" he longed to actualize. He was, therefore, theoretically powerless to prevent sociology's absorption into the projects of the bourgeois French state.

The political discredit[25] and cognitive dissonance that Durkheimianism suffered as European society, convulsed by war and upheaval, refused to settle down in the manner predicted and prescribed, only hastened the process of internal metatheoretical decomposition. The vector of humanist faith, as an authentic operant, was evacuated from the matrix, and appropriated instead by the generation of Nizan, Sartre, Merleau-Ponty, and Kojève from the side of its Germanic articulation. The vector of science that emerged from the wreckage, although committed at first, by way of demythologizing ethnography, to the elaboration of a "new humanism," was essentially apolitical and formalist—the ground, in fact, for the temporary resurrection, over the corpse of Aristotle, of Pythagoras and Plato.[26] However, divorced from all fideistic enthusiasms and increasingly prepared to press the demythologizing, antiteleological thrust of positivism to its logical conclusion, rationalism's negative moment gained the upper hand; and at the Derridean catastrophe point the will to believe modulated into the nihilism of refusal, and therewith the master-override of French rationalism—the injunction to conjoin faith and reason in the medium of both—became completely unhinged.

From a transformist perspective, while there can be no return to the naive forms of humanism and scientism that structuralism has conceptually demolished, the current campaign to liquidate the last vestiges of Judeo-Christian and Aristotelian logocentrism can hardly be considered a satisfactory point of arrival. But how can the demythologizing argument be brought to the stage of a wise transvaluation? After the annihilation of positivist certitudes, is it possible yet again to reinstitute the matrix of reconciliationism, and thereby reformulate French rationalism's dislocated project?

Such an issue can hardly be broached without first taking cognizance of the one attempt that has been made to revise the positivist synthesis directly in light of its post-Durkheimian deconstruction.

The peculiarity of that attempt—in Althusser's structuralist "intervention"—is that it was conducted as a doctrinal polemic on the terrain of Marxist-Leninist politics. As such, Althusserianism had the merit of introducing a transformist element into positivism's homeostatic formulations, and conversely of making the quasireligious character of his Communism more self-conscious. However, this was at the price of enclosing the positivist system in another dogmatism which, in addition, occluded the full nature of the maneuver.[27] Moreover, Althusser's failure to provide a convincing resolution of Durkheim's aporias revealed not only the familiar problems of ideological circularity but also the deeper flaws within French rationalism's antimetaphysical metaphysics that have brought that tradition to its current post-structuralist impasse.

For Althusser, as for Durkheim and Comte, the lynchpin of a fully positivized world-view was the establishment of social science; and the scientificity of the latter depended on fashioning a social ontology emancipated from all trace of ideological projection. Althusser's metatheoretical strategy was to excise the hypermentalism of Comte, Durkheim, and Marx by reconceptualizing the social in terms of the Marxist categories of practice and social formation, and the cultural instance they problematized as the moment of that contradictory ensemble's ideological reproduction.[28] Then, in order to erase Marxism's own teleological and essentialist elements, he rethought the resultant totality as a complex structure of structures whose conjunctural deployment and historical unfolding represented the overdetermined effects of relational play immanent and transcendent to the individual and collective subjects who acted it out.[29]

Quite apart from the Marxist simplifications, Althusser's corrected ontology was reductive in two striking respects. First, by recasting praxis as decentered production, Althusser regressed to a pre-Marxist objectivism in whose terms the politics his social science was intended to serve could not be thematized without contradiction. Secondly, his topography of the social circumscribed all its "relatively autonomous"[30] instances within the self-identical boundaries of a singularly defined social formation. The first reduction flowed from the requirement that the social (in Althusser's terms: the "continent of History") be defined as an autonomous, scientifically demarcated order of being, the second from a confusion of social reality as a general medium of human existence with the totalities conceived, on the basis of both common sense and biological analogy, to be the composite elements of its material order.

The problem is not just that these dimensional reductions preempted

144 □ ANDREW WERNICK

the search for a truly complex ontology, but that the sociological realism which left its Aristotelian traces in them, and which from Comte to Althusser has ontologically anchored the whole anti-Aristotelian campaign, was itself fundamentally misconceived. The language-object that structuralism uncovered at the culmination of French rationalism's attempt to expunge teleology (and with it, human purpose) from an objective specification of sociohistorical being, is the *reductio* of that impossible project: an object that makes objectivation inconceivable.

In order to escape the dilemma, a way needs to be found to reincorporate the censored dimensions of subjectivity, praxis, and biology into the texture of social ontology without reduction and without recourse to the magic of entelechy. This can only be done if social reality is conceived *ab initio* as a multidimensionally complex order of being, simultaneously experiential and penetrated by a host of processed alterities, and within which no single overriding mode of causality prevails. By definition, such an entity—if entity is the right term—cannot be grasped in the homogeneous image of a substance, still less a substance comprehended exclusively in the medium of its inert determinacy. And until that Aristotelian shadow is dispelled, post-structural rationality will continue to rotate on the ontological spot.

A second major flaw in Althusser's totalization was its mystification of the fideistic dimension of the political and epistemological commitments his ontological operation was designed, in the last analysis, to shore up. At the political level, it may be said that at least the Comtean transcription implied that Marxism had a fideistic element: the Communist eschaton immanent to the class struggle and ecclesiastically expressed by the Party. However, his dogmatization of that faith precluded its problematization, and led only to its aprioristic theoreticist and pragmatist displacement.[31] Thus, for all his corrective insistence on the inescapable presence of ideology, both as a general dimension of social reality and as an axiological element within the transformist project itself ("real humanism"),[32] Althusser's discussion of the latter focused entirely on its "unprecedented" positivity and, unlike Comte and Durkheim, not at all on its equally irreducible religious character. In addition, "real humanists" would object that Althusser's Marxist homologue of positive religion was vitiated even as a faith—both by the Gulag that lurked in its anti-individualist and productivist version of the human project and by its unreconstructedly centralist, hierocratic, and bureaucratic ecclesiology.

At the epistemological level, the inconsistency of Althusser's oc-clusion of the fideistic is perhaps more self-evident. By insisting that the real object is outside the "knowledge relation" and that no guar-antees of truth exist beyond the historically developing practices and languages of science, Althusser adopted the conceptualism that had already punctured positivism's assertorial mode, but without accept-ing or even facing its relativizing consequences.[33]

A more consistent epistemological posture would have been to frankly accept the fictional and heuristic character of his social on-tology, and then strive to refine and clarify his provisional cognitive commitments through a process of successive approximation that re-mains ever open to reflexive metatheoretical overhaul. A parametric corollary would have been to substitute the porous criterion of "reasonableness" for the more hardened, univocal one of rational necessity in enlightened humanism's justificatory rhetoric. Of course, such "reasonableness" would be flaccid without the nerve to make cognitive, axiological and indeed practical commitments. Transform-ism itself demands it. Even in its provisory form, therefore, an en-gaged rationality retains its scholastic metastructure as a *fides quaerens intellectum*, albeit one that is penetrated by faith on both sides of the equation.[34]

Althusserian dogmatism no less than post-structuralist hyperrela-tivism has eschewed this Habermasian compromise because they are similarly fixated (triumphantly or dismissively) on the Cartesian equation of scientific knowledge with certitude: a conception of rea-son that ultimately derives from the scholastic desire for an intellec-tual method to secure its absolute fideistic ground. At the minimum, any revival of the reconstructed reconciliationist paradigm will have to recognize that the road back to apodicticity is foreclosed by the insight that the *ratio* of scientific realism itself subsists in faith.

But more is required to correct the Anselmian paradigm than just softening the demands it makes on rationality. The ontological de-centering that is neo-Kantianism's flip side has reduced the human subject—individual and collective—to the status of a "signifier with-out a signified," and to believe in contemporary post-structural reason is to accept the conceptual "death of Man." Habermas, in line with the essentialist underpinning of the German *episteme*, has tried to evade the dilemma by refiguring the human *telos* as a formally deriv-able communicative ideal. But the problem of theorizing and valoriz-ing the subject for whom the ideal exists remains unsolved. Althusser, for all his dogmatism, got much closer to formulating the problem by attempting to assimilate "theoretical anti-humanism" within a still avowedly humanist political ideology. But his reference to an "ideology which will depend on science this time"[35] was highly elliptical, and in uncritical Comtean manner seemed still to presuppose a continuous discursive logic between the contradictory terms the phrase proposed to conjoin.

The issue was first grasped in all its tense contradictoriness by Nietzsche. For him, the transvaluation implicit in any final move to extinguish the fading idols of Hebraic and Hellenic antiquity was predicated not only on the resurrection of the human will, but also on the courage of that will not to be wholly taken in by the commitments we dare to make.[36] Even in pursuit of the redemptive, the passion for truth once demythologized must embrace irony: the only conceivable mediation between bad faith and no faith.

In addition to the existential implications (quasifascistically explored by Nietzsche himself), the enigma of an activist, humanist faith saturated with irony presents a completely new dilemma for the reconciliationist impulse. Where once reason had enjoined the Christian and later the humanist faithful to theorize their Absolute, now—going much further in reverse than negative theology ever did—post-structural rationality insists that even in the midst of a transformist commitment transcendental notions are to be rejected as the purest illusion.

In effect, in the Nietzschean finale of a disintegrating positivism, modern reconciliationism, whether Cartesian or Hegelian, has discovered not only that its credalist conception of faith was mirrored in the false ontology of an exteriorized Absolute, but that its very notion of a coherent consciousness had all along been profoundly undialectical. The way toward a higher reconciliationism lies in dropping the strained doctrinalist mode, Marxist or otherwise, so as to grasp this new, and in Nietzsche's sense Buddhized, *dispositif*[37] of faith and reason, attitude and cognition, that French rationalism, through its structuralist dislocation, has now encountered.

NOTES

1. V. Descombes, *Modern French Philosophy* (New York: Cambridge University Press, 1979), p. 12 *et seq.*

2. J. Derrida, "Structure, Sign, and Play" in R. Macksey and E. Donato, eds., *The Structuralist Controversy* (Baltimore: The Johns Hopkins University Press, 1972), p. 249. It should be noted that Derrida's equation of structuralism with structural linguistics is not the only available meaning for the term. For an alternative, deriving from the mathematical conception of systematicity, see J. Piaget, *Structuralism* (New York: Basic Books, 1970). In this paper, I refer exclusively to the former.

3. In the English-speaking world, the different phases of the French tradition have

generally been considered in isolation from one another. The current Durkheim "revival" is leading to an improvement, however. For an excellent recent account of structuralism's relation to the Comtean tradition, see C. P. Babcock, *Lévi-Strauss: Structuralism and Sociological Theory* (London: Hutchinson, 1975).

4. Lucien Goldmann's neo-Lukácsian analysis of the three major European epistemic traditions poses the problem but reduces the differences between them to the variant political sociology of the French, German, and English, "bourgeois revolutions." See L. Goldmann, *Immanuel Kant* (London: NLB, 1971), pp. 31-49.

5. "As far as you are able, join faith and reason." The last sentence of a letter from Boethius to Pope John I. See J. Pieper, *Scholasticism* (New York: McGraw-Hill, 1964), pp. 37-38.

6. *Ibid.*, p. 149. See also D. Knowles, *The Evolution of Medieval Thought* (London: Longman's, 1962), pp. 311-26.

7. L. Wittgenstein, *Tractatus Logico-Philosophicus* (London: Routledge & Kegan Paul, 1949), vii.

8. The synthesis of induction and deduction within scientific method has never been so straightforward as either Enlightenment social theorists thought or as twentieth-century critics of scientistic system-building have believed. For an example of the latter, see M. Horkheimer and T. Adorno, *Dialectic of Enlightenment* (New York: Herder and Herder, 1972), p. 7: The Enlightenment's "ideal is the system from which anything and everything follows. Its rationalist and empiricist versions do not part company on that point."

9. Marx's well-known account of German idealism in *The German Ideology* (New York: International Publishers, 1947), pp. 3-6, refers to the effects of "backwardness" but not to the impact of the Lutheran theological tradition.

10. Durkheim saw this faith as an indispensable element, along with political upheaval, in the precocious development of French sociology. See his essay "Sociology," in Kurt H. Wolff, ed., *Essays on Sociology and Philosophy by Emile Durkheim et al.* (New York: Harper, 1960), especially p. 383.

11. The key mediating figures in France were Renouvier and Boutroux. See S. Lukes, *Emile Durkheim: His Life and Work* (London: Allen Lane, 1973), pp. 54-58.

12. The classic discussion of eighteenth-century rationalist ideology remains Carl L. Becker, *The Heavenly City of the Eighteenth Century Philosophers* (New Haven: Yale University Press, 1932).

13. The issues engaging Dilthey, Windelbrand, and Rickert were ontological as well as in the narrow sense methodological. For a good discussion see Thomas Burger, *Max Weber's Theory of Concept Formation* (Durham, N.C.: Duke University Press, 1976).

14. See, for example, H. Marcuse, *Reason and Revolution* (New York: Oxford University Press, 1941), pp. 323-29.

15. For an ultra-individualist but insightful examination of the similarities between Comte and Hegel, see F. A. Hayek, *The Counter-Revolution of Science* (New York: Free Press, 1955), pp. 191-206.

16. This term, originally developed by Gaston Bachelard in *La Formation de l'esprit scientifique*, was taken over by Althusser, in his words, "to designate the mutation in the theoretical problematic contemporary with the foundation of a scientific discipline." L. Althusser, *For Marx* (London: NLB, 1969), p. 32 *et seq.*

17. For Durkheim's most direct discussion of his differences with the classical Positivists, whom he subsumed under the more general rubric of "scientific socialists," see E. Durkheim, *Socialism*, ed. A. Gouldner (New York: Collier, 1962).

18. For the Durkheimian program, see especially E. Durkheim, *Suicide* (New York: The Free Press, 1951), pp. 361-92.

19. The importance of the medical-organismic metaphor to Durkheim's methodology is

made most explicit in ch. 3 of *Rules of Sociological Method*. The deificatory element in his social ontology was not fully related to epistemological issues until his *Elementary Forms of the Religious Life*. For a discussion of how this latter leads to logical dilemmas, see T. Parsons, *The Structure of Social Action*, vol. I (New York: The Free Press, 1968), pp. 441-50.

20. Durkheim's attempt to sociologize Kant's moral theory is explicit from the outset: "Briefly, in one of its aspects, the categorical imperative of the moral conscience is assuming the following form: *Make yourself usefully fulfill a determinate function*." E. Durkheim, *Division of Labour in Society* (New York: The Free Press, 1933), p. 43. For a summary of his modification of Kant's epistemology, see *Elementary Forms of the Religious Life* (London: Allen and Unwin, 1968), pp. 9-20 and 427-31.

21. "It is from the cause that the effect draws its energy, but it also restores it to the cause on occasion, and consequently it cannot disappear without the cause showing the effects of its disappearance. [footnote]: . . . this reciprocity of cause and effect might furnish a means of reconciling scientific mechanism with the teleology which the existence, and especially the teleology of life implies." E. Durkheim, *Rules of Sociological Method* (New York: The Free Press, 1964), pp. 95-96.

22. See *Individual and Collective Representations*, in the collection of Durkheim's essays entitled *Sociology and Philosophy* (London: Cohen and Weston, 1965).

23. See C. Lévi-Strauss, *Structural Anthropology* (New York: Basic Books, 1967), ch. I.

24. See *Division of Labour*, pp. 346-49; *Elementary Forms*, pp. 424-27; and Durkheim's Dreyfusard pamphlet, "L'individualisme et les intellectuels," in Emile Durkheim, *On Morality and Society: Selected Writings*, ed. Robert N. Bellah (Chicago: University of Chicago Press, 1973).

25. "Whether it be mathematics or collective representations, everything in Durkheimianism leads to social harmony. Bourgeois philosophy tries very hard to conceal the war raging throughout society, a war it does not dare declare—beneath the celestial vale of an imaginary peace, a peace it is incapable of establishing on earth." P. Nizan, *The Watchdogs* (New York: Monthly Review Press, 1971), p. 156.

26. H. Lefebvre, *Au delà du structuralisme* (Paris: Éditions Anthropos, 1971), pp. 261-78.

27. Althusser dropped hints about his Comtean preoccupations in the introduction to *For Marx* (Allen Lane, 1969). There, in a diatribe against the poverty of French bourgeois philosophy, he refers to "its relentless hostility to the only mind worthy of interest that it produced, Auguste Comte" (p. 25). When pushed by political pressure to recant, he sidestepped this genealogical connection and declared "*Nous avons été Spinozistes*." *Éléments d'auto-critique* (Paris: Hachette, 1974), p. 65.

28. This operation is outlined in his essay "Ideology and Ideological State Apparatuses" in *Lenin and Philosophy* (London: NLB, 1971).

29. See the essays "Contradiction and Over-determination" and "On the Materialist Dialectic" in *For Marx*.

30. This concept originates with Durkheim: ". . . once a basic number of representations have been thus created, they become, for the reasons which we have explained, partially autonomous realities with their own way of life." E. Durkheim, *Sociology and Philosophy*, p. 31.

31. The transition from the "theoreticist" definition of philosophy as the "theory of theoretical practice" to the pragmatist definition of it as "class struggle in theory" is noted in the preface to the Italian edition of *Reading Capital*, included as a foreword to the English edition (London: NLB, 1970), pp. 7-8, and elaborated in the title essay of *Lenin and Philosophy*.

3 2. See *For Marx*, pp. 242-46.

33. Althusser's twist is to rework knowledge as production. See *Reading Capital*, pp. 40-43, for a direct discussion of his epistemology as a concatenation of Spinoza and Marx.

34. Goldmann's approach is to link a Blochian philosophy of hope with the Pascalian notion of faith as a wager. In the twentieth century, historical catastrophe has had the effect, if one follows Goldmann, of *hiding* the transformist Absolute. See L. Goldmann, *Immanuel Kant*, pp. 165-79.

35. The phrase occurs in Althusser's reflection on Gramsci, *Reading Capital*, p. 131.

36. Nietzsche's critical irony, it should be emphasized, had a self-consciously positivist edge: "It is not the victory of science that distinguishes our nineteenth century, but the victory of scientific method over science. History of scientific method, considered by Auguste Comte as virtually philosophy itself. The great methodologists: Aristotle, Bacon, Descartes, Auguste Comte. The most valuable insights are arrived at last; but the most valuable insights are methods." Aphorisms 466-69 in *The Will to Power* (New York: Vintage, 1968), p. 261.

37. "Buddhism is the only really 'positivistic' religion history has to show us, even in its epistemology (a strict phenomenalism), it no longer speaks of 'the struggle against *sin*' but, quite in accordance with actuality, 'the struggle against *suffering*.'" F. Nietzsche, *The Anti-Christ*, in combined edition with *Twilight of the Idols* (Harmondsworth: Penguin, 1968), p. 129.

Chapter 8
Structuralism as Syncretism: Institutional Distortions of Saussure
Marc Angenot

Ni lu ni compris
Aux meilleurs esprits
Que d'erreurs promises

Paul Valéry, *Le Sylphe*

In any given discipline—and particularly in those blurred, fuzzy sectors of knowledge made out of conflictual traditions, as literary studies are—we find a number of concepts, notional tools, circulating, or (to write more cautiously) a number of *keywords* whose definition, scope, and relevance are continually refashioned. The success of these words and notional compounds is sometimes perceived as a sort of collective need, a collective impulse of the scientific, or indeed ideological, community—however great is in fact the disagreement as to the extension and use of these terms.

It is probably healthy and salutary not to take for granted the presence of these keywords, their migrations and possible metamorphoses, to trace back what epistemological avatars they underwent, under what ideological constraints they are transposed from one intellectual stream to another, and occasionally into different linguistic and cultural communities. Such an inquiry brings into question all the major problems of historical epistemology and the sociology of intellectual life. These problems are not easy to deal with, especially if one grapples with contemporary phenomena, not only because of a lack of perspective but also because contemporary social sciences in "liberal" societies are made up of a number of theoretical traditions both intricate *and* incompatible to a degree, where currents of eclecticism constantly tend to neglect or conceal unavoidable confrontations.

Any systemic inquiry, however, into the way major cognitive paradigms of our century have appeared and evolved, have been coopted, trivialized or even defaced—and also *why* and *where* these distortions and defacements took place—would take much time and many pages to expose and illustrate. I shall deal here only with a quite specific case bounded by a limited time span. I propose to take the field of literary criticism and cultural studies in France during the so-called structuralist age, i.e., in the sixties and early seventies, and to confine my discussion to the way Ferdinand de Saussure's linguistic thought has been received and interpreted by scholars in literary and cultural studies.

It is not my purpose either to vindicate Saussure's thought or to "reveal" what Saussure had finally in mind, nor to try to correct some interpretations of his theories and substitute a supposedly authentic reading. However, I do imply that there actually is in Saussure's linguistic thought a consistent set of linguistic concepts and an operative potential that those linguists who are situated in his direct theoretical heritage have attempted to clarify and elaborate in different ways. My aim is to formulate general hypotheses about the way Saussure has been used during the period in question. I shall not aim to be polemical, although some of my contentions may take a polemical turn on account of false perspectives and smokescreens spread by structuralist verbiage. I believe that we usually do not know how notions and paradigms are being parachuted, borrowed, or recycled in our own fields of research. Hence, in writing about Saussure in French literary structuralism of the sixties, I expect in fact to be writing about all of us, in a way.

The reader will recall that most of the works considered today as representative of French literary scholarship were published during the sixties: Barthes's, Bremond's, Greimas's, Kristeva's, Genette's, Todorov's major books, as well as the most renowned works of Lévi-Strauss, Lacan, Althusser, and Foucault, at the periphery of that field, all of them labeled "structuralist" at a given moment. The majority of today's major cultural journals were launched during that period, such as *Tel Quel* (1959), *Communications* (1964), *Change*

(1968), and, in the early seventies, *Poétique* (1970) and *Littérature* (1971). Publishers like Didier and Larousse even took the risk of marketing journals of linguistics, like *Langages* (1966) and *Langue Française* (1969), and making them fashionable to a degree, which was the last thing to be expected from a journal of linguistics. In the late sixties also appeared a number of works by Derrida, Baudrillard, Serres, Deleuze, and Lyotard that are considered as tolling the passing-bell of structuralism—works that nonetheless still make an extensive if "perverse" use of structuralist phraseology.

All these works and journals, in spite of their differences, had a conspicuous common point: they quoted Saussure. They referred abundantly to his *Cours de linguistique générale* (CLG); they made wide use of his phraseology and that of the linguistic schools that are considered his intellectual heirs. So my question is: how do we deal with this extensive and constant reference to a general linguist, a bad prophet in his own country, who up to the fifties had exclusively, if deeply, influenced non-Francophone linguists and literary theoreticians? What was Saussure's epistemological role in the setting of French structuralist literary criticism? In what way have his theories been integrated, criticized, or dynamized by them? After all, as Genette wrote, "structuralism being a linguistic method *par excellence*," there is perhaps nothing surprising in seeing Saussure reverently referred to.[1] I suspect that the matter is not so simple.

One should first look back from the structuralist era to Saussure himself. Let me just remind the reader of a few important and already paradoxical data. Ferdinand de Saussure taught a course in general linguistics at the University of Geneva in 1907, 1908, and 1910. However, when we talk about the *Cours de linguistique générale* as such, we are not talking about something Saussure would have written, wholly or in part. We are referring to an amalgamation of course notes edited by three of his former students in 1915 (Saussure having died in 1913).

We know today that the three editors—Bally, Sèchehaye, and Riedlinger—displayed more good will than scientific rigor and even philological prudence. They built up a text made of an astonishing number of reflections and interpolations. Some of these interpolations have been unavoidably read as Saussure's genuine thought. L. Hjelmslev seems to have found his road to Damascus with the final sentence of the *Cours*: "The unique and *only* true object of linguistics is language considered in itself and for itself."[2] Unfortunately, this sentence was never written or uttered by Saussure. L. J. Calvet, on the other hand, has shown that the confusing equations "*signifiant* = acoustic image" and "*signifié* = concept" are also inter-polations of the editors.[3]

The status that Saussure himself granted his course is rather uncer-tain: he destroyed his notes before his death. Saussure possibly con-sidered that the theses orally expounded in his seminar were a gnoseo-logical framework both fundamental *and* insufficiently developed, a set of elementary theses in all their starkness, deprived of adequate theoretical elaboration. That is the way the *CLG* has been conceived by linguists like Trubetzkoy, Jakobson, Hjelmslev, Buyssens, Martinet, and Prieto—and that is why each, in his own way, endeavored to build around the *Cours* a more consistent theoretical apparatus.

The other major historical problem is related to the migration of the *CLG*: that is, the fact that Saussure's paradigm took forty years to travel from Geneva to Paris. French linguistics at the time, under the hegemonic influence of Antoine Meillet, opposed insuperable ob-stacles to Saussure's acceptance and discussion. That is why Saussure began migrating *eastward*, as it were, and found a first institutional landing point in Russia during the first world war. There, the *CLG* provided a strong theoretical source of inspiration both to the Moscow Linguistic Circle (Bogatyrev, Jakobson) and the formalists-to-be of the Opoiaz (Šklovskij, Ejkhenbaum) and later to the scholars of the Leningrad Institute of Art History (Tynjanov, Tomaševskij, and Vinogradov). Tynjanov and Jakobson's meditations on Saussure are fundamental elements for the development of Russian formalism. On the other hand, Saussure came to be polemically criticized and re-jected in the late twenties (but at least understood in a pertinent light) by the major literary scholar of our century, Mikhaïl M. Bakhtin, who published with V. N. Vološinov in 1929 his *Marxism and the Philosophy of Language*. In the thirties, a migration began westward and, once again in Prague, Saussure became a major source of reflec-tion for Mukařovsky's semiology of the arts. In other words, Saussure is an important source for three significant literary reflections between the World Wars, that of Jakobson and his group, Bakhtin and his cir-cle, and Mukařovsky. At the same time, Saussure's *CLG* became the "Bible" of two major schools of linguistics: Prague's phonology and Copenhagen's glossematics. In French-speaking countries, however, his influence remained almost nonexistent, except in Brussels with Eric Buyssens. He eventually came back to French linguistics (a hard-ly fashionable discipline just after World War II) with Gougenheim, Martinet, Mounin, and later the Argentinian Luis Prieto, who cur-rently occupies the chair of linguistics at Geneva.

The above survey is obviously drastically simplified. It is simply aimed at showing how singular the international fortune of the *CLG* has been. I am moving toward the sixties, when Saussure ends his epistemological cruising, returning to France on the shoulders of the Russian Jakobson, the Lithuanian Greimas, the Dane Hjelmslev, and the French (but French ethnologist) Lévi-Strauss, himself initiated to Saussureanism in the United States. By the time it becomes *de rigueur* to read and draw inspiration from Saussure in France, it is clear that this Saussure is bound to be read through his cosmopolitan tribulations and through layers of superimposed mediations.

A convenient date to serve as a starting point may be found in the first French attempt at applying Saussure to cultural phenomena, i.e., Roland Barthes's *Mythologies,* published in 1957. It should nevertheless be noticed that, to a large extent, Saussure's international influence and the critiques he underwent remained partly concealed to the French scholars: in 1957, neither Hjelmslev, nor the Russian formalists, nor Propp, nor Bakhtin were translated into French. They come to be translated, one by one, as the structuralist fad develops. As for Mukařovsky, who had taken the trouble to write many of his early essays directly in French, the effort did not pay at all, and he remains neglected to this day.

In fact, in the mid-sixties, the word "structuralism," applied to Saussurean linguistics, was also a kind of synonym or nickname for Lévi-Strauss's anthropological theories[4] —not counting Jean Piaget's epistemology, which was little known in France. For a while, the break with conventional approaches to literature was also acknowledged through another synthetic label: "la Nouvelle Critique." This polemical entity was misleading: Mauron's psychocriticism, Goldmann's sociology of literature, and the structuralists-to-be were seen as components of a tactical alliance against an alleged rearguard of positivists and literary historians. René Picard's little pamphlet against Barthes, Weber, and Goldmann appeared to confer a sort of justification on this aberrant assemblage.[5] (Apart from its polemical character, the idiom "Nouvelle Critique," itself derived from "nouveau roman," should also be considered from a sociological point of view as the model for later expressions like "Nouvelle Philosophie" and, more recently, "Nouvelle Droite"—idioms in which marketing practices are always combined with ideological misapprehensions.)

Some years later, around 1968—one has only to reread dozens of monographs and special issues—Barthes, Todorov, Genette, Kristeva, Foucault, Althusser, Lacan, Greimas, Bourdieu, Sollers, and so forth, in the most glorious confusion, are all considered structuralists. A semantic inflation had occurred, embracing in a catchall term this so-called structuralist generation, to the point of grouping in a suspect way almost *all* the accredited representatives of the social sciences, philosophy, and the literary disciplines. Around 1969-70, even more suspiciously, a rapid and discernable relinquishment of the word "structuralism" is to be observed, compensated by a sudden inflation of "semiotics." But that is another story.[6]

During the late sixties, the primary task of every student of the arts, encouraged by the doubtful unanimity of the academic media, was *to go and read Saussure*. Usually, this meant a few chapters — one-fifth of the *CLG*. However, the reading always went wrong for some reason. The student had the unpleasant feeling that he was to play the part of the little boy in Andersen's tale. He had been promised that the foundations of modernity were to be unveiled to his eyes, yet he was faced with a text both simple and obscure, remarkably unfit for any immediate use in literary analysis. He did not find anything that, as a whole, was tangible and palatable, as it were. In sum, as an operative paradigm, Saussure's thought escaped him almost necessarily.

It should be said here that there was in fact, in these few pages that constituted the structuralist vulgate, thinking matter for any nonlinguist scholar. By saying so, I am not offering my own interpretation, but I am synthesizing the cognitive nucleus that all those linguists from Trubetzkoj to Prieto have effectively extracted from the obscurities of the *CLG*. What we find in Saussure is a gnoseology, a paradigm for a theory of knowledge based on the following axiom: that linguistic praxis does not operate with sounds to communicate about things but with classes determining the identity of sounds, classes whose relevance is not immanent but determined by other classes determining the identity of messages. Hence, Saussure's basic notions: "point of view," "value," "difference," "syntagm," "paradigm."

It follows that Saussure's gnoseology was definitely the opposite of the one that came to be formalized by Lévi-Strauss, for instance, or Barthes et al. — cognition being in his opinion related to a point of view that is itself determined by a specific human praxis. In such praxis, the identity of classes serving as tools is only differentially known because their relevance is validated in *another* system, that of classes determining aims or goals. This amounts to saying that there is no immanent taxonomy for any set of objects or phenomena, that relevance is teleological, i.e., external to the set under scrutiny. In a word, Saussure was to a certain degree the antistructuralist *par excellence*, at least in regard to the sense which that word seemed to carry in French ideology of the 1960s.

But for the student there was an easier way out: to take eclectically, one by one, all the binary oppositions found in the book: language/speech, signifier/signified, synchrony/diachrony, syntagm/paradigm, without worrying much about their interconnectedness and their role in a scientific model. Certainly this dismemberment entailed an equivocation, a trivialization of Saussure. Isolated from their context, these oppositions were becoming both flat and confusing, innocuous and inoperative. But at least they seemed ready to serve.

This leads me to a proposition: contrary to what happened before the Second World War in Slavic countries, there was no global consideration of Saussure by anyone outside linguistics in France, either to work *with* him or to reject his epistemology. What happened was a dismemberment, a fragmentation of his thought, with a loss of its operative potential and an absence of recognition of its inherent limitations. Such dismemberment was already at work in Lévi-Strauss; literary scholars simply contributed to speeding up *ad absurdum* and *ad nauseam*. In other words, if it is true that, for instance, Prague phonology would not have existed without Saussure, in French structuralism, although he was constantly if wrongly quoted by critics of all allegiances, Saussure served no critical purpose; he remained Greek to most scholars, misunderstood as a scientific whole.

I am not implying at all that through this process of dismemberment French scholars missed something of which they could have made good use. Given the orientations of the time, it may even be contended that they were on other tracks, mostly looking after problems to which Saussureanism did not provide a key. Even so, following on the proposition above, the question of his success remains—that is, the success of a phraseology made out of a dozen terms, and a doxography made out of another dozen quotations. This success, which seems to be in inverse ratio to his cognitive integration, is what interests me here.

If Saussure remained a dead letter for most of the French structuralist scholars, if at the most he was only a kind of distant stimulator for theoretical conjectures fundamentally alien to his point of view, we must still ask ourselves what role he played in spite of everything—what was his function in intellectual life? In order to provide hypothetical answers to this question, a preliminary contention as to the nature of French structuralism must be expressed.

I contend that French structuralism never existed as an *episteme*, or even as a regulating hegemony determining an axiomatic common denominator of scientific research. I might be stating the obvious, but I thereby deny a major theme of special issues and monographs devoted to the rise of structuralism. In consequence, French structuralist preaching may be aptly described as a covering apparatus concealing confused skirmishes of incompatible points of view, and also serving as a label for major attempts at syncretism. In structuralist literary criticism, I contend, actual borrowings from Saussure and functionalist linguistics remained minimal and rudimentary. On the contrary, ingredients taken from both Marxist and Freudian traditions were already more substantial. The salvage and recovery of those antiquated knowledges coming from Aristotle and Quintilian, called rhetoric, poetics, topics, and tropology, played an even more considerable role. César du Marsais's *Traité des tropes* (1713) certainly was more influential and more useful to many critics than Saussure ever was. At best, the latter served as a ritual reference aimed at irradiating the tropes of classical rhetoric with his "modernity." Finally, the most important ingredient that determined the actual regeneration of French criticism was the influence of Russian formalists and postformalists (like Bakhtin), in spite of the small number of translations available at the time.

I will not question here the influence of Lévi-Strauss's anthropology and Lacan's psychoanalysis, insofar as they can be seen as mediators between literary criticism and Saussure. I shall content myself with saying that I am in agreement with those (like Umberto Eco and Luis Prieto) who show that Lévi-Strauss retained only *some* elements of the phonological paradigm and covered them with a specific idealist philosophy. As for Lacan, it should be obvious that his reference to Saussure does not correspond either to an internal reshaping of the former or to an actual critique of Saussureanism but to a simple absorption, literally extravagant, of Saussure's terminology into his own reflection, a reflection not only alien to Saussure's thought but also, for better or worse, diametrically opposed to his.

I can now try to answer my previous question by formulating *seven* hypotheses regarding Saussure's actual role:

1. If Saussure remained a dead letter, he also became a password, a phantasmatic common reference for doctrinaires and scholars who most of the time did not have much else in common. He provided a sort of *phraseological cement* linking, in an atmosphere of good feelings, of "entente cordiale," scholars who were in fact seeking their ways in divergent directions.

If my conjectures are correct, Saussure was nothing but a token or a pledge of nonaggression at a time when, on the contrary, contradictions between twentieth-century theoretical traditions were stirring up and when actual obstacles and aporias were multiplying. This pledge of nonaggression, like any covenant of that kind, was also a pact of mutual support against common enemies: positivistic literary studies, empiricism, dogmatic Stalinist Marxism, and the still prominent heritage of critical neo-Hegelian synthesis. This is why no actual consensus was required for using any Saussurean term. It was not important that the *signifier* was perseveringly confused with the material signal, with the phonation, with the word considered apart from its meaning, with libidinal investment in speech, with the denotation of any phenomenon considered as a means for human praxis in relation to a goal, or with the first element in any deductive, inferential, or presuppositional relation. This is why the *signified* was indifferently taken for meaning, message, psychological or ontological reference, class of empirical objects, nonverbal reality referred to in a given statement, and so on. This is why the concept of the "arbitrariness of the sign" was likely to lead to curious new repudiations of Cratylism, this "arbitrary character" being conceived by some quite nonnegligible scholars as an adequate but somewhat belated rejection of the idea of a natural link between "words" and "things." This is why the concept of *value* in Saussure was hooked to the concept of value (*Werte*) in Freud, and to the same term in Marx, leading to curious disputes about the surplus-value in Saussurean value, in a sort of merry-go-round of ideological syncretism.

It should be added that this atmosphere of entente cordiale, of irenism, was something new in the republic of scholarship. It curiously differs from the atmosphere of violent, and somewhat Byzantine, polemic that spans, for instance, the history of modern German or Slavic scholarship.

2. Given the fuzzy and disparate character of the syncretic diffusion of Saussurean terminology, any *re*interpretation of his thought offered a facile effect of originality. This effect was induced by the malleability of Saussure's fragments and the absence of regulation regarding their use.

3. Saussure also provided a conventional mark of scientificity, considering that, at the time, the search for some sort of scientificity in literary studies was seen as mandatory. Such a requirement was to a certain extent a legacy of Russian formalism; more importantly, it was related to a new concept of academic prestige in the humanities and social sciences.

4. If Saussure provided a way of concealing profound discordances among scholars, he also served, perhaps most significantly, as a major component of the attempts at syncretism that characterize the structuralist epoch. He was not only a "common place"

for academics sharing neither goal nor methodology; he became also a purely illusory means of overcoming epistemological obstacles in the path of a general theory, a *théorie d'ensemble*.[7]

This syncretism was (and still is) particularly at work in literary studies. On one hand, this field was becoming a remarkable Babel of voices, and cognitive fragments indiscriminately extracted from historical materialism, psychoanalysis, philosophy, logic, and linguistic or philological traditions were more or less adroitly pasted up together as if their coexistence raised no question. On the other, literary scholars had become institutionally more prone to syncretism. One should probably put this contention the other way round: in the intellectual division of labor of liberal "postindustrial" societies, literary criticism is meant to become this common place, this place of the "no matter what," a monkey antic of old humanism, where digests of all philosophical and scientific paradigms are discharged and recycled.

Let me try to define "syncretism" in the sociology of knowledge. It is not a simple and sometimes commendable eclecticism, i.e., the choice at random of procedures and concepts refashioned following preestablished cognitive aims. Syncretism is a *factitious amalgamation of dissimilar ideas or theses that look compatible only insofar as they are not clearly conceived*. It is "*Vereinigung ohne Verarbeitung*" (Eisler): accumulation without reworking.[8] It leads to a euphoric confusion, determined by a sort of horror of incompatibilities; it results from a synoptic labor aimed at creating a false impression of totalization. By talking of syncretic tendencies, in the sense defined above, as the dominant trait of literary studies during the last twenty years, I am again stating the obvious. I believe, however, that the phenomenon has not been adequately acknowledged, and I therefore submit the present hypotheses as a starting point.

The label "structuralism" and the reference to Saussure thus had the role of serving for a specific time to provide a degree of self-regulation to this cranky aggregate. The phenomenon is not new in the tradition of bourgeois philosophies: a striking parallel could be drawn with late nineteenth-century sociohistorical Darwinism represented in France by G. Le Bon, G. Le Dantec, V. Pareto, G. Vacher de Lapouges, *e tutti quanti*. I trust that I am not reflecting the ideological confusion I try to describe by suggesting that all the works published over the structuralist era fall into the categories of syncretism, false synthesis, and neurotic repetition of epistemological breaks that occurred elsewhere and elsewhen. I nonetheless suggest that syncretism was (and still is) the common horizon of literary scholarship. It should perhaps be added that nowhere is it more evident than in university teaching, where a typical misconception of pluralism encourages the student to combine and absorb passively all the major currents of scholarship and philosophy.

5. These attempts at syncretism, for which "structuralism" provided a name, were overdetermined in the French sixties by the inability of France to keep pace with the great intellectual movements of the twentieth century. Insofar as most of the major Slavic, German, and Anglo-Saxon scholars had never penetrated French intellectual life and were not translated, their sudden and random "discovery" speeded up the process of syncretization. It should be remembered here that Wellek and Warren, who make considerable use of Saussure, had been translated in all European languages and in Japanese, Korean, Hebrew, and Gujarāti, before a French translation was undertaken in 1971. For lack of translations, those scholars like Greimas, Todorov, and Kristeva, who were able to cope with Balto-Slavic languages, were destined to play an important role of intermediary. Meanwhile, Ferdinand de Saussure, belonging to the Francophone realm, provided a sort of jingoistic solace, as being after all a major inspirer of some twentieth century theories.

6. As a major ingredient of what I claim as syncretism, Saussure himself was syncretized: amalgamated with Peirce, for instance, as if the two thinkers were naturally complementary, but also juxtaposed with Strawson, Frege, Ogden and Richards, or Chomsky, especially since the concept of reference, axiomatically absent from Saussure's thought, was seen (in a typical syncretic way) as *missing*, and therefore generously added to his system—in much the same way that Marxo-Christians were satisfied with discretely interpolating the "human soul" into Marx, in order to complete historical materialism.

7. Finally, syncretized and simplified as it might have been, Saussure's thought also became an obstacle, insofar as it seemed to provide not only a method but also a (fetishized) paradigm for a semiotics of nonverbal phenomena. Perhaps one should not say "Saussure's thought," but simply refer to the reliance on, and direct transposition of, any linguistic paradigm to other types of semiosis.

Nowhere is this more obvious than in the so-called "semiology of icons" as it developed (or tried to develop) for the last 15 years in France and Italy. This label is itself a good example of syncretism: "semiology" coming from Saussure, "icons" from Peirce, and the expression being applied to the study of simulacra like painting, photographs, and movies—a purely empirical grouping that, as we know, does not exactly correspond to what Peirce had in mind when he defined the category of "icons."

I recently surveyed the theoretical attempts in the Franco-Italian realm at constructing a semiotics of images, with or without reference to *l'iconicitá*.[9] To limit myself here to Saussure's import in this field, I believe that, far from helping anyone, linguistic fetishism became a serious epistemological obstacle. Roland Barthes, the jack-of-all-trades of his generation, was among the first to embark on a "semiology of images" for which he provided in 1964 an essay in *Communications* that was to be read and taught as a major breakthrough.[10] Barthes, having decided to produce "a semiology of images," immediately asks himself the following question: "Is analogical figuration (i.e. the copy) able to produce actual systems of signs?" We must stop at this first sentence, since all difficulties are eluded: the analogical character of images is laid down a priori; analogy is equated with the concept of "copy"; far from asking how there is meaning *as to* the image, Barthes formulates a question doubly biased on the side of linguistics: whether this meaning is made up of "signs" and to what extent it is "systematic" or "codified." I skip over more and more nebulous elaborations to get at what Barthes terms a "spectral analysis of the messages" contained in an advertisement for Panzani spaghetti: "Its signifier is the compound of tomato, fish, and tricolored shades (. . .) its signified is Italy, or else *italianity*." This is intuitively right —of a kind of intuition anyone could come to without a conceptual apparatus—but all the problems that a semiotician would normally address are confused and mishandled.

If one were asked to provide only one example of theoretical inconsistency, this famous statement about "iconic messages" (sic) would be sufficiently symptomatic of Saussurean dismemberment. Barthes, moreover, is not the most inconsistent of all. One has to read the epigones of structural semiotics to fathom the depths of irresponsibility and verbalism. Carontini's and Peraya's *Projet sémiotique*,[11] a handbook widely used by students, is a piling-up of Saussure, Peirce (revised by Morris), Ogden and Richards, Greimas, Kristeva, Barthes, and Eco; and for good measure, some glimpses of Derrida, Lacan, and Althusser. This ambiguous cocktail is baptized "le projet sémiotique" (in the singular), and the reader is unable to find the least discrepancy between Saussure and Lacan, Peirce and Kristeva.

It is risky to try to *explain* the development and success of structuralist syncretism. It can be seen as a substitutive simulacrum to

Marxism, understood as an encompassing framework for the social sciences. The dogmatic stagnation of offical Marxism, the slight prestige of French critical Marxists, and the absence of any alternative "bourgeois" consensus are elements that may help one understand the phenomenon. It is perhaps trivial to note that structuralism also corresponded with a sudden and rapid development of universities and especially of the humanities in academic structures. Such an inflation of literary studies seems inversely related to the decrease in influence of literature in high culture. There is also, as we noticed, the total collapse of more conservative philological methods and the need for glamorous and modern ways of dealing with cultural phenomena, notably those phenomena that were far from possessing any academic legitimacy, such as movies, TV, photographs, comics, and mass literatures. Henri Lefebvre, Fredric Jameson, and others have rightfully questioned and criticized structuralist triumphalism in all these respects.[12]

Liberal ideologies being always somewhat manic-depressive, forms of anaxiological skepticism evolved in the late seventies from the structuralist euphoria. This current of skepticism corresponds with the ideological stampede, isomorphic with political despair, of today's survivors of French ideology.[13]

NOTES

1. *Figures I*, 149. Trans. by the present author.

2. *CLG* (Paris: Payot, 1915, republ. 1967), p. 317.

3. L. J. Calvet, *Pour et contre Saussure* (Paris: Payot, 1975), pp. 26 ff.

4. See, for instance, the special issues of *Les Temps Modernes*, 246(1966), and *Esprit*, 360(1967). The best study on structuralism from an epistemological point of view remains Jean Piaget's *Le Structuralisme* (Paris: P.U.F., 1968; trans. as *Structuralism*, New York: Harper & Row, 1970). About structuralism considered as ideological fashion, see, for instance, Roger Crémant [pseud], *Les Matinées structuralistes* (Paris: Laffont, 1969).

5. René Picard, *Nouvelle Critique ou nouvelle imposture* (Paris: J.-J. Pauvert, 1965); with replies by Roland Barthes, *Critique et vérité* (Paris: Éditions du Seuil, 1966), and J.-P. Weber, *Néocritique et paléocritique* . . . (Paris: J.-J. Pauvert, 1966). On Lucien Goldmann and literary structuralism, see several of his essays gathered in *Marxisme et sciences humaines* (Paris: Gallimard, 1970).

6. It should be remembered that U. Eco's fundamental works in semiotics are posterior to 1970 and therefore escape our inquiry.

7. I am thinking here of *Tel Quel*'s *Théorie d'ensemble* (Paris: Éditions du Seuil, 1968). An extensive study of *Tel Quel* ideologies and notably theories of *l'écriture* remains to be done.

8. See J. Lalande et al., *Vocabulaire technique et critique de la philosophie* (Paris: P.U.F., 1926, republ. 1976), *verbo* "Syncrétisme."

9. Marc Angenot, *Critique de la raison sémiotique* (Montréal, 1980). Mimeographed.

The text refers to the semiotic theories of Barthes, "Groupe mu," Eco, Greimas, Kristeva, Lindekens, Metz, Porcher, and so on.

10. "Rhétorique de l'image," *Communications*, 4(1964), 40-51. The translations that follow are by the present author.

11. Carontini and Peraya, *Le Projet sémiotique* (Paris: Éditions Universitaires, 1971).

12. See, for instance, Henri Lefebvre, *Position: contre les technocrates* (Geneva: Gonthier, 1966), and Fredric Jameson's major works from *The Prison House of Language* (Princeton: Princeton University Press, 1972) to *The Political Unconscious* (Ithaca: Cornell University Press, 1981).

13. See Vincent Descombes and Jean Piel, eds., *L'année politico-philosophique: le comble du vide* [special issue of Critique, no. 392] (Paris: 1980), and François Aubral and Xavier Delcourt, *Contre la nouvelle philosophie* (Paris: Gallimard, 1977), among several polemical essays on the present state of affairs in "French ideology."

Chapter 9
Text and Context:
Derrida and Foucault on Descartes
Robert D'Amico

Structuralism remains an important hypothesis because it is an extreme hypothesis. The structuralist strategy intended to bring about a unified scientific development in the social sciences, not by imposing a common philosophical position (for example, materialism, behaviorism, empiricism, etc.), but solely at the level of a specific kind of formalization or method. Cultural formations were to be studied as systems of signs, such that an economy, kinship system, or even type of cuisine would be analyzed not in terms of its function, purpose, or utility for some culture but only in terms of how as a system it orders and establishes regularities. These cultural forms were to be seen as kinds of "texts" having both a semantic and syntactic dimension, and it was their syntactic level that could be given a formal representation. Therefore the subject matter of investigation and discovery would be the properties of such sign systems, their rules or regularities, with the possibility of revealing universal principles of ordering that cut across cultural diversities and empirical irregularities.

Some have concluded that, to the extent that the structuralist enterprise has failed or been abandoned, the initial objection to its exclusive emphasis on objective ordering at the expense of subjectivity has been confirmed. Specifically, the failure of structuralism and its attempt at a scientific method for the study of culture has been linked to the rise of the opposite strategy found in historicism and theories of interpretation. By historicism or interpretation theory I mean, roughly, theories in which it is held that the study of culture cannot be scientific as the result of an essential methodological difference and not simply a practical limitation. For the historicists, subjective beliefs or intentions are the key to understanding culture, and such comprehension is distinct from a scientific explanation. The inclusion of subjective interpretation in the account of the object suggests that the failure of formalization in the cultural "sciences" follows upon the recognition that formalism is an interpretive position, and one that is itself a cultural expression.

Though I think this debate is significant on its own terms, my reference to it here is only to introduce what I see as an attempt to pass beyond the exclusive alternatives stated above. If we are stuck with the term "post-structuralism," I understand it to refer to those who have tried to examine why we approach culture in precisely these alternatives of structure and history and not others. If the effort at formalization and semiotic modeling of culture has failed and there are, on the other hand, still reasons to believe that an intentional or subjective account is also inadequate, then perhaps the problem does concern these assumptions shared by structuralism and historicism in their common analogy of the cultural object as being "read" like a text. By their common analogy I mean that for structuralism the "object" we study is actually a systematic arrangement of signs, while in historicism every cultural object, like every text, has an excess of meanings and interpretations that can never be systematic or complete but only contextually understood.

The rest of this essay concerns suggestions for steps outside our present alternatives in an exchange between Jacques Derrida and Michel Foucault over a passage from Descartes—an exchange concerning the nature of a text and of textuality itself. This is a still useful exchange that occurs at an early moment in the development of post-structuralism. Both thinkers have been concerned with the metaphysics hidden within the analogy of the text and the view that such a metaphysics sets the parameters of our thinking concerning the social sciences. But I have chosen their exchange because it has the further advantage of giving us a specific concrete problem situation or example to discuss and therefore gives substance to these relatively abstract disputes. Although I have been emphasizing the wider connotation in structuralism of the word "text" as it can be applied to such non-booklike things as economic systems, the theoretical problems remain the same for even traditional textual objects and, in a short study, a focus on a traditional text allows us to avoid certain other problems that arise in dealing with more complex cultural objects.

The dispute has its origins in a brief analysis of Descartes's *Meditations* in Foucault's first major work, *Histoire de la folie*. We must recall that even though Foucault's name is now associated with this new, vague term "post-structuralism," owing to his own criticisms of structuralism, at the time of *Histoire de la folie* Foucault's work was considered a strong application of the structuralist method to historical research. Though Foucault's study was not formal in the strict sense of the term, he tried to examine a vast amount of material by isolating certain relatively abstract transformations in the classificatory and constitutive levels of prescientific theories of mental illness. The gloss on Descartes in Foucault's book comes within the discussion of major institutional and social changes in the treatment of the mad. It is this background, rather than the issues of philosophy, that Foucault suddenly rediscovers in Descartes's treatment of madness and skepticism. Such a structural linkage between different "discourses" raised a breath of historicism in Foucault's otherwise structuralist problematic. I believe that it was Derrida who first showed clearly the presence of this historicist tendency and that their exchange concerning this criticism led Foucault, in spite of his attitude in the debate, to change his approach radically. It is Foucault's modified views that I compare with Derrida's in the conclusion to this paper. To assist following the important points of both Derrida's and Foucault's "reading," I will quote the relevant passage from Descartes in full before turning to their respective expositions.

But it may be said, perhaps, that, although the senses occasionally mislead us respecting objects minute and those so far removed from us to be beyond the reach of those observations, yet there are many other presentations the truth of which it is impossible to doubt; as for example, that I am in this place, seated by the fire, clothed in a winter dressing gown, that I hold in my hands a piece of paper, with other such intimations. But how could I deny that I possess these hands and this body, and in that way escape being classed with persons in a state of insanity (*insanis*), whose brains are so disordered and clouded by dark bilious vapours as to cause them to assert that they are monarchs when they are in the greatest poverty; or clothed (in gold) and purple when destitute of covering; or that their heads are made of clay, their bodies of glass, or that they are gourds? But they are mad (*sed amentes sunt isti*) and I would be no less extravagant (*demens*) if I were to follow such examples.

Though this may be true, I must nevertheless here consider that I am a man, and thus, consequently, I am in the habit of sleeping and representing to myself in dreams those same things, or even sometimes others less probable, which the insane think are presented to them in their waking moments. . . . I cannot forget that, at the same time, I have been deceived in sleep by similar illusions. . . . I perceive so clearly that there exist no certain marks by which the state of waking can be distinguished from the state of sleeping, that I feel greatly astonished, and in amazement I almost persuade myself that I am now dreaming.[1]

Descartes excludes the traditional skeptical examples of madness while shifting the privileged example of systematic doubt to the dream. At the same time, in its historical determination, Foucault treats this textual strategy as only a philosophical expression of new social practices excluding and removing the mad from the public sphere of social life through confinement and legal disqualification. Foucault takes as his project in the book, one that can be seen at the microlevel in the passage we are considering, an investigation of the moment at which reason must exclude that which is other than itself, that which is unreason. At that moment reason, in objectifying unreason or madness, constitutes itself as the reason of inquiry, and it is on the basis of such a separation that the concepts of a scientific attitude are constituted. However, for Foucault the problem is to grasp such a separation without utilizing the very concepts that now overlay and presuppose the original separation.

No concepts of psycho-pathology will be allowed to play the organizational role — it is a matter of speaking of this debate between reason and non-reason without supposing a victor. . . . Then will appear the domain in which the man of reason and the man of madness separately but not yet separated produce the dialogue of their rupture. . . .[2]

Therefore, we have in the *Meditations* a moment in which epistemological questions about madness no longer concern the philosopher. The *Meditations* argue that the threat of madness no longer concerns philosophy, since confusion and error are not part of madness. Truth and error could not be part of madness, since they are signs of reflection and thought. To be in error is to think, and to be mad is simply not to think and therefore not to doubt. The "certainty" of the mad, which the skeptics had traditionally used against philosophers, is turned back upon them when Descartes argues that precisely because the mad never doubt they therefore never think. Finally, philosophers, even when they say things that are, as Descartes says, "extravagant" or mad-appearing (Am I asleep?), are in fact thinking. Therefore, unlike the mad, the philosophers as thinkers are not determined by their own metabolism—the black vapors that Descartes designates as the physical cause of the madman's illusions.

Descartes has therefore shifted the epistemological problem from what kind of objects are present to our mind to what kind of subject thinks. In that context, madness is simply the absence of thought, and that is why Descartes can dispense with it in such cavalier fashion. While the philosopher raises problems of the fallibility of perceptions because those are problems of epistemology, madness simply falls to the level of an empirical disorder.

In the economy of doubt there is a fundamental disequilibrium between madness on one side and dream and error on the other. Their situation is different in relation to both truth and inquiry; dream and illusion are surmounted through the very structure of truth; but *madness is excluded by the subject who doubts.*[3]

Among the many forms of illusion madness traces one of the paths of doubt most frequently cited during the sixteenth century. . . . Descartes banishes madness in the name of that which doubts and which can no more be mad than not think or not exist. . . . The problematic of madness . . . is modified in an almost imperceptible but nevertheless decisive manner. . . . Non-reason during the sixteenth century formed a sort of open peril which could always menace and compromise the relation of subjectivity and truth. The path of Cartesian doubt seems to testify that for the seventeenth century the danger is conjured away and madness is placed outside of the domain where the subject secures its rights to the truth . . . madness is exiled. If a man can always be mad, thought, as the sovereign exercise of a subject compelled to perceive the truth, cannot be insane. A line of division is traced which goes far toward making the familiar Renaissance experience of a rational Unreason impossible. Between Montaigne and Descartes an important event has occurred.[4]

Foucault calls his book a structural study of the history of madness because the complex of notions, institutions, scientific concepts, juridical-police measures, images, etc., are treated as a systematic ordering without concern as to whether they refer to a real object or not. Therefore Foucault's concern is not to uncover the origins of a scientific study of madness, nor to ask what was being studied under the name of madness, but rather to ask how madness became an "object" for the sciences, how it replaced or displaced older problems in medicine and physiology, and finally, how madness became a legal and institutional problem. Foucault's hypothesis is that, in these complex systems by which persons talk about, confine, define, and categorize such entities as madness, we will discover that which constitutes such an object from a precategorical experience. Therefore no privilege is given to the scientific concept, nor are prescientific objectifications of the phenomena treated as obscure and confused attempts at science. Rather, each level by which the "object" is carved out of experience is treated as autonomous, as wholly ordered or ruled on its own terms.

Since what Foucault calls the silence of the mad is inaccessible to any system of knowledge and always concealed by the objectification of madness in knowledge, Foucault argues that his history follows not the concept of madness but the historical decision that separated reason and unreason and therefore set the stage for a new science of abnormal behavior. It is this decision, this exchange of sense and non-sense, that Foucault calls the "elusive root and original confrontation" that the book strives to uncover in the sedimentation of knowledge and opinion. A structural study of the ordering of knowledge and opinion is the technique, and therefore in the passage from Descartes we find, when it is fitted into the structural study of the whole, an elliptical, unconscious formulation of this decision by which madness is handed over to medicine and therefore "disqualified" from serious discourse.

Let us turn to those passages in which Foucault tries to defend and locate the position of his own work. In raising a question concerning the intent of his book, Foucault seems to attach the study of madness to a larger, more profound question concerning the very possibility of meaning. Foucault argues that the constitution of meaning always requires an exclusion.

[T]he perception that western man has of time and space lets appear a structure of refusal, through which one denounces a speech as not being language, a gesture as not being productive (*n'étant pas oeuvre*) a figure as not having the right to take place in this history. This structure is constitutive of that which is meaning and non-meaning, or rather this reciprocity by which they are linked to one another. . . . The *necessity of madness* throughout the history of the West is linked to this movement of decision which detaches from the background noise and continuous monotony a significant language which completes itself and transmits itself in time; briefly, this decision is linked to the *possibility of history*.[5]

Foucault then draws the conclusion that every concept of madness, especially the medical or scientific concepts, is the result of some "capture," objectification, and consequent "repression" of the mad.

The perception which tries to know the mad in their savage state belongs necessarily to a world which has already captured them. The liberty of the mad is only understood from the heights of the fortress which imprisons them.[6]

Thus this "savage state" or untamed experience of madness, before all objectification, is what Foucault seeks, and he seeks it at the moment of the decision that separates reason and unreason. But is this decision itself historical or the condition of all that is historical? Foucault seems to answer that if madness, in whatever form it occurs, is simply *l'absence d'oeuvre*, then all the historian can hope to discover is:

the perpetual exchange, the obscure common root, the original confrontation which gives meaning to the unity as well as opposition of sense and non-sense.[7]

If Foucault is right, the historian discovers that which makes knowledge possible, the preconditions on the basis of which history can be seen as rational.

Here we see in its philosophical form one defense for the use of the structuralist method. Instead of looking at intellectual history as the search for the positive content of terms or concepts, or what certain concepts were referring to, we investigate, on the other hand, what makes concepts possible. One vision of structuralism is that it is an approach or vantage point that allows one to take a vast quantity of documents and find within them a unifying order or set of rules. If such rules were to be discovered they would, so it is claimed, allow a body of documents to "represent" or designate some particular object. The historian who uses the structuralist method, then, at least according to Foucault, does not make the error of prejudicing an analysis by already accepting the decisions of the historian's present as to questions of reference and meaning. The structural study uncovers the preconditions of meaning and reference and then historicizes those preconditions or constitutive acts.

Now what is particularly interesting about Foucault's defense of this procedure in his book—and Derrida is the only one to have pointed this out, to my knowledge—is that he combines a commitment to a structural study with a historicist conception of the relationship between the text and the world. By "historicist," I mean that Foucault seems to hold to a relationship of "reflection" or conditioning between Descartes's text, for example, and the actual juridical, political, and economic event of mass confinement and hospitalization of the mad in France before the Revolution. Descartes's *Meditations* reflect the repression and disqualification of the mad carried out by the police.

In an extended and penetrating criticism of the passage on Descartes, Derrida has raised some basic questions about Foucault's approach and the relationship between structural and historicist methodologies.[8] In *L'Écriture et la différence* Derrida argues that even though Foucault has drawn our attention to a "strategy" within the *Meditations*, the reading or interpretation of the text on the part of Foucault rests on an unexamined and unquestioned historicism running throughout the book and at the basis of the very project of the book.

Derrida finds the root problem in the very project of a history of madness. How, Derrida asks, can a history of the relationship between madness and reason be written if Foucault is going to claim to suspend the "privilege" given to reason over unreason? In the very use of language and meaning the privilege has already been given to reason so that, apart from silence, such a history fails on its own grounds. The problem, as Derrida sees it, is that Foucault is attempting, on one hand, to ask what makes meaning and reason possible while, on the other, hoping to locate some particular event or series of events in which this "decision" can be localized. The demand for its historical location and even the suggestion of certain historical factors or causes of the decision—such as Foucault's discussion of the economic and political reasons for the confinement of the mad—are what Derrida calls the historicist bias of the book.

For Derrida there is a philosophical question that is being avoided both with the appeal to structuralism and the unreflected historicism in Foucault's book. The division between sense and non-sense is a precondition for the possibility of meaning and therefore historicity; it is the root of historicity itself. The problem here is not one that can be localized in Descartes's *Meditation* or any historical event, because it is what allows us to constitute history as a domain of inquiry and to isolate events, causes, and meanings within that domain. It is a question of the disposition that makes texts and therefore history possible. To claim to put into question the authoritarianism inherent in our reason and its power of exclusion, if that is what Foucault claims he is doing, would be a hopeless and impossible task since, Derrida argues, it would deny itself at every moment that it communicated its results or gave meaning to its experiences.

What is the source and status of the language of this archaeology, of this language which must be understood by a reason which is not classical reason? What is the historical responsibility of this logic of archaeology? . . . Is it sufficient to organize a closed shop against the instruments of psychiatry in an effort to recover an innocence and break all complicity with the rational and political order which holds madness captive? Psychiatry is only a delegate of this order, one delegate among many . . . *all* our European languages, the language of all those who participate . . . is part of the delegation of that project Foucault defines under the title of capture or objectification of madness. Nothing in language and no one among those who speak it can escape the historical culpability —if there is such a thing and it is historical in the classical sense—over which Foucault seems to hold court. But it is perhaps an impossible trial since the hearing and the verdict ceaselessly reiterate the crime by the very fact of their utterance.[9]

Derrida situates his reading by arguing that positioning a text within a historical context must be preceded by an "internal, rigorous and exhaustive analysis" of the discourse of the text itself (the "sign itself" as he says) so as not to falsify the text with its contextual determination. In this particular example, Derrida argues that Foucault, aside from some suggestive insights, has blinded himself to the text through the imposition of an extra-philosophical problematic.

With regard to the passage in question, Derrida notes that it begins with a "perhaps" (*Sed forte*). This "perhaps" is missing from the original French translation. The madness hypothesis therefore is not in fact brushed away by decree or inattention as the overdetermined historical act that Foucault describes. Derrida holds—in what he calls a classical interpretation—that the whole paragraph that follows the "perhaps" is not Descartes's own objection but that of a nonphilosophical novice who is protesting such radical philosophical questions and doubts. The *sed forte* is a pedagogical and rhetorical part of a *feigned* objection. Descartes is echoing an imaginary nonphilosopher who says: "But of course we are sane men, there are limits to what we can doubt." Descartes then pretends to acquiesce to this *natural attitude*; he feigns agreement only the more radically to dislodge his imaginary interlocutor with the dream example.

The dream is introduced then as an experience more universal and common to all men than madness, an experience resistant to the *dogmatism of the natural attitude*. Thus, Derrida argues, rather than retreating from madness, the example of sleep radicalizes the analysis. In contrast to Foucault's suggestion of a complicity of exclusion between the philosopher and the medical or judicial structures, Derrida sees the "extravagance" of the mad rejected for pedagogical and rhetorical reasons—i.e., its weakness as an instrument of doubt. Madness is not *total enough* (whereas all men sleep) and it allows for the naturalistic response (but we who are speaking, we are sane).

In addition, there is a second "perhaps" later in the first *Meditation*, namely that which introduces the *genium malignum*.[10] Here, in Derrida's interpretation, is the total madness that was *apparently* excluded from the text. What Descartes strategically feigned to avoid— a total deception in which the world takes on the quality of the phantasms of the asylum—is introduced when the naturalistic attitude has been divested of its last defenses.

I have already noted that Foucault considers Descartes's attitude toward madness to be rooted in the Cartesian ontology. Descartes denies that the inability to determine criteria that distinguish with certainty between sleep and the waking state is similar to the doubts that may be raised about our knowledge when confronted with a man who believes himself made of glass. Doubt is only radical and philosophical in the dream example. The reason for the asymmetry of these two examples, according to Foucault, is that for Descartes madness is a fault *only of the body*; it is therefore not an epistemological issue (as the dream is) because it cannot be entertained by the *Cogito*. It has, as a phenomenon, been excluded from mind (the black vapors of Descartes's medical analysis indicate a physiological explanation) and, as the impossibility of thought, madness is *other than* the *Cogito*.

But this is the aspect of Foucault's treatment that Derrida finds so problematic and unreflective. Derrida is convinced that Descartes's argument that madness is an "ailment" or *thing* of the body (rather than of the *Cogito*) is a pedagogical or textual strategy, but not an effect in the text of social and historical "overdeterminations." Foucault seems to be arguing that, when the experience of Unreason is turned into a mental illness, there is a general repression of the mad, which extends into theory (Cartesianism, in this case). The exclusion of the mad from the world of reason is replicated in philosophy, just as their legal confinement follows from the definition of the mad in medical and clinical terms.

This issue of historicism, as Derrida calls it, raises the following questions: Does a philosophical text exhibit an unconscious exclusion determining and even superseding the movement of its argument? Is Descartes's text a small fissure in an overdetermining extratextual historical rupture? Are these texts, especially those of philosophy, merely clumsy seismographs registering shifts in what Foucault calls monumental history? While Derrida agrees that the text imposes itself, its own closures and forces, on the writer and reader, not the reverse, he in this context defends what he calls the truth *en droit* of Descartes's reasoning. In Derrida's view, one must not be carried away by the discovery of reading as closure and strategy. For even after the discovery that all philosophical texts have this closure built into them, one is still forced to use the language of philosophy to continue to speak about it. On one hand, we can view ourselves as caught within the text, but Derrida emphasizes that the text is not merely a metaphor of some broader social power of exclusion. Foucault, on the other, has tried to do both—he wants to swamp the text with the force of social practices and at the same time see the decision of excluding unreason as the source of historicity itself, as the source of the text itself.

Foucault says, "*La Folie, c'est l'absence d'oeuvre*" . . . But the *oeuvre* begins with the most elementary discourse, with the first articulation of meaning, with the phrase, with the first syntactic beginning of an "as such" since to make a phrase is to manifest a possible meaning . . . [the phrase] carries in itself normalcy and meaning no matter what the state, health or madness of those who offer it. . . . In the poorest syntax the logos is reason and a reason already historical. And if madness is in general outside of all factual and determined historical structure then madness is in general and in essence silence.[11]

Derrida's rejection of the historicist account leads him to a radical interpretation of the control over doubt in the *Meditations*. In fact, Derrida argues that Descartes's text is parallel to Foucault's own reflections on the relationship between reason and unreason. Descartes's strategy to deal with doubt seeks a point of reference prior to all meaning and reason, and such a zero point of reflection is what makes philosophical discourse, or any discourse, possible. Descartes did not, in Derrida's view, demonstrate a historical prejudice in his rejection of the case of madness (making Descartes an unwitting ally of the police), but grasped an exclusion that is at the very nature of discourse and language. Foucault's misreading is then, Derrida concludes, only a part of Foucault's lack of reflection on the very project of his book and the failure of his "archaeology of silence."

Since the *Cogito* no longer concerns the objectivity or content of thought, Descartes was correct in seeing madness as a matter of indifference. The problem Descartes posed, and Foucault poses without realizing it, is that of radical exclusion. The *Cogito* is what is left over when everything I think is doubted, and therefore, as that which survives radical exclusion, it reveals what makes the act of exclusion and doubting possible. Descartes places the *Cogito* outside the separation, or prior to the separation, of reason and unreason. All efforts to enclose this moment within a historical set of concerns miss its essential point. Any historicist reduction, Derrida argues, will try to erase precisely this difference, which must precede historicity because it is its precondition and will erase what is Descartes's genuinely radical level of inquiry.

The *Cogito* at the end of the first meditation—what Derrida calls its "hyperbolic extension"—as it allows reason and unreason to determine themselves, is the critical moment in the text. For Derrida, the "exclusion" in the *Meditations* is not where Foucault places it but precisely here, where Descartes retreats from the total hyperbole and guarantees the *Cogito* in God. It is God that saves the *Cogito* from its hyperbole and from the mad silence that must stand as an ever-present possibility. God protects the *Cogito* from insanity. The Foucaultian interpretation only applies at that moment (which is not strictly speaking historical) where Descartes must confine the *excess* of the *Cogito* so as to *organize* a *philosophical discourse*. Descartes must prevent the *Cogito* from "choosing" the absence of the *oeuvre*; he must preserve the possibility that it can *say its choice* and continue to be a speaking subject.

Derrida's point is to show that God actually represents the identification of the *Cogito* with *parole*—that is, with the self-transparent act of speech contained in the performative-like utterance, "I think, therefore I am." For Derrida, this series of identifications between speech, *Cogito*, and God is a fundamental structure in the relatively autonomous history of philosophy, which he designates as "logocentrism," or the metaphysics of presence that reiterates itself continually throughout the history of the philosophical text.[12] Thus, Descartes's text is not to be read as the theoretical reflection of a social practice ostracizing the mad but as a repetition of the philosophical act whereby writing and the text itself are excluded from the self-presence of speech.

God is the name and the element of that which makes possible an absolutely pure and absolutely self-present self-knowledge. From Descartes to Hegel and in spite of all the differences that separate the different places and moments in the structures of that epoch, God's infinite understanding is the other name for the logos as self-presence. The logos can be infinite and self-present, it can be *produced* as *auto-affection* only through the *voice*; an order of the signifier by which the subject takes from itself into itself, does not borrow outside of itself the signifier that it emits and that affects it at the same time. Such is at least the experience—of consciousness—of the voice; of hearing (understanding)-oneself-speak (*s'entendre-parler*) that experiences, lives and proclaims itself as the exclusion of writing, that is to say of the invoking of an "exterior," "sensible," "spatial" signifier interrupting self-presence.[13]

For Derrida, obviously, the text does not function simply as a latent expression of something outside itself. That which appears external to the text, as its reference, is produced by the resources of the text itself. Therefore, appeals to historical conditions and setting up a relationship of reflection between the text and such conditions are only the effects of the metaphysical traps within writing and the presence of the word.

Foucault has not sidestepped this line of criticism in Derrida's article, and in his reply to these criticisms he focuses on the fundamental issue of historicism. Foucault claims that the question raised by the attacks on referential unity in the text (and here Foucault and Derrida agree) is whether there is anything anterior or exterior to the text. Foucault claims we are in the midst of a traditional question: is philosophical discourse itself conditioned? If there is something inaccessible to the text, something extratextual that determines and constrains the production of discourse, then philosophy cannot claim to be a foundational discourse. Foucault argues that Derrida has tried to preserve for philosophy its old autonomy and has revived the classical function of criticism, namely, to protect philosophy from its determination by social and historical forces.

Foucault begins by arguing that in designating the dream as more "universal," Derrida really erases the double function of the dream in the discourse of the *Meditations*. A "meditation" functions both as an argument of logic *and* as an exercise or demonstration. Descartes discredits the example of madness at the level of an "exercise." The dream as frequent, accessible to all men, and repeatable *suits meditation*—its appropriateness allows the "training" to continue. In other words, it does not put the whole enterprise of philosophic inquiry into question, nor hold up the meditative discourse. Thus it is this structure inherent in the "meditations" as a discourse that leads Descartes to choose the *customary* over the *extravagant.*

This is what Foucault meant when he argued that madness, for Descartes, concerns not the objects of thought but the *subject who thinks*. The dream example has the unique privilege of allowing me to entertain strange fantasies, and even leads me to the "astonishing" realization that there are no criteria for distinguishing being awake and being asleep, but without in any way preventing the *Meditations* from continuing. *Age ergo somniemus*—this supposition not only does not affect the enterprise of a "search for truth," but it leads the inquiry on, in the form of the dream example. The dream provides the unique example in which the subject who thinks is disturbed, astonished, troubled, and led to doubt, but never *in doubt* of being able to carry on the philosophical inquiry.

Foucault, in defending this reading, considers the vocabulary distinguishing the account of madness and the dream. His point is that there is a textual difference there that supports the view that the two examples have a different function and status within Descartes's discourse. The discussion of madness resorts to a vocabulary of comparison in which I contrast my experiences with those of the mad, while the discussion of the dream uses the vocabulary of memory; I recall, I remember, I realize. In the dream example, the events concern present experiences (my hand, the fire), whereas, in madness, another "scene" is created of phantasms (bodies of glass, heads of clay). Whereas the dream example leads to a kind of proof that no criteria can distinguish it from being awake, the madness example is simply put aside as "extravagant." Though it would be "extravagant" to entertain the possibility of being mad, the possibility of being asleep can be the object of reflection. The difference here is that one threatens to disqualify the very project of reflection itself and therefore must in turn be disqualified from a "meditative" inquiry.

For Foucault, then, there are two parallel but different "exercises" in the *Meditations—demens* and *formiens,* which both Descartes and Derrida unsuccessfully try to reconcile. Foucault argues that a discursive analysis shows that the two forms of doubt are not—as they are presented in the text—continuous. This hidden or repressed separation is what Foucault calls the "exclusion"—an exclusion that has a historical or extraphilosophical origin.

For example, our attention should be drawn to the fact that Descartes uses three terms for "madness"—*insani, amentes,* and *demens. Insani* is significant because it is taken from medical terminology and refers to a victim of illusions arising from vapors in the brain. However, after that example, Descartes then uses the terms *demens* and *amentes* at the crucial moment in the passage where he "excludes" the example of madness for purposes of doubt. These terms are *juridical* and designate a category of people who are incapable of religious, judicial, or civil duties and responsibilities. Therefore *amentes* and *demens* are terms of disqualification, of lack of capacity. Unlike feigning sleep, pursuing the extravagances of the mad has the added deficiency of disqualifying the subject as a qualified inquirer. *Demens* signifies the inability to continue the end of discourse, and hence the need to avoid and exclude this possibility. *Dormiens* sustains the continuity and qualifications of the subject as one who meditates.

Thus it is not the case, as Derrida "classically" supposes, that madness is a *weak or inferior* example; rather, the dream and madness examples *confront one another,* on Foucault's interpretation, and are systematically opposed in the differences articulated in Descartes's discourse. It is a choice between *two exercises* or examples, only one of which sustains the discursive practice of meditation and allows the thinking subject to be modified by a discourse.

It is necessary to pay attention to the very title "Meditations"—Every discourse, whatever it is, is constituted through a whole of utterances (*ensemble d'énoncés*) which are each produced in their time and place as discursive events. In the case of a pure demonstration these utterances are . . . linked . . . according to formal rules—the subject in this case is fixed, invariant and neutral. A meditation, on the other hand, produces as part of its discursive event utterances which carry with themselves *modifications* of the subject who grasps these statements (*sujet énonçant*)—the subject, that is, passes from incertitude . . . to wisdom. . . . Briefly the meditation implies a subject modifiable by the very effects the discursive event itself produces—a demonstrative meditation.[14]

Thus a meditation has a double structure—its propositions form a system and its exercises form a special kind of subject who can state the truth. However, between these stuctures there are gaps where, Foucault argues, the exercises and propositions cross, where the illusion of an unbroken system breaks open. This is precisely what we see in those pages on dreams and madness, and it is this event that philosophies repress by denying the determination of the extratheoretical practices on their text.

Derrida proposes a voice behind the text, the nonphilosopher with whom Descartes will have a dialogue and whom Descartes will lead to radical doubt. However, Foucault argues, is this not the very exclusion we have been describing? Of course it is more subtle than Descartes's simple rejection of extravagance. But, in giving the weak position to the nonphilosopher, Derrida's reading of Descartes allows the dream example to disarm the interlocutor as well as disqualify him (he is *not* a philosopher). Derrida has to insert the *voice behind* the text, to read this into the text, so as to again give the *double* lecture of the *Meditations* its appearance of unity and coherence. Derrida, to conceal the gaps, must therefore exclude that which would exclude the discourse—which is done through the unqualified voice of the naive nonphilosopher (mysteriously appearing behind the words of the text).

The same holds for Derrida's attempt to treat both the *genium malignum* and the *Cogito* as the moment when Descartes does confront the issue of madness in its total, hyperbolic state. But here Foucault argues that the *Cogito* and *genium malignum* are precisely able to be controlled, voluntary exercises of the meditating subject because of the exclusion already noted to assure the structure of the *Meditations* as a discourse. For Foucault, the significance of this text is its effort to qualify the kind of subject who has the right to think and question; a qualification with great historical import, though that is concealed through a discursive strategy. This strategy, however, can be deciphered when it is seen in the context of the social practices that determine it, but not when it is treated as a "sign in itself."

It is not simply as a result of inattention that the classical interpreters, before Derrida and like him, have erased these passages of Descartes. Today, Derrida is the most decisive representative of this system whose ultimate manifestation is the reduction of discursive practices to textual traces alone—[reductions such as] the invention of voices behind the text, so as not to have to analyze the mode of implication of the subject in a discourse. . . .

I will not say that this is a metaphysics, *the* metaphysics, or its closure, which is hidden in such "textualization" of discursive practices. I will not go so far; I will say that this is a small historically well determined pedagogy . . . which teaches the student that there is nothing outside of the text but that within it, in its intersections, its spaces, and in what is not said resides the source (*réserve*) of its origin; there is no point in looking elsewhere, for right here, certainly not wholly in the words, but in the words as erasures (*comme ratures*), in their grid (*grille*), "the meaning of being" speaks itself. A pedagogy which, conversely, gives to the instructor this unlimited sovereignty endlessly to respeak (*redire*) the text.[15]

It would seem that the most important conclusions to be drawn from the Foucault-Derrida exchange concern the ontological status of texts, writing, or discourse, and the metaphysical framework that shapes our readings. First, as regards the text itself, this approach effaces the distinction between the original and its readings. The aim of the reading, contrary to all naive realisms, is not the purity of the original, not the full meaning of what the author created, but the operation and functioning of the text itself as text—as it is reiterated and reproduced. Texts do not face directly onto the world but are embedded in networks of practices, and their operations as texts within the intertextual universe of the secondary languages of criticism are what Foucault calls the "rules" discoverable in a discursive formation. The discovery of such rules, strategies, or whatever they are called is not to be seen as the truth of the given discourse, and is designed against those deep and traditional metaphysical closures that support the pursuit of certainty of reference.

Second, texts as objects that have independent objective relations with other objective formations function in part to exclude, repress, transgress, deny, and close off. In such ways any given text deploys a politics or ethics. In emphasizing the disqualification of the mad in his *Meditations*, Descartes is not telling us something about himself, nor is he marshaling valid arguments, according to Foucault. Rather, Descartes's text itself deploys a strategy, a classification which, independently of its author, is also a disqualification and exclusion that sets up a hierarchy of values and possible practices available as such once the text exists as a text. These practices or strategies are *in* the text to be discovered and utilized; they are not in Descartes. They are as much a part of the text as an object as the discovery of the difference between composite and prime numbers is *in* the number system and not simply in the mind of whoever grasps the distinction.

Contrary to interpretation theories, it is precisely this objective status and functioning of the text that makes reading possible, not the subjective consciousness of the reader or author. But, on the other hand, contrary to structuralism, the text is not a natural object; it does not have a "mute" relationship to itself and its world.

What will happen to the study of texts if we reject the metaphysical traditions still present in historicism and structuralism, along with their by-product, the search for a "true reading"? There are differences finally in Foucault's and Derrida's answers as we have already seen. But at a minimum they agree that we cease looking for some transcendental vantage point by which to assess and judge different systems of representation. What we then have left to us are the effects of discursive systems as they allow representations to work. We do not learn about mankind, consciousness, meaning, or any ultimate referent of our discourses and texts. If some of Derrida's arguments are taken seriously by Foucault, as I believe they are in his later writing, then their efforts converge only to the extent that discourses or texts are treated as objects in the world, not anterior spaces for transparent representations either of objects or beliefs. Foucault, unlike Derrida, does not think that this "objective" view of texts is solely a theoretical achievement, or that political criticism is doomed to the status of a metaphysical surrogate.

Discourse has its own rules of appearance, but also its own conditions of appropriation and operation: an asset that consequently, from the moment of its existence . . . poses the question of power: an asset that is by its nature the object of struggle, a political struggle.[16]

The position I have constructed from the exchange between Derrida and Foucault is indeed a strange and difficult way to think about the history of theory. We have long tended to think of texts as the mere vehicles for what philosophers used to call ideas and then called consciousness. Traditionally, the obstacles to truth lay not in the texts themselves but somehow in the readers and authors—the texts were the windows through which a critical gaze examined the issues. It seems that now not only has the philosopher lost a "natural" language but, further, the languages of criticism and the literary function of the text fill the gap left by the disappearance of pure philosophical inquiry. A sign of such recourse in theory to the critical or second languages is that both Derrida and Foucault, in their treatment of Descartes, concern themselves with the literary effects and symptoms of the text, not the traditional issues of sound philosophical argument. Between Derrida and Foucault there is no traditional philosophical dispute, which is why the debate is elusive. What is left is the absence of older certainties.

We can turn Derrida's question back upon himself. What is the status of his texts? As readings, do they reveal the mechanisms of other texts or simply of themselves? If we are forced to avoid the word "represent," because of these criticisms, how finally do we even say what it is one reading does for another text or another reading? Are we being driven, as in traditional skepticism, to an ultimately inexpressible position which remains, as always, the only escape from metaphysical tangles? Of course, I do not mean that these questions have failed to occur to either Derrida or Foucault. Each in his own way has virtually discussed nothing else—it is the single note of their works. But their conclusions, if I understand them, are precisely skeptical. There is a fundamental limitation or impossibility at the heart of thought and representation—we cannot both represent and represent ourselves representing.

Perhaps it is not useless to reiterate that while these problems remain unanswered, the older certainties remain unavailable. Once every reading is strategic, none can claim innocence and none can rely on intrinsic privilege. One might then ask, in frustration, if there is finally no way to read a text, no way even to judge a reading? If "anything goes," why do texts not simply reduce to black marks on a page? The answer is that texts are not the kinds of objects we have traditionally understood them to be. A text or discourse exists not through the systematic exclusion of misreading—quite the reverse. To use Karl Popper's phrase, a text objectively exists, not just at the moment it is correctly read, but quite autonomously in "its dispositional character of being understood or misunderstood or misinterpreted, which makes a thing a book."[17] Can such reflections assist further investigations? Certainly, the most promising directions of inquiry cut across our traditional dichotomy between the sciences and the humanities in an interesting fashion. Such studies, however, are likely to forego not only the search for a privileged discourse or foundation for thought but also the traditional humanist expectations of finding the answer to our innermost fears and hopes.

NOTES

1. Descartes, *Oeuvres philosophiques* Tome II (1638-42), ed. F. Alquié (Paris: Garnier, 1961), p. 178 (Latin) and pp. 405-6 (French).

2. M. Foucault, *Folie et déraison: Histoire de la folie à l'âge classique* (Paris: Gallimard, 1961), p. i. There is a second edition of this work, which eliminates the orignal preface and

adds two appendices called "La Folie, l'absence d'oeuvre" and "Mon corps, ce papier, ce feu" under the title simply of *Histoire de la folie* (Paris: Gallimard, 1972). Since there will be quotes from both editions, they will be designated as *Folie et déraison* and *Histoire de la folie* respectively in the following footnotes. The English translation, *Madness and Civilization*, trans. Richard Howard (London: Tavistock, 1967) is an abridged translation of *Folie et déraison* but does not include any of the passages discussed in this article. An interesting study of the Foucault-Derrida exchange, which puts emphasis on its relevance to literary theory, is Shoshana Felman, "Madness and Philosophy *or* Literature's Reason," *Yale French Studies* No. 52 (1975), 206-28.

3. Foucault, *Folie et déraison*, p. 55.

4. *Ibid.*, pp. 56-57.

5. *Ibid.*, p. vi.

6. *Ibid.*, p. vii.

7. *Ibid.*

8. J. Derrida, *L'Écriture et la différence* (Paris: Éditions du Seuil, 1967). The essay on Foucault is "Cogito et histoire de la folie," pp. 51-96.

9. *Ibid.*, p. 58. Foucault says of his own style of writing in the study on madness: "it was necessary to maintain oneself in a sort of relativity without recourse. . . . A language without support was therefore necessary: a language which could enter into the play but still permit an exchange. . . . It was a matter of safeguarding at all costs the *relative* while being *absolutely* understood." *Folie et déraison*, p. x.

10. Descartes, *Oeuvres philosophiques*, pp. 181, 412.

11. Derrida, *L'Écriture et la différence*, p. 48.

12. The full discussion of Derrida's attack on metaphysics as a tradition can be found in *Of Grammatology*, trans. Gayatri Chakravorty (Baltimore: The Johns Hopkins University Press, 1976).

13. Derrida, *L'Écriture et la différence*, p. 98.

14. Foucault, *Histoire de la folie*, p. 593.

15. *Ibid.*, p. 602.

16. M. Foucault, *Archaeology of Knowledge*, trans. A. M. Sheridan-Smith (New York: Pantheon, 1972), p. 120.

17. See Popper's *Objective Knowledge: An Evolutionary Approach* (Oxford: Clarendon Press, 1972), especially chs. 3 and 4.

Chapter 10
Breaking the Signs:
Roland Barthes and the Literary Body
John O'Neill

In my view, any strictly Platonist or historicist attempts to grasp the
shift from structuralism to post-structuralism involve "misreading"
what each analytic strategy brings to literary and semiological criticism. There can be no general estimate of this yield apart from what
one can ground in the practice of individual thinkers such as Roland
Barthes, whose encounter with the lively intellectual movements of
his day is continuously revised or "revisioned" from work to work.
Situated between Lévi-Strauss and Derrida, and with some reference
to Lacan and Foucault—though lacking the stamina of all of them—
Barthes's itinerary consciously, if not indulgently, takes us over the
difficult ground lying between a *science of literature* (structuralism)
and the *permanent revolution* or *atopia of language* (deconstructionism). Thus, at one level, it seems best to think of structuralism and
deconstructionism as absolutely relative analytic strategies. Where
thought is settled, its objects achieve an individual and reified status
—one might say, they acquire a reality and a morality that it is hard
to question. Yet things and relationships, realities and values, are
never quite solidary. They may be placed within larger frames of
space and time that suspend their individual weight, refloating them
as changing values of an underlying structure, pattern, or myth. For
a time, thought will again be trapped in fascination with the per-
manence and universality of structure freed from evanescent detail.

Inevitably, however, every structure seems to oscillate, and, never having achieved perfect closure, once again to open up to the tide of history, social change, and individual appropriation. All human institutions seem to reveal a similar cycle, as may be seen from the great testaments of Vico, Hegel, and Marx. This is not to deny, of course, that at a different level of ideological and historical concreteness it may be appropriate to view structuralism and deconstructionism as a continuous strategy, project, or tradition.

At first sight, literature as an institution might appear to be indifferent to such observations. After all, literature is demonstrably the work of individuals creating artifacts whose power to describe human reality, society, and nature resides in a competent use of language. Literary realism combined with literary individualism seems to capture the essence of our literary institutions. Such, at any rate, was the case until it could be argued that these were merely oppressive fictions of the literary establishment. To destroy such an establishment, literary structuralists began to find texts without authors, as well as intertextuality and the coproductivity of writing and reading freed from linguistic realism. The excitement of these discoveries very quickly, if not from the very start, hastened structuralism into post-structuralism — or deconstructionism. As a matter of fact, something very similar occurred in the social sciences. Here the constructivist attack upon positivism could not be controlled by phenomenology, whose formalism quickly yielded to a variety of deconstructionist strategies in pursuit of the social production of meaning and order.[1] We cannot investigate these connections here. Yet, in following Barthes's itinerary, we shall be very close to these developments, at least as they influenced the life of a figure who met them with different degrees of enthusiasm, practicing and revising their precepts according to his own best sense:

> In short, structuralism will be just one more "science" (several are born each century, some of them only ephemeral) if it does not manage to place the actual subversion of scientific language at the center of its programme, that is, to "write itself." How could it fail to question the very language it uses in order to know language? The logical continuation of structuralism can only be to rejoin literature, no longer as an "object" of analysis but as the activity of writing, to do away with the distinction derived from logic which turns the work itself into a language-object and science into a meta-language, and thus to forego that illusory privilege which science attaches to the possession of a captive language.[2]

Structuralism and Demythologization

Although Barthes on two occasions at least seems to have espoused what he later saw as the myth of the scientificity of literature, even

his most structuralist studies appear as mocking, self-consuming artifacts. In *Le Système de la mode* (1967), for example, he submerges
himself in the world of women's fashion, apprentices himself to the
fictions whereby those who, like himself, seek to be loved cover
themselves in words, fabrics, and fabrication. This world of fashion
prefigures the world of La Zambinella, in which truth and appearance
are no more solid than male and female. Like a child, or like Michelet,
he wanted to get into the secret of words, into the secret of women,
to assume their fascination before a public. Hence *Le Système de la
mode* will appear to be a forsaken intellectual enterprise unless we
understand its forbidden motive, its pleasure in the erotic spaces between the flesh and the word, between the exoticism of the language
of clothes and the language of science when juxtaposed:

Is not the most erotic portion of a body *where the garment gapes*? In perversion
(which is the realm of textual pleasure) there are no "erogenous zones" (a fool-
ish expression besides); it is intermittence, as psychoanalysis has so rightly stated,
which is erotic: the intermittence of skin flashing between two articles of clothing
(trousers and sweater), between two edges (the open-necked shirt, the glove and
the sleeve); it is this flash itself which seduces, or rather, the staging of an ap-
pearance-as-disappearance.[3]

In every case, language and the flesh exceed the attempt to classify
and organize them. On Barthes's account, it is as though language can
no more be completely classified than a woman can ever be fully
dressed: hence the failure of structuralism. By the same token, neither
language nor a woman can ever be completely stripped: hence the
impossibility of deconstructionism and of demystification. With
women, as with language, style is taken to be everything: it held
Barthes in endless fascination. This, however, anticipates Barthes's
itinerary, and we should now follow him without the privilege of his
continuously revised program.

In his preface to the 1970 edition of *Mythologies*, Barthes provides
the retrospective standpoint from which this phase of his work is to
be considered. It represents a combination of Saussureanism and
semioclasm, that is, an attempt to break the signs, to demythologize
by means of a detailed analysis of the sign system that fulfills the
ideological function. Later on, Barthes abandoned the "euphoric
dream of scientificity" with which the current state of linguistics
seduced semiology and literary criticism. His *Système de la mode* is
exceptional for the attempt to devise an abstract, monological system of clothing signs that never steps outside the world of women's
fashion into the social and economic system upon which it is floated.
By contrast, in *Mythologies*, Barthes never pursues the analytic strategy at the expense of the critical task of unveiling the operation

whereby bourgeois myths naturalize the objects, events, and relationships that underwrite the status quo, essentializing it and removing it
from historical and political change. Here we can present only a single
example given in some detail rather than try to capture the variety
of topics pursued in *Mythologies*. The example is that of a magazine
cover which, during the Algerian war of independence, shows a black
soldier saluting the French flag.[4] In formal semiological terms the
elements of the myth of imperial France may be analyzed in terms of
the accompanying schema:[5]

	D.1. SIGNIFIER Photographic image	D.2. SIGNIFIED Negro Saluting French flag	
Language	D.3. SIGN C.I. SIGNIFIER		C. II. SIGNIFIED Colonialist nationalism, militarism
Myth	C. III. SIGN		

The image presents a self-sufficient whole, in which the Negro's
salute and the greatness of the French Empire overlap and leave no
room for anticolonialism. The signified is swallowed in the signifier,
and an unhistorical sign closes the circuit of meaning to constitute an
irreproachable myth of imperialism. In order to deconstruct the myth
in this case, it is necessary to perform the following "readings":

(a) By focusing on the empty signifier, the reader allows the black
     soldier saluting to stand as a *symbol* of French imperialism.
     This is the standpoint of the journalist who must find a form
     for the concept he has to convey.
(b) If the reader focuses upon the full signifier, distinguishing de-
     notation and connotation, the myth is decoded and the black
     soldier becomes an *alibi* for French imperialism. This is the
     standpoint of the mythologist engaged in deconstruction.
(c) If the reader responds to the signifier as an inextricable whole
     of denotation and connotation, the black solider is the very
     presence of French imperialism. This is the naive standpoint
     of the reader of myths.

Myths escape decoding by bypassing language, avoiding the critical
unveiling or liquidation of their meaning by *naturalizing* it so that
the reader remains in the natural attitude, so to speak, of the myth

consumer. Because language is never at the zero degree, it cannot avoid feeding myths:

Now in a fully constituted myth, the meaning is never at zero degree, and this is why the concept can distort it and naturalize it. We must remember once again that the privation of meaning is in no way a zero degree: this is why myth can perfectly well get hold of it, give it for instance the signification of the absurd, of surrealism, etc. At bottom, it would only be the zero degree which could resist myth.[6]

From this standpoint, Barthes considers that in *Writing Degree Zero* he had in fact been concerned with the demythologization of literature. We may indeed take this to be the case for the light it throws upon his later work and, in particular, on the much bolder critical strategies devised to carry out his project. The symbiosis between language and myth is such that it is impossible for literary criticism, linguistics, or structuralism to avoid their own mythologies. Barthes was aware, of course, of having succumbed to these mythologies in his proposals for a science of literature, that is, the most general discourse upon the plurality of meanings ever attributed to a work. In practice, he withdraws from such a project in favor of the exploration of the ties between the literary text and the *literary body.*

The Question of Style

With the benefit of Lacan's powerful revision of Freud, Barthes found himself turning away from the politics of criticism toward the pleasures of the text. How this shift was accomplished may be seen from his transformation of an early, if awkward, terminology in which he distinguished the two modes of transitive and intransitive writing— the work of the *écrivant* and of the *écrivain*. Throughout the classical period, there existed an official discourse shared by the writer (*écrivant*) and the preachers. These were "transitive" men whose task was to instruct and explain without any concern for the reflexive features of language, which they assumed to be an unambiguous instrument of communication. This separation of language and literature arose from the suppression of rhetoric, and it lasted until Mallarmé, Proust, and Joyce—those "intransitive" men—restored the reflexivity and productivity of language to the author (*écrivain*), making him inseparable from the act of writing:

. . . the modern verb *to write* is becoming a sort of indivisible semantic entity. So that if language followed literature—which, for once perhaps, has the lead—I would say that we should no longer say today "*j'ai écrit*" but, rather, "*je suis écrit*", just as we say "*je suis né, il est mort, elle est éclose.*" There is no passive idea in these expressions, in spite of the verb *to be*, for it is impossible to transform "*je suis écrit*" (without forcing things, and supposing that I dare to use this expression at all) into "*on m'a écrit*" ["I have been written" or "somebody wrote me"]. It is my opinion that in the middle verb *to write* the distance between the writer and the language diminishes asymptotically. We could even say that it is subjective writings, like romantic writing, which are active, because in them the agent is not interior but *anterior* to the process of writing. The one who writes here does not write for himself, but, as if by proxy, for a person who is exterior and antecedent (even if they both have the same name). In the modern verb of middle voice *to write*, however, the subject is immediately contemporary with the writing, being effected and affected by it. The case of the Proustian writer is exemplary: he exists only in writing.[7]

So conceived, the author (*écrivain*) withholds himself from the social commitment of language and official literary discourse: the best an author can do is to be responsible to literature as a failed commitment, neither true nor false. In practice, or in our age, writer and author are rarely separable identities, and we find ourselves engaged in writing for our own sake as well as that of society, simultaneously using a language we seek to emancipate from common usage, earning a living in universities, laboratories, and bookstores while half-excused from life.

Yet Barthes also conceives of the author as a productive worker, forging a native language whose strength lies in his own body, from which language acquires a surplus value beyond anything the writer could intend because he is wholly given up to the immaterialism of language and the body.[8] Such a concept of language and embodiment required Barthes's later theory of the text and, in particular, the method of fragmentary writing that became the very mark of Barthes's pleasure in and of texts.[9] We are required now to abandon the notion of the literary work as a sort of Newtonian object and to conceive of it as an endlessly relativized text between texts — as intertextuality.

Viewed from this perspective, the text loses its essential significance and becomes a radically symbolic play of language whose efficacy involves us in a hermeneutics and psychoanalysis of the polyvalent meanings from which it is woven. The literary game of influence is thereby exhausted and must be replaced by a materialist criticism, analogous to Freud's interpretation of dreams, following Lacan. Such a practice equalizes reading and writing after their long subordination. It also liberates the author from the Oedipal contract which, so to speak, underwrites all the literary conventions of the readerly text,

but not the text of pleasure, which is engendered only through différance à la Derrida.[10]

From the very start, in *Writing Degree Zero*, Barthes was concerned
with the writer's freedom and commitment within the quasinatural
environment of language and literature. At this stage, namely, prior
to his encounter with structuralism and Saussurean linguistics, language is represented as a historical burden, a collective legacy, apparently only to be overthrown in an act of literary violence, reject-
ing realism in favor of magic, placing poetry beyond prose. Since
Barthes's argument presupposes familiarity with Sartre's *What Is
Literature?* (1948), it may be well to recall that essay briefly.[11]

The intention of Sartre's survey of the history of literature is not
to separate its future from its past or near-present. Indeed, Sartre is
not surveying the history of literature in any ordinary sense at all. It
is only in the light of a literature that is for-itself that its separation
from its modality as action identifies it as having been a literature of
hexis and consummatory destruction. The task of literature is to reveal the human situation in order to surpass it toward a community
of freedoms. Its proper history is internal to the ideal relationship of
generosity and freedom that it forges between the writer and the
public. In the past, literature fell into the category of consumption
because it had adopted a metaphysics in which being and having were
identical. Thus literature professed to offer through indulgence the
fulfillment of being, the appropriation of being through the spectacle
of being. By contrast, the literature of praxis starts from the metaphysical assumption that being is appropriated only through the act
of making itself. The literature of praxis is always a literature *en situation.* It inserts itself into the world of gestures and instruments that
reveal the world in the act of transforming it. The writer engaged in
such a task must create what Sartre calls a total literature, which is
simultaneously a literary and political activity in which the writer
and the reading public communicate man to man, on the model of a
socialist society.

Thus we are in language as we are in the body; that is, as a vehicle
of expression, an excarnation of particular purposes or detotalizations
of the total human project. In speech we unveil the world, name its
objects, and describe the situations in order to transcend them. According to Sartre, it is the poet who does not pass beyond words to
the practical utilities that they furnish. To the poet these connections
are purely magical. He uses words to produce word-objects or images
of the world, but not to express a certain situation like the writer of
a political pamphlet who intends to transform the situation in the

light of his description. Every creation of the genuine artist, far from being a finished object, opens on to the entire world, calling forth the freedom of his public.

The artist's creation, therefore, appeals to a kingdom of ends for which terror and beauty are never simply natural events but simultaneously an exigency and a gift to be integrated into the human condition. Whenever the artist is separated from his public, his work loses its quality as an imperative and is reduced to a purely esthetic object. In turn, the artist is forced to substitute the formal relationship between himself and his art for the relationship of commitment and transcendence between the artist and the public. Under these conditions, works of art function not as outlines of the total man, but as treasures whose scarcity is the measure of the absolute poverty of man, whose eternity is the denial of human history.

Not yet having embraced structuralism, Barthes appears to be uncomfortable with the closure in various historical modes of writing — revolutionary, bourgeois, Marxist, even the writings in *Les Temps Modernes*. Barthes's objection is that political commitment violates the necessary ambiguity of language, the fundamental inability of the writer who respects language to push it to either pole of society or the individual. As we shall see, he never really altered this view, even though he realized it kept him out of politics. Yet he admired Brecht enormously, even as a political writer. What he loved in Brecht was his ethical combination of intellectual clarity and pleasure, of theatrical distance, judgment, and enjoyment. Barthes was absolutely overwhelmed by *Mother Courage*. "Basically, Brecht's greatness, and his solitude, is that he keeps inventing Marxism."[12] Above all, Brecht's formalism dissolved the "petty bourgeois realism" of socialist art, as well as its morality, unable to adapt to its own history. He established the productivity of the gestural and theatrical signifier while simultaneously setting it in an ideological context that did not overwhelm its autonomy, its constitutive ambiguity. In Brecht Barthes saw that fundamental respect for the suspense of language that he himself observed and loyally cultivated:

One could say that literature is Orpheus returning from the underworld; as long as literature walks ahead, aware that it is leading someone, the reality behind it which it is gradually leading out of the unnamed — that reality breathes, walks, lives, heads toward the light of meaning; but once literature turns around to look at what it loves, all that is left is a named meaning, which is a dead meaning.[13]

With regard to bourgeois writing, he objected to its use of the narrative past (the preterite) to confer a universal reality upon events and characters (in the third person) who were otherwise imaginary and local fictions. Above all, the bourgeois novel is a mythological device for suppressing existential history in favor of society:

This is strictly how myths function, and the Novel—and within the Novel, the preterite—are mythological objects in which there is, superimposed upon an immediate intention, a second-order appeal to a corpus of dogmas, or better, to a pedagogy, since what is sought is to impart an essence in the guise of an artefact.[14]

Unlike Sartre, Barthes seems to have understood from the very beginning the significance of modern poetry for the autonomy or productivity of language. He never accepted the realist view of language and thought, or the classical euphoria in the clarity of ideas and unencumbered prose. He saw in these assumptions the subordination of Nature to Society, and the very same violence in which Marx saw the essence of Capitalism. He positively ridicules the practices of socialist realism. Yet he was unwilling to conspire with Mallarmé's murder of language or with Camus's degree zero writing, for example, because he refused to believe in any successful escape from language and its responsibilities.

Writing therefore is a blind alley. The writers of today feel this; for them, the search for a non-style or an oral style, for a zero level or a spoken level of writing is, all things considered, the anticipation of a homogeneous social state; most of them understand that there can be no universal language outside a concrete, and no longer a mystical or merely nominal, universality of society.[15]

Barthes saw in the proliferation of literary language a utopian quest for an Adamic language that might name things prior to all divisions and all conflicts. While he may never have been tempted to the political versions of that vision, I believe that, in spite of his apprenticeship to a transcendent structuralism, this utopia of language remained a personal vision. It deepened with that carnal knowledge that characterizes his later writings. Yet, here again, there are powerful beginnings of this development in *Writing Degree Zero*, contained in certain distinctions drawn by Barthes which he employed to underwrite his differences with Sartre. Where Sartre opposed language and style in analogy with the contrast between collective determination and individual decision, Barthes needed a further distinction to avoid the pitfalls of an instrumentalist view of language upon which he felt Sartre fell back.

As a matter of fact, we can see that Barthes's usage differs from Sartre's even with respect to the two terms they seem to share in the chapter each wrote called "What Is Writing?" Barthes is concerned with the productivity of language as a historical phenomenon whose historicity is given a quasinatural form in the literature of any given period of society. Although he already has certain structural linguistic formulations of this phenomenon, he is basically concerned with the ethical question it raises. Yet, like Merleau-Ponty later,[16] he is unwilling to resolve the problem in a Sartrean decision, to politicize language as preeminently a social object. Most men dwell in language without making its usages thematic and can never hope to expropriate all of its wealth. Much of the time a writer will similarly trust the great scaffold of his language even when trying, as he must, to overreach it. Indeed, the writer must, so to speak, suspend himself between two languages—between the common language into which he is born and a second language, or *style*, which is, so to speak, his body language, the resonance of his sounded being to which he must listen if his *writing* is to be productive of something else than the commonplaces of language and *literature*, which is language pointing to its official mark as *belles lettres*:

> A language is therefore on the hither side of literature. Style is almost beyond it: imagery, delivery, vocabulary spring from the body and the past of the writer and gradually become the very reflexes of his art. Thus under the name of style a self-sufficient language is evolved which has its roots only in the depths of the author's personal and secret mythology, that subnature of expression where the first coition of words and things takes place, where once and for all the great verbal themes of his existence come to be installed.[17]

Here we can see that Barthes's attachment to what he calls the "great verbal themes of his existence" is rooted in a deeper phenomenology of language than anything Sartre espoused. Indeed, this original remark strikes the theme of all Barthes's later investigations into everyday mythologies, the structural semiotics of fashion, his study of Michelet, Sade, Loyola, Fourier, Balzac, and himself. As yet, his linguistic body, so to speak, is given a deterministic formulation that will later relax under the influence of Lacanian psychoanalysis, opening the *literary body* to the defiant pleasures of the text, resolutely set against the literary and political establishment of his day. Barthes, in my view, never lost sight of the writer's solitude, which derives from his obligation to listen to and cultivate the literary sensibilities that are his unchosen and therefore uncommitted being-in-the world.

Style, then, is the writer's resistance to society and politics and not a Sartrean will. Style is indifferent to society and choice; nor is it a literary instrument:

> It is the decorative voice of hidden, secret flesh; it works as does Necessity, as if,

in this kind of floral growth, style were no more than the outcome of a blind and stubborn metamorphosis starting from a sub-language elaborated where flesh and external reality come together.[18]

In Barthes's view, style is outside the pact between the writer and society. It utterly precedes the writer's choice of language, being a marriage of thought and body conveyed in rituals of metaphor and gesture that are the natural product of time and the condensation of living. Between language and style so conceived, Barthes locates the distinctive function of writing (*écriture*). The writer links language to society in accordance with its great historical epochs, which he may celebrate or reject. But although the writer conceives of his freedom as a historical project, it remains a utopian use of language that forever falls back upon its own society. Barthes, therefore, ultimately separates himself from Sartre's literary project, remaining, like Merleau-Ponty, a philosopher of ambiguity:

Writing is an ambiguous reality: on the one hand, it unquestionably arises from a confrontation of the writer with the society of his time; on the other hand, from this social finality, it refers the writer back, by a sort of tragic reversal, to the sources, that is to say, the instruments of creation. Failing the power to supply him with a freely consumed language, history suggests to him the demand for one freely produced.[19]

How Barthes understood the body of language and style may be seen from his discussion of Michelet's historical writing. As we know from *Mythologies*, Barthes was fascinated by the smooth, sleek, silken surfaces of things, of toys, food, and automobiles—above all, of women dressed, undressed in never-ending fashion, clothed in words, exalted, impenetrable, glossy and glorious.[20] Language of women, for women, in service of women, a service which Barthes allowed himself to enter like Michelet, whom Barthes studied like himself. No conventional biography results: what is undertaken is another display of the procedures and insights of what I elsewhere call *homotextuality*[21] —that is, literary conduct displayed in the corporeal practices of writing and reading that exceed both a plain physiology and any reduction of textuality to sexuality.

Barthes's life of Michelet is concerned only with the incarnations of the man who lived and wrote history, who could not live apart from writing history, and whose own life set the parameters of the *History of France*, each otherwise incomplete. Accordingly, the man is presented as voluminous like the very histories to which he devoted his life. By the same token, he had always to worry that his strength should last, his days be long enough to match the histories he was making. Thus, his body became the battleground of history, so to speak; he devoured history and was eaten away by history's demands upon his strength:

> Michelet's sickness was migraine, a mixture of dizziness and nausea. Everything was like migraine to him: the cold, a storm, spring, the wind, the history he was narrating.[22]

Michelet's body never ceased to struggle under the massive, encyclopedic historical corpus that he pitted himself against. He was always at work, long hours, at grips with immense projects from which, if he were ever free, he feared to die. He therefore lived off history's own lifeblood like a parasite, suffering its calamities and exuberances—above all, its deaths. He made himself a corpse of history, donned its masks, and moved in and out of its stages, always approaching an end he needed to delay in order to confer upon it its proper due:

> Work—history in other words—being a nursery place where every weakness was assured of its value; his migraines settled there, that is, were rescued and endowed with meaning. Michelet's whole body becomes a product of his own creation and he established in himself a surprising sort of symbiosis between the historian and history. The nauseas, the dizzy spells and the depressions no longer come only from the seasons and climates; it is the very horror of narrative history that provokes them: Michelet has "historical" migraines.[23]

History was Michelet's body. He devoured it, he lived from it. He could do this because whether from the origin of reptiles, the Battle of Waterloo, or the feeding of English infants, he regarded history like Vico, as itself a living corpus, a body in which we have our very humanity:

> Michelet described with predilection all the intermediate stages of matter, savouring those ambiguous zones of development, where silex gives place to wheat, then to the French who feed themselves from it; where the plant extends itself into an animal, the fish into a mammal, the swan into a woman (Leda in the Renaissance), the dew into a stone, the goat into a prophet (the Moses of Michelangelo); where a child's brain is nothing else than the milky flower of the camelia; where man even can substitute himself for the woman in the transhumanisation of marriage.[24]

Michelet, writes Barthes, loved the world's body, its waters from which the fish are born and everything slippery, sliding, and silkenlike a woman's body, a woman's skin. Like the world's body, Michelet's history is also gendered and moves in accordance with the rhythms of birth, life, and death. History's body is male and female. The world-woman is moved, overthrown, and renewed by history's heroes. The two figures in Michelet's web are Grace and Justice, or Christianity, the woman as environment, and Revolution, the male as forceful entry, overthrow, rebirth. History is flesh. Thus the ultimate task of the historian is to discover the principle of corruptibility in the living flesh of each historical period. Here, again, we connect with the portraits of history, with history-as-portrayal, written into the faces, the eyes, modes, and posture of its principal actors. Men are historical because they are embodied, humored, fleshed, and fed.

Fragmentation, Perversity, and the Pleasure of the Text

From the very beginning, Barthes struggled to break the signs, to proliferate meanings, to exceed structure, classification, and stereotypes. With every step away from the conventional mode of writing, with each transgression of the codes of established literary criticism, as in *On Racine*, and above all in *S/Z*, he pushed writing back into the text of pleasure, back into the textual body that underwrites the atopia of meaning. Thus the liberated text became increasingly an icon of the liberated body, without center, hierarchy, or division:

Who knows if this insistence on the plural is not a way of denying sexual duality? The opposition of the sexes must not be a law of Nature; therefore, the confrontations and paradigms must be dissolved, both the meanings and the sexes be pluralized: meaning will tend toward its multiplication, its dispersion (in the Theory of the Text) and sex will be taken into no typology (there will be, for example, only *homosexualities*, whose plural will baffle any constituted, centered discourse, to the point where it seems to him virtually pointless to talk about it.[25]

He therefore employed literary criticism to disperse a work, to multiply its meaning through hundreds of fragmentary comments, each indulging its own purpose, and altogether excessive, like the countless stars of the night sky. In fact, every work of Barthes prefigures Barthes on Barthes, deepening the reflexive pleasure toward which he pushed reading and writing. Barthes's fragments are therefore deliberate play, promiscuous and excessive openings and foreclosures of literary desire drawn from nowhere, *hors-texte*, incomprehensible to the conventional commentator. He slipped through classifications, oppositions, and divisions of logic, drifting in language, ignoring alibis, the natural, the narrative as much as law, sex, and marriage. This resolute inability to master his ideas according to the divisions of the day rendered him incapable of violence and therefore incapable of politics. If Barthes's writings nevertheless collect, they do so as a personal encyclopedia of topics indulged for their own sake, as pleasurable incidents in a life compelled to find meaning. The futility in this compulsion to meaning is exonerated only through the author's surrender to the tide of words washing up their own meanings for him to decipher—like a child on the beach.

Barthes wanted to use political philosophy and scholarship generally in the same way. That is, he would surround himself with them and then, with an eye on his own body, pick and choose among them what suited him. In this, the mirror image is essential. He saw language; first the language of others, then his own language naked, and then several languages from which to keep his writing in love with his own body:

The *corpus*: what a splendid idea! Provided one was willing to read *the body* in the corpus: either because in the group of texts reserved for study (and which form the corpus) the pursuit is no longer of structure alone but of the figures of the utterance; or because one has a certain erotic relation with this group of texts (without which the corpus is merely a scientific *image-repertoire*).[26]

Writing, then, would become an atopia; it would consist of sentences whose sexuality would not be phallocentric expressions of the violence between the sexes (in accordance with legal convention), and it would be quite unpreoccupied with conquering meaning, mastering it, reducing it to a system or to a calculus. Such writing would be dedicated to foreplay and postponement rather than consummation. Therefore he wrote introductions, sketches, outlines, histories of writings—rhetoric, stylistics, unfinished, unfinishable works, mock systems of intelligence and pleasure.

In every case, he struggled to escape the conventional scenarios that it was his misfortune to see in the words around him. His body's capacity for seeing words deprived him of his political body: he did not enjoy the abstract disembodied discourse of politics. There was nothing for him to try on, nothing to touch, nothing that suited him in it. Political gestures did not suit his corporeal style. He lacked convictions because he could not use language to convince himself—let alone others. In short, he was unable to make a scene, since the essence of such staging is the violence in ordinary language:

. . . violence always organized itself into a *scene*: the most transitive of behavior (to eliminate, to kill, to wound, to humble) was also the most theatrical, and it really was this kind of semantic scandal he so resisted (is not meaning by its very nature opposed to action?); in all violence, he could not keep from discerning, strangely, a literary kernel. . . .[27]

ROLAND BARTHES AND THE LITERARY BODY □ 197

The Literary Body and the Body Politic

In the last analysis, Barthes remained pessimistic about our chances of limiting violence either at the collective level or in our individual lives. The only way he saw to resist society was to retreat from it, to struggle against death and disintegration as a writer. Here he hoped to sow seed, to be regenerated among other writers and thinkers. What appealed to him in his position at the Collège de France was that it is an institution outside of power (*hors-pouvoir*). At the same time, like Foucault, he did not see power in monolithic terms but as consisting of innumerable social strategies. He therefore considered that he could attack and displace power wherever it lodged in the discourse of domination and servility. For this reason, he hoped for a plurality of language without subordination, free from the conventinal *topoi* in which power sediments. Barthes's dream of a language in which knowledge and pleasure might circumvent the language of power remains a literary fantasy. This is not to say it should be set aside as worthless. Rather, it needs to be combined with the kind of analysis of discourse production attempted by Foucault, Bourdieu, Habermas, and Paulo Freire,[28] and even Barthes's own studies of mythology.

While we can concede the antiestablishment pathos of Barthes's theory and practice of literary pleasure, and its post-structuralist direction, it is necessary to be clear about its political and sociological limitations. Barthes really did not concern himself with anything but the faults of political writing (its stereotypes, realisms, false antitheses, and violence). He seems to have forgotten his own contributions to a sociolinguistic analysis of political discourse. Any future work would, in my view, have to consider how the literary community is located within the larger communicative community as both an ideal speech *atopia* and as a practical pedagogy working at the level of literary initiation. Cultural politics would then be less a matter of artistic sublimation than the work of decoding the discursive production of th body politic upon three institutional levels—family, work, and personality. Thus it may be said that the counterculture has prematurely identified political emancipation with the level of the *libidinal* body politic in terms of cultural and sexual emancipation of the personality, but without any strategy for connecting with the reproductive level of the *bio-body* and the working level of the *productive* body politic. Thus literate, middle-class, bourgeois counterculture

198 □ JOHN O'NEILL

fails to connect with working class and family culture, and thus fails
to situate the literary community and libidinal emancipation within
the broader project of emancipation strategically articulated to embrace the different levels and larger communicative community of a
resurrected body politic. Barthes's literary deconstruction, like so
much else in the counterculture, ironically remains locked within the
establishment of knowledge and culture. Since most revolutionary
regimes have been peculiarly puritanical in practice, it is hopelessly
ill-conceived to imagine that there is any *direct* social nexus between
polymorphous perversity and socioeconomic emancipation. Indeed,
as Foucault reminds us, the link between power and sexuality in the
modern biopolitical economy is endemic.

It seems best, therefore, neither to neglect nor to abandon the
struggle to situate the problematics of the literary body and its community within the larger body politic. We must, however, refrain from
the imaginary extrapolation of the ideal language or speech community to the total political community. We must learn to deal with a
Babel of tongues. The humanities and the social sciences produce discourses that are mutually hostile and far from intelligible to the lay-
man. We lack contexts in which the variety of institutional and practical discourses can confront one another to practice translation and
dialogue. The university and the media are the institutions where this
exercise is currently located. But media differ widely in their pedagogical possibilities, and both university and media are increasingly
instruments of mass culture. Nevertheless, it remains true that the
university, notwithstanding the external and internal constraints on
its engagement with the larger issues in the polity, is the institution
of last resort when it comes to the production of emancipatory
knowledge and subversive discourse.

Barthes did not ignore these issues. We may not share his response
to them. But we should recognize Barthes's personal courage and his
resolute freedom in the pursuit of his craft and the creation of his
own corpus:

If I managed to talk politics with *my own body*, I should make out of the most
banal of (discursive) structures a structuration; with repetition, I should produce
Text. The problem is to know if the political apparatus would recognize for very
long this way of escaping the militant banality by thrusting into it—alive, puls-
ing, pleasure-seeking—my own unique body.[29]

I think Barthes did not believe that any political regime could
tolerate the pleasure of the text. Yet like many others he considered
the writer's freedom an essential institution in any occasion of a

good society. Inasmuch as this freedom must be fought for within the literary community, he may be considered a radical. That he was unable to find the linkage between literary emancipation and a broader social emancipation merely reveals the present political condition of all intellectuals.

NOTES

1. John O'Neill, "From Phenomenology to Ethnomethodology: Some Radical 'Misreadings,'" *Current Perspectives in Social Theory*, I (1980), 7-20.
2. Roland Barthes, "Science versus Literature," in Michael Lane, ed., *Introduction to Structuralism* (New York: Basic Books, 1970), p. 413.
3. Roland Barthes, *The Pleasure of the Text*, trans. Richard Miller (New York: Hill and Wang, 1975), pp. 9-10.
4. Roland Barthes, "Myth Today," in *Mythologies*, trans. Annette Lavers (London: Paladin, 1973), pp. 116-34.
5. Rosalind Coward and John Ellis, *Language and Materialism* (London: Routledge & Kegan Paul, 1977), p. 28.
6. *Mythologies*, p. 132.
7. Roland Barthes, "To Write: An Intransitive Verb?" in Richard Macksey and Eugenio Donato, eds., *The Structuralist Controversy: The Languages of Criticism and the Sciences of Man* (Baltimore and London: The Johns Hopkins University Press, 1970), p. 143.
8. Roland Barthes, *Le Grain de la Voix: Entretiens 1962-1980* (Paris: Éditions du Seuil, 1981), p. 190.
9. John O'Neill, "Homotextuality: Barthes on Barthes, Fragments (RB), with a Footnote," in Gary Shapiro and Alan Sica, eds., *Hermeneutics: Questions and Prospects* (Amherst: University of Massachusetts Press, 1984).
10. Jacques Derrida, *Writing and Difference* (Chicago: University of Chicago Press, 1978).
11. John O'Neill, "Situation, Action and Language," in *Sociology as a Skin Trade: Essays Towards a Reflexive Sociology* (New York: Harper and Row, 1972), pp. 81-95. See also Dominick La Capra, *A Preface to Sartre* (Ithaca: Cornell University Press, 1978), ch. 2: "Literature, Language, and Politics: Ellipse of What?" La Capra shows how Sartre later rethought his position in the light of Barthes's views.
12. Roland Barthes, "The Tasks of Brechtian Criticism," in *Critical Essays*, trans. Richard Howard (Evanston: Northwestern University Press, 1972), p. 74.
13. Roland Barthes, "Literature and Signification," *ibid.*, p. 268.
14. Roland Barthes, *Writing Degree Zero and Elements of Semiology*, trans. Annette Lavers and Colin Smith (Boston: Beacon Press, 1970), pp. 33-34.
15. *Ibid.*, p. 87.
16. Maurice Merleau-Ponty, *The Prose of the World*, trans. and intro. by John O'Neill (Evanston: Northwestern University Press, 1973).
17. Barthes, *Writing Degree Zero*, p. 10.
18. *Ibid.*, p. 11.
19. *Ibid.*, p. 16.
20. Michel Butor, "La Fascinatrice," *Les Cahiers du Chemin*, 4 (15 octobre 1968), 20-55.
21. See O'Neill, note 9, above.
22. Roland Barthes, *Michelet par lui-même* (Paris: Éditions du Seuil, 1954), p. 17.
23. *Ibid.*, p. 18.

24. *Ibid.*, p. 31.

25. *Roland Barthes by Roland Barthes*, trans. Richard Howard (New York: Hill and Wang, 1977), p. 69.

26. *Ibid.*, p. 161.

27. *Ibid.*, p. 160.

28. John O'Neill, "Decolonization and the Ideal Speech Community: Some Issues in the Theory and Practice of Communicative Competence." To appear in John Forester, ed., *Critical Theory and Public Life*, forthcoming.

29. *Roland Barthes by Roland Barthes*, p. 175.

Chapter 11
La Greffe du Zèle:
Derrida and the Cupidity of the Text
Charles Levin

*There is no tenet in all paganism which would give so fair
a scope to ridicule as that of the* real presence; *for it is
so absurd, that it eludes the force of all argument.*

David Hume

*The dead letter often has greater influence than the
living word.*

Kierkegaard

Discretionary Theoretics

*For a ground becomes accessible only as meaning, even if
it is itself the abyss of nonmeaning.*[1]

It is hard to imagine metaphysics, that ambiguous, invidious stratification of discourse, without writing. But Derrida is subtle. First we
have to draw a distinction between the Book and the text—or, more
fundamentally, between the "natural totality," which the book as a
totality of signifiers presupposes, and *writing*, the presupposition
of the text, whose "disruption . . . aphoristic energy . . . and

difference" have been neutralized by the "Western tradition" (apparently all of philosophy). Writing has been subordinated precisely because it is the necessary medium of the metaphysical tradition. "Logocentrism, this epoch of the full speech, has always placed in parantheses, suspended and suppressed for essential reasons, all free reflection on the origin and status of writing . . ." (*G*, 43).[2]

It is a little surprising, though, to see these references to "essential reasons" and "free reflection" in Derrida; but then, as he so often emphasizes himself, we can never entirely cleanse "this language" of its undesirable implications, which ultimately shackle reflection, only to lead "it" willy-nilly where "it" does not want to go. Writing can always escape reflection in the end. This would be one of the "essential reasons" why it has been, and presumably remains, an uncomfortable subject for a *logocentric* tradition. Because it transcends the immediacy and the nominalism of a pluridimensional *con*text, writing always overflows our intentions, our *meaning* (in the veridirectional, positivist sense). This is all the more true if we admit with Derrida that an *ethic* of writing would be a critique of what he calls the "proper": we cannot be the "proprietors" of the texts we are creating. To write is to disseminate, to bequeath without naming the beneficiaries, and this negates not only property in authorship, but the authority of proper meanings. Conversely, there is always a certain impropriety about reading: interpretation is always, in a sense, inappropriate. This is as it should be. The general element of indicating, of pure pointing, is never identical with the element of expression in language (*SP*, 17f).[3]

Reflection has habitually overlooked—or suppressed—the materiality of language, its dependence on the physicality of a medium, its rootedness in the earth: "Heavy serious, solid earth, the earth that is worked upon, scratched, written upon" (*WD*, 304, n. 23). The "trace" of language is impermeable to dialectic, it cannot be surpassed or "overcome" or negated, because all these operations of reflection rely on language, and language relies on a mark, a repeatable gesture —the trace. The indication of a meaning must indicate itself in order to indicate. We must read the writing in order to get at the truth, but if this writing is not the truth itself, then we have already fallen from a state of Grace, into the irremediable lapse of the trace.

What is logocentrism? According to Derrida, it is the immemorial attempt to escape this condition. "The (linguistic) sign is always the sign of the Fall" (*G*, 283): metaphysics conceives the written sign as a *re*presentation of speech, hence, in the extreme, not as language at all, but as an indication of language. Language itself would be elsewhere, or rather, writing would be elsewhere; the spoken word, the *Logos*, would be *present*. Truth, beauty, and other perfections would be the modes of presence, immediacy; speech, as opposed to the delay and spatial transfer, the metaphoricity of writing, would be their ideal expression.

The doctrine of logocentrism proposes speech as the preeminent form of presence, and presence as *the* form of truth and meaning. According to Derrida, this is the core doctrine of Western metaphysics, an apparently inescapable reference of philosophical language, which always slips through, however coiled, however dissembling, however transparent, however deferred the reference may be. And yet this reference contradicts language; it contradicts the always differing and always deferring spatial and temporal *process* of language, the necessity of physical arrangement, which Derrida, punning, signifies with the term *différance*—a term that he apparently does not intend to "mean" anything. Language is *gramm*atical: it is an organization of traces, and the trace of an organization.

But if language is never pure meaning, it always aspires to be so, and thus wars against itself. This is history, the history of an externalizing process that has no original or ultimate interior, an *archia* or *telos*; yet it recedes and approaches, and *only* does so. It is never "present." In a gesture reminiscent of Marshall McLuhan, Derrida will counsel that this indeterminate but crucially determining fact of *extension* can never finally be transcended. It can only be understood better, and thus mitigated:

Emancipation from this language must be attempted. But not as an *attempt* at emancipation from it, for this is impossible unless we forget *our* history. Rather, as the dream of emancipation. Nor as emancipation from it, which would be meaningless and would deprive us of the light of meaning. . . . Rather, as resistance to it, as far as possible. In any event, we must not abandon ourselves to this language. . . . (*WD*, 28)

Thus, history is never finally manifest. (Does this mean that history can never be secular? Is it inevitably a theology, even if a negative theology? Derrida seems to reply "yes." In this respect, history and language are alike: "Language cannot make its own possibility a totality and *include* within itself its own origin and its own end" (*WD*, 95). Or rather, the *possibility* of history resides in language, language as writing. Meaning is not foreseeable. "To write is to be incapable of making meaning absolutely precede writing. It is thus to lower meaning while simultaneously elevating inscription" (*WD*, 10).[4] But not inscription *for* posterity's sake, Derrida would caution.

He is not concerned primarily with the technical prerequisites of history, but with their metaphysical analogue (*G*, 8). Historicity is not the ability to record facts, but the fact of being able to record, which has no meaning in itself: it is "the excess by which every philosophy (of meaning) is related, in some region of its discourse, to the non-foundation of unmeaning" (*WD*, 309, n26); "the nonbasis of play upon which [the] history [of meaning] is launched" (*WD*, 276); "an absolute unknowledge from whose nonbasis is launched chance, or the wager of meaning, history and the horizons of absolute knowledge" (*WD*, 268). By being an apparently heterogeneous field, by allowing the possibility of this play, a différance, writing makes "history—that is, meaning" (*WD*, 254) possible as well. But it also produces a countermovement to history, and "today such a play is coming into its own, effacing the limit starting from which one had thought to regulate the circulation of signs" (*G*, 7). But this double meaning of nonmeaning is, by definition, ambiguous, a neoplasm of pleonasm:

Dissemination opens, without end, this difficulty/tear [*accroc*] of writing that resists resewing, the place where neither meaning/direction [*sens*], even plurivocity, nor *any form of presence* fastens the trace a-graphically [*agrapher*]. Dissemination intercourses, works through [*traite sur lit*], the point where the movement of signification binds the play of the trace in thus producing history. (*Dis*, 33)

Derrida determines structuralism itself as an ideological moment of logocentric metaphysics by *disseminating* its ontology of difference everywhere. He wants the "richness implied by volume" to displace the structuralist "simultaneity of a form" (*WD*, 25). But by volume, Derrida does not mean to imply a language referring beyond itself, implicating itself in otherness. This, for him, would amount to a "rather precious continuist prejudice" (*G*, 69). What Derrida means by volume is an "indefinite extension" on a homogeneous plane—the ideal space of "inscription." The "simultaneity of a form" is not dissolved in the *aqua regia* of a pluridimensional space-time that exceeds the absorptive power of language; it is rather stretched out unendingly in an ideal space of digital reproducibility and interrelationality. It is a network curved back into itself by the weight of its own terms. What Derrida wants, in fact, is a structure without limit, in which the "meaning of meaning . . . is infinite implication, the indefinite referral of signifier to signifier" (*WD*, 25)—in which the concept of play replaces the concept of system and fissures the concept of boundary. The immobility of arbitrary terms will no longer be motivated by the structuralist rule of law, will no longer cower beneath the legislative authority of structure; it will be charged with the life of an *un*moti-vated play, which "before attempting to understand all the forms of play in the world" would be first of all "the game of the world" (*G*, 50) itself.

Reading Derrida, we are confronted, more and more directly, with the fundamental and honest indecision of a project that wants to shake language free of reification, yet recognizes that success would eliminate difference and make all language the same. Language was born in chains and everywhere it is free: but there is no break, episte-mological or historical; there is no permanent deconstruction; and deconstruction will not lead to the withering away of the Logos.

"My justification would be as follows," writes Derrida: Saussure's subordination of writing to speech

already gives us the assured means of broaching the deconstruction of *the great-est totality*—the concept of the *episteme* and logocentric metaphysics—within which are produced, without ever posing the radical question of writing, all the Western methods of analysis, explication, reading, or interpretation. (*G*, 46)

This "greatest totality," which is borrowed partly from Heidegger and partly from Husserl, "those two Greeks" (*WD*, 83), will be a constant source of embarrassment. Derrida will ask: Is totalization "useless," or simply "impossible"? (*WD*, 289) The answer is ambigu-ous, because Derrida, not unlike a certain version of Hegel, forgets that a unitary *principle* of movement is also absolute:

What I want to emphasize is simply that the passage beyond philosophy does not consist in turning the page of philosophy . . . but in continuing to read philos-ophers *in a certain way*. (*WD*, 288)

This endlessness, however, this inability to turn over a new leaf—which, Derrida shows, has always determined the illusion of totality as a forgetting, hence a repetition and a reification, a denial rather than an openness to history (*pace* Lukács)—this "nontotalization" always pre-supposes a totality. *Which* philosophers do we continue to read "*in a certain way*?" Metaphysical philosophers. Logocentric philosophers. Philosophers of the ontotheological tradition. Those who are trapped in a certain language. In other words, all philosophers, the *totality* of philosophy, and "all the Western methods," and so forth.

But: "If totalization no longer has any meaning, it is not because the infiniteness of a field cannot be covered by a finite glance or a finite discourse, but because the nature of the field—that is language and a finite language—excludes totalization" (*WD*, 289). Like Hegel, Derrida can only dispose of infinity's badness in the name of a *good infinity*, a finite infinity, a sprightly *language*. And this detotalization, this by now archetypal rebellion against "ontotheology" in the name of a process, this relativization of the absolute, is done from the absolute standpoint of a movement, a movement that is everywhere, like God hearing the world's prayers: "Nontotalization can also be determined in another way: no longer from the standpoint of a concept of finitude as relegation to the empirical, but from the standpoint of the concept of *play*" (*WD*, 289). This play, as différance, actually opens the possibility of deconstruction. But in it, Derrida is only deferring indefinitely the question of the "blind spot," the gaping vortex, around which his own discourse is organized. How can this movement, this play, this "disruption of presence" (*WD*, 292), be a *standpoint*, a position?

The Metaphysics of the Discrete

But it is not the purpose of critical thought to place the object on the orphaned royal throne once occupied by the subject. On that throne the object would be nothing but an idol. The purpose of critical thought is to abolish the hierarchy.

Adorno, *Negative Dialectics*[5]

As Derrida himself explains: "Différance is the systematic play of differences, of traces of differences, of the spacing through which elements relate to one another. This spacing is the production, active and passive . . . of intervals without which the 'full' terms would not signify, not function" (*Pos*, 39). If the movement of différance is comparable to the "always already" of a dismantling of the structure of the sign, of the opposition and separation of signifier and signified, the sensible and the intelligible, it nevertheless also *presupposes*, as *already in place*, the same structuralist theory of meaning (*SP*, 139f).[6] It is the discombobulation of that theory, its shakedown—what Derrida refers to as a solicitation.[7]

Likewise, if the concept of the trace is presented as a kind of material *prerequisite* of language, it still presupposes "the structure implied by the 'arbitrariness of the sign' " (*G*, 47). "The instituted trace cannot be thought without thinking the retention of difference within a structure of reference where difference appears *as such* and thus permits a certain liberty of variations among the full terms" (*G*, 46-47). But if the trace cannot be thought without difference (i.e., without structuralism), difference cannot be thought without *dif-férance*, which in turn cannot be thought without the trace. "The 'unmotivatedness' of the sign requires a *synthesis* in which the completely other is announced as such . . . within what it is not . . . the trace, where the relationship with the other is marked." The trace is a *synthesis.* "Why the trace? . . . It is a question of producing a new concept of writing. We might call it *gram* or *différance.* The play of differences presupposes in effect syntheses and references which prevent there ever being a simple element which is present in itself and refers only to itself. Whether in the order of spoken or written discourse, no element can function as a sign withot referring to another element which is itself not simply present. This chaining [*enchaînement*] means that each 'element' is constituted with reference to the trace in it of the other elements of the chain or system. Nothing, in either the elements or the system, is anywhere ever simply present or absent" (*Pos,* 37-38).

In consequence of this argument, Derrida will be able to show that structuralism has misunderstood itself, failed to develop the potentiality of its own concepts. He will explode the structuralist "combinatory," or rather (more "properly"), *extend* it indefinitely. Meaning will still be determined by a totality of differences, but a totality which is never totalized, which is *in principle* untotalizable. For how can a system of differences have *natural* boundaries? On the other hand, an *arbitrary* boundary would not be a boundary, from the point of view of the *absolute* (i.e., for Derrida, from the perspective of language itself).[8] The totality is not a Book: "rather, this chaining, this tissue, is the *text* which is only produced in the transformation of another text" (*Pos,* 38). The synchronic unities of structuralism, (the "presence" for example, of the sign [only in speech?]), ultimately depend on the assumption of a center (an intentionality of consciousness, a meaning, for example) which "closes off play," where "the permutation or the transformation of elements . . . is forbidden" and "the substitution of contents, elements or terms is no longer possible" (*WD,* 279). But structuralism cannot account, on its own terms, as Derrida will show, for such a center, which would really be an anthropomorphic projection, or an Archimedean point that miraculously escapes a determinate system in order to institute it.

Derrida, as we know, calls this lapsus "logocentrism"; and its paradigmatic form of repression is the "exclusion of writing" (*G,* 45). In the logocentric schema, the idea of a center and of an original unity could be preserved in the shadow of writing as a "representation" and an "image" of the spoken word. But the Saussurean theory of the sign itself undermines the possibility of "two distinct systems of signs"—of writing in subordinate opposition to speech (*G,* 45; *Pos,* 28). Derrida will insist, however, that with the deconstruction of internal limits, the "play of difference" loses exterior boundaries as well: "Play must be conceived of before the alternative of presence and absence. Being must be conceived as presence or absence on the basis of the possibility of play" (*WD,* 202)—unlimited play.

This possibility of play may doubtless be traced back to Claude Lévi-Strauss's "floating signifier," which he had derived in part from something in the "human condition":

since his origin man has disposed of an integrality of signifier of which he is hard pressed to discover the proper allocation of signified. . . . There has always been an inadequation between the two, accessible to divine understanding alone, which results in an overabundance of signifiers in relation to the signifieds on which they can place themselves.[9]

This "overabundance" allowed Lévi-Strauss to develop his theory of *bricolage*; but from the same surplus of elements, Derrida could argue that, in principle, "every discourse is bricoleur." If there is never really an author, as Lévi-Strauss himself has sometimes insisted, but only a rearrangement of terms, another configuration of signs, then even Lévi-Strauss's "engineer" is "a myth produced by the 'bricoleur' "; from which it follows that "the very idea of *bricolage* is menaced and the difference in which it took on its meaning breaks down" (*WD,* 285). Interposed like a gatekeeper between the text and the play of the world, even bricolage, which has randomness and chance built into it, is doubtful. Even reading is suspect.

What Derrida needs is an irreducible concept, a concept that somehow works on itself alone, reduces itself, and thereby escapes the subject-object dichotomy of metaphysics. The concept would, of course, be difference itself, if it were not for the direct implication of meaning that arises from difference. But this secondary function can be erased by claiming the priority of difference in space-time (*Pos,* 37-39), in other words, by coining *différance*:

We've got a circle here, because if we distinguish rigorously between language and speech [*langue et parole*], the code and the message, the schema and usage, etc., . . . we do not know where to begin or how something begins in general. . . . We thus have to admit, before any dissociation of the type *lange/parole,* code/message, etc., . . . a systematic production of differences, the *production* of a system of differences—a différance—in whose effects one can eventually, by abstraction and according to determined motives, circumscribe a linguistics of *langue* and a linguistics of speech, etc. . . . . Since nothing is present or in-different, nothing precedes différance and spacing. (*Pos*, 40)

Différance does not reunite structuralist dichotomies after the fact; it precedes them, makes them possible. But it is difficult to grasp how différance, which would have discontinuity and absence and delay within itself, can do more than reflect a great chain of being and its source—God—in a Mirror of Difference. *Différance* has no subject to refer it, and refers to no subject. It is, in fact, only the structuralist dream of transcendence: an antireferential space in zero time—the epitome of the Same. Différance, in short, is the unmoved mover refracted by an inverted ontology: a sort of unplayed playing (*SP*, 159).

To say that différance is originary is simultaneously to erase the myth of a present origin. Which is why "originary" must be understood as having been *crossed out*, without which *différance* would be derived from an original plenitude. It is a non-origin which is originary. (*WD*, 203)[10]

The paralysis of structuralism leads us back to différance, but différance does not allow Derrida to escape the circle of structure-event that inspires deconstruction. An ontology of difference does not circumvent structure, *it is produced by it*. If speech is only an articulation, that is, a setting in motion of differences, then it must draw substance from a previous structure. This Saussure had already established. But the structure itself must have been articulated beforehand. In desperation, Saussure granted precedence, arbitrarily, to a constitutive act of differentiation: speech.[11] In a sense, he was choosing the priority of the deed over the Logos, an old nineteenth-century prejudice he could not quite shake. But Derrida still calls this a logocentric gesture because it implies an original presence, the presence of an origin, an *archia*, or as Sartre used to say, an essence that precedes existence. Impossible. Yet Derrida himself quibbles on this point, for does he not refer us to a production, "a very old philosopheme of production" (*Spurs*, 77)—namely, if I may use a double, but not ontological genitive, the *production* of différance?[12]

In a classic metaphysical flourish, Derrida has invoked the *same difference*—for it is precisely with the concept of spacing that he proposes to fill the void, the *space*, generated by the "unmotivated, but not capricious" (*G*, 46) polarities of structuralist thought.

What différance means, then, is that structural synchrony will now, by virtue of a new definition, contain diachrony within itself, as trace. It is as if the content of Zeno's paradox could be separated from its form, so as to have the beauty of the paradox without the absurd conceptual result.[13] Just as Zeno had assumed that time was made up of a succession of discrete instants in themselves stationary, structuralism must *in every case* justify its reduction of the continuous to the discrete, the analogue to the digital; for without this reduction, it can constitute neither the sign nor structure.[14] The field must be cut up (*découpé*), before it can be submitted to structuralist activity. But in a crucial sense, structuralist activity *is* this "discretionary" procedure, raised to the order of ontological determination. The result is a pure, signifying field, a serial array of discrete signifiers, which can then be brought back into relation with each other only within the structuralist delimitation of what is possible, and more importantly, only in terms of what structuralist reading (or *bricolage*) can regulate.

If Derrida seeks to replace structural opposition with the play of différance, thereby demonstrating that no discrete term can be "present" to consciousness, he has not dissolved the hegemony of structure; he has only deferred the problem of infinite regress that haunts it. He asks, in effect, that if each instance is fully present in itself, how can they all be joined together, except by a meaningless act of mental summation? It follows that the isolated term must *contain* traces of the others, as we have already seen. But for Derrida, the trace still has the analytic character of discreteness, hedged around as it is by the "harsh law of spacing" (*G*, 200), separated out with the regularity of the interval. The question is no longer raised: *"who* established this structure of differentiation that makes the 'effect' of speech (writing is never defined as an 'effect') possible?" The trace, this unit of "synthesis and referral," is simply sprung back into motion by virtue of différance, the postulated synthesis of *langue/parole*, structure/event, synchrony/diachrony, etc., which is somehow not itself an origin, or the presence of an origin—just an initial "production."

And since the trace is never traced back to the diacritical reduction that *actually* produces it, it remains "given" (if no longer present). In this way, the signifying chain of the logocentric, which originates in the articulation of a presence, is conscientiously reversed, so that it *begins with an inscription*—a procedure that neatly reinforces the structuralist logic of contiguity and the metaphysics of the discrete. This gesture, a familiar one, conveniently eliminates consciousness from the equation, if it desires;[15] and replaces it with the blank sheet, the space, the interval and margin—a kind of extroverted *tabula rasa*.

The hardcore Derridean doctrine, which emerged reluctantly in the late 1960s as a positive revision of structuralism, can be seen as a kind of recapitulation of the standard logocentric debate in Western philosophy: the transition from skepticism to rationalism to empiricism. Each establishes its argument from a general condition of uncertainty and nonpresence, and attacks the problem head on by reducing the issue of being alive and aware-of-something to a sign relation. The Cartesian refusal to capitulate to skepticism, which all twentieth-century French philosophers, including Derrida, have attacked, proposes a transcendental consciousness as a moment of transparency within the general semiosis. Empiricism, recognizing that the tautology of a consciousness present to itself and prior to perception is not sufficient to warrant a constitutive subject, tries to deconstruct this presence, although empiricism always implies the same transcendence of consciousness by treating the world as a congeries of perceptual traces: after all, something must stand behind perception to organize it, as Kant pointed out. But empiricism was original in conceiving this "something" not as an entity but as a blank upon which certain standardized and arbitrary forms of significatory relation could, in effect, *write*. Locke's doctrine of contiguity and the associationism that ensued have both resurfaced as textual strategies. And Derrida's debt to these themes emerges quite clearly when one realizes that his principle of spacing, which overtly symbolizes the mediate distance between traces and the discreteness of the textual field, is only a structuralist displacement of this seventeenth-century background consciousness, an avatar of a secular myth about God's significant absence from the world.

In this respect, différance is clearly also a kind of "materialist" analogue of the standard Heideggerian and Sartrean nothingness, which also attempted to escape the rationalist-empiricist antinomy by attacking the notion of mind as a system of signifying conventions (or a semiosis). This is an active nothingness that "carries a signification of productive, positive, generative force" (*Pos*, 108-9, n. 31). But Derrida's graphomorphic impulse also reaches back to an earlier phenomenalism in which the nothingness of consciousness was still passive, receptive, a blank sheet. Empiricism in particular wanted to analyze experience into manageable units that could then be pressed into relations of contiguity. Like Derrida, this strategy functionalized "ideas" by "explaining" them as relational effects of passively acquired "impressions," perceptual traces. The trace here is quite obviously a spiritual descendant of the positivist "sense-impression." It resurrects the empiricist critique of language and naive realism in terms of a similar, ambiguous conception of the given as a pure atomic state, a kind of abstracted immediacy working in tandem with a doctrinal deferment of the sensual whole. It was, in a sense, the empiricists who first argued that the play of similarity and contiguity was in principle perpetual in order to rule out referentiality. Only now, in Derrida, this associationism has been revised in differential terms, and the play takes place on paper.

On these grounds, it is entirely possible to challenge the deconstructionist dogma that the *signified* has been the privileged term in metaphysics; for if the "meaning" and the "referent" can be conceived as having traditionally claimed seniority over their "representations" (signifiers), logic has nevertheless always concerned itself with the formal coherence of these representations, and this coherence has always lobbied at the expense of a speculative, and above all, a *scandalous* referent. Even if the putative secondary of the signifier in philosophy is granted, it does not automatically follow that the structure of the sign can be applied nonviolently to all philosophical discourse as an integral unit. In insisting on a parallel identification of the signifier with the sensible, the signified with the intelligible, Derrida is able to construct an anachronistic history of philosophy by straightening its lines into a structuralist problematic which is his own and which occludes the other concerns of these philosophies.

But, as we shall see, it is in haunting organized discourse that "speech" and "presence" have continually undermined the *logistics* of a certain writing, of Plato's graphomorphic Ideas,[16] of Rousseau's autodidactic moralism, or of Lévi-Strauss's tabular projections onto the "primitive" mind. The veridirectional *authority* of the Voice has always been a ventriloquism, and this voicing of something inscribed, or writing of something voiced elsewhere, has nothing to do with speech and exchange. The internal, polar relationality of the sign does not count (for) much in speech, the discreteness of the signifier, necessary in writing, is not necessary in speech, and the symbolic exchange[17] of the experience of the other is irreducible. In writing, this "presence" mocks the elements of writing, and reveals the ineffectuality of merely rearranging these elements after they have already been condemned to fungibility by an economy of the discrete.

If we imagine (with Heidegger) an onto-theo-logy stemming from Plato, if not earlier, and conceive its problem entirely in terms of the issue of immediacy, then Western logocentrism boils down to an argument over whether the presence of truth is sensible or intelligible. On this view, empiricism is already a deconstruction, for it replaces the reification of "form," "cause," "substance," "telos," and "origin" with the reification of sensory experience, and demonstrates that all ideas, even, in the end, its own ideas, are purely speculative "effects" of a "material" process of imprinting. But Derrida never concerns himself with this *difference* within the history of "presence"—his work thrives on confounding all claims for immediacy, gathering them on the same plane, and assigning them an identical import. Without this simplification, he would never have been able to insist on the univocity of the metaphor of speech, or to dismiss the powerful, graphomorphic tradition stemming from the Pythagorean and Platonic *ratio*, or to overlook its connection both with the rationalist model of a discontinuous, repeatable world, and with mystical hermeticism. Nor would he have been able to describe the apparent privilege accorded to writing in *this* logocentric tradition as a mere "metaphoric sense," which does not affect his interpretation of the real meaning, the "common sense" of "repressed" writing in that tradition (*G*, 17).

Since the account of meaning exclusively in terms of the differences between discrete elements produces not only the problem of infinite regress, but the problem of how to reunite the terms that have been separated out, together with the problem of the impossible "presence" of such a term (the terms, like their reconciliation, being only deduced, never experienced); and since these problems are then solved by an appeal to the same difference (in its synthetic form, as différance), the whole concept of the trace begs the structuralist question: it always refers us back to the opposition of structure and event. After all, what is the trace, if not some sign of movement within the neutralized universe of the text?—the protension-retention of Husserl's "internal time consciousness" objectified and reduced to a signifier? But this sign can only be the movement it signifies, which has been bracketed out by the imposed serialization of différance. As I shall attempt to show, this *petitio principii* suffuses the whole supporting framework of Derridean discourse.

The Political Economy of the Discrete

I use "totalitarian" in the structuralist sense of the word, but I am not sure that the two meanings do not beckon each other historically. (WD, 57)

The irony of deconstruction is that, having created its object, logocentric thought, in its own image—the reflection of an autotelic writing—it proceeds to parody "ontotheology" in its conduct of every encounter with its examples. In spite of himself, Derrida deploys a hermeneutic, an interventionist hermeneutic that ruptures the opacity of its texts, and realigns them according to an already established theme. Deconstructionist interpretation is an economic invasion, a systematic attribution and distribution of values that decontextualizes the subject discourse by scattering its community of terms and substituting an arena of productive relations.

Deconstruction normalizes everything it encounters. Anything unique, or utopian, or even mad in the Western canon is subjected to a kind of ponderous ridicule that rolls the text out on a referential plane where nothing is in principle different and everything refers to everything else. As this transformation takes place, we are presented with language in its fundamental guise—a language to which, by virtue of an invoked necessity that is never explained or reconciled with play, everything must conform. Saussure's reduction of the continuous in speech is turned against his "phonologism" (G, 29f; 44f); Lévi-Strauss's semiotic is turned against his nostalgia, which is made to appear as a kind of naive anarchism (G, 101-40); Rousseau's paranoia is turned against his dream of the Festival (G, passim). The network always defeats community as social form, as an "originary" social form. Even Foucault's schematisms are used to discredit his critique of rationalism.[18] It is always language itself, by its nature, that performs this function—a language in which "there is no praise, by essence, except of reason" (WD, 43); in which "all History can be . . . the history of meaning, that is, of Reason," something that "Foucault could not fail to experience" (WD, 308, n. 4).

Discourse and philosophical communication must carry normality within themselves. And this is . . . not a defect or mystification linked to a determined historical structure, but rather is an essential and universal necessity from which no discourse can escape, for it belongs to the meaning of meaning. (WD, 53)

Language becomes "the reasonableness of reason, of philosophy, of Hegel, who is always right as soon as one opens one's mouth in order to articulate meaning" (WD, 263). It turns into a kind of homeostasis, a totalitarian feedback perpetually aligning the oscillation of terms in a logocentric configuration, where perception is reduced to speech, and speech to an ontological fantasy. And since this language, the only language, is the "greatest totality," difference is really impossible except as a kind of excess that spills over, runs away, into silence. Change, or anarchic feedback, leads to the destruction of language itself.

Since it is a certain sliding that is in question . . . what must be found . . .

is the point, the *place in the pattern* at which a word drawn from the old language will start, by virtue of having been placed there and by virtue of having received such an impulsion, to slide and to make the entire discourse slide. A certain strategic twist must be imprinted upon language; and this strategic twist, with a violent and sliding, furtive movement must inflect the old corpus in order to relate its syntax and its lexicon to major silence. (*WD*, 264)

This passage to silence resembles a prospectus of deconstruction itself. The "meaning of meaning" as normality is confronted with the meaning of meaning as "the indefinite referral of signifier to signifier" whose "force is a certain pure and infinite equivocality which gives signified meaning no respite" (*WD*, 25). Language is always already the totality and its failure, presence and its deconstruction, Logos and Physis, eternal recurrence and difference, necessity and chance. It is the Scylla of Charybdis, the fluidity of reification: a Kybernetic Pass. And we are condemned to live inside this diapoly of language because deconstruction only confirms its identity with language in the two moments of textual intervention: the "broaching" and the sliding. The text is broached by means of a calculated reversal of valences:

On one hand, we must go through a phase of *reversal*. . . . In a classical philosophical opposition, we are not dealing with a peaceful coexistence, but a violent hierarchy. One of the two terms commands the other (axiologically, logically, etc.), holds the superior position. To deconstruct the opposition is first of all, at a given moment, to reverse the hierarchy. (*Pos*, 56-57)

The moment of tactical reversal is, of course, rigorously structural. Its condition, the *sine qua non* of the whole operation, is the isolation and delimitation of textual components, a kind of arresting of play. The signifier, as a strategic ally in this "economy" of deconstruction, becomes a "positive lever" (*Pos*, 109). Lip service is paid to "pure and infinite ambiguity," but in order to prise apart the seams of the text, Derrida must designate a still point, a factor, a constant multiplier; this is the operational center of deconstruction, which is often described as the "blind spot" of the text on the model of psychic condensation. "The broaching of deconstruction, which is not a voluntary decision or an absolute commencement, does not take place just anywhere, or in an absolute elsewhere. A broaching, truly, it emerges [*s'enlever*] according to lines of force and forces of rupture which are localisable in the discourse to be deconstructed" (*Pos*, 109).

Derrida actually believes in these lines and forces and their delimitation; they are not unlike the forces and relations of production, in that their contradiction explains everything before it happens. Everything in the text can be subjected to a prior economy, a political economy of the discrete that antedates the deconstructor and ensures his success:

Rousseau says A, then for reasons that we must determine, he interprets A into B. A, which was already an interpretation, is reinterpreted as B. After taking cognizance of it, we may, *without leaving* [my emphasis] Rousseau's text, isolate A from its interpretation into B, and discover possibilities and resources there that indeed belong to Rousseau's text, but were not produced or exploited by him, which, for equally legible motives, he preferred to cut short by a gesture neither witting nor unwitting. (*G*, 307)

Here, in this propaedeutic to structuralist ventriloquism, Derrida reveals how the moment of sliding coincides with the reversal, in codetermination, as a kind of unraveling of the "broaching" itself. "Writing", writes Derrida, "is the impossibility for a chain (of signifiers) to repose on a signified that will not throw it back in order to be placed in a position of signifying substitution" (*Pos*, 109-10). But Derrida is careful to insist that his frequent recourse to the concept of the signifier is "deliberately ambiguous" (*Pos*, 109), asserting that even his own Cluster of Signifieds—trace, play, difference, différance, dissemination, graft, supplement, writing, "etc.," *including* the Signifier itself—escapes any "conceptual strategy" that would "momentarily privilege them as *determinate* signifiers and even as *signifiers*, which, according to the letter, they are no more" (*Dis*, 284).

Now this indeterminacy, which, according to Derrida, is sustained in his own work, is achieved by virtue not of a special intention, but of a "common law" (*Dis*, 284). Presumably it would be a kind of fidelity to this "law" that averts, during the phase of reversal, an unfortunate peripety in which the very term "signifier" "leads us back to or holds us in the logocentric circle" (*Pos*, 110, also 81). Thus, a kind of flight occurs at the very moment of specification in the text, according to a familiar economy of the "always already." Like the reversal, this discombobulation is never voluntary, although it is construed as an extremely calculating "double writing" that "marks the distance" between the reversal and "the irruptive emergence of a new 'concept,' a concept of that which no longer allows itself, has never allowed itself, to be understood in terms of the anterior regime" (*Pos*, 57). But it is, paradoxically, an organized *economy* (not a play) that truly escapes the determinate system:

Our intention here is not, through the simple motions of balancing, equilibration, or overturning, to oppose [certain concepts to others]. Quite the contrary. To counter this simple alternative, to counter the simple choice of one of the terms or one of the series against the other, we maintain that it is necessary to seek new concepts and new models, an *economy* escaping this system of metaphysical oppositions. This economy would not be an energetics of pure, shapeless force. The differences examined *simultaneously* would be differences of site and differences of force. If we appear to oppose one series to the other, it is because from within the classical system we wish to make apparent the noncritical privilege naively granted to the other series. . . . Our discourse irreducibly belongs to the system of metaphysical oppositions. The break with this structure of belonging can be announced only through a *certain* organization, a certain *strategic* arrangement which, within the field of metaphysical oppositions, uses the strengths of the field to turn its own strategems against it, producing a force of dislocation that spreads itself throughout the entire system, fissuring it in every direction and thoroughly *delimiting* it. (*WD*, 19-20)

But it is precisely the somewhat arresting *escape* of meaning Derrida describes that also *traps* us in language, for it "engages in its own *economy* so that it always signifies again and differs" (*WD*, 25). Deconstruction is the internal time consciousness of language. It forever retains and protends while trying to focus on an instant.

And this fatality of deconstruction is really the impossibility of rescuing this instant, or signifier, or trace, or gram from the structure of the sign. The signifier cannot escape, or lead to escape, because this structure is precisely "axiological, logical, etc." (*Pos*, 56) or "violent" determination as such, and as structure it is *totally indifferent* to the location of diacritical marks. It ensures only that there be such distinctions, and that there be clear spaces between them, to mark them off. Rousseau called this the "calculus of intervals," which he believed "deprive(s) language of its vital, passionate quality which made it so singable." In their abstraction, signifier and signified are interchangeable; as Roland Barthes pointed out, it depends on the direction of their sliding whether they produce ideology or metalanguage,[19] metaphysics or its deconstruction.

All the terms that make up the Derridean Cluster of Alibis (speech, presence, origin, *telos*, consciousness, etc.) and the Cluster of Signifieds (writing, différance, etc.), are subject to an economy of abstraction and reconfiguration that makes them determinate *referents* of grammatological discourse. But nowhere is this repressive labor of the sign more evident than in Derrida's scriptural strategy, an Old Testament strategy in which the Subject never speaks directly, but captures the discourse of the others, and finally submits them to the role of *portes-parole*:

What does Rousseau say without saying, see without seeing? That substitution has always already begun; that imitation, principle or art, has always already interrupted natural plenitude; that having to be a discourse, it has always already broached presence in différance; that in Nature it is always that which supplies Nature's lack, a voice that is substituted for the voice of Nature. But he says it without drawing any conclusions. (*G*, 215)

Derrida is able to privilege the economics of deconstruction because he has assumed the identity of language and metaphysics; deconstruction is then only the same, timeless struggle of language to apotheosize itself: it is the self-consciousness of the Logos. In this respect, it never really gets Derrida beyond Hegel. By opposing the servility of writing to the authority of the Voice, Derrida simply polarizes the continuum on which all forms of communication are generically related as human potentialities, while fusing exactly what is opposed in writing and speech, so that speech is invaded by the work of the sign,[20] and writing takes on the ambivalence of speech. This is a perpetual game, or play, in which "the truth of the master is in the slave; and the slave become a master remains a 'repressed' slave. Such is the condition of meaning, of history, of discourse, philosophy, etc." This servile consciousness, in its endless elaboration and deferral and regret of the origin is none other than writing, the *arche-écriture*:

The master is in relation to himself, and self-consciousness is constituted, only through the mediation of servile consciousness in the movement of recognition; but simultaneously through the mediation of the thing, which for the slave is initially the essentiality that he *cannot immediately negate in pleasurable consumption, but can only work upon, "elaborate"; which consists in inhibiting his desire, in delaying the disappearance of the thing.* (*WD*, 255) (my emphasis).

This is the cupidity of the text, its desire of desire itself, and therefore of delay of the satisfaction of desire, its fear of the ephemerality of speech, and therefore its refusal of reciprocity. Its bureaucracy. Its cosmophagy.

The Administration of the Discrete

The grammatologist least of all can avoid questioning himself about the essence of his object in the form of a question of origin. (G, 28)

Heidegger believed that the Logos principle and the Physis principle had originally been merged in pre-Socratic thought, or at least that their "relatedness" had been properly recognized until Plato autono-mized the Logos, and inaugurated "metaphysics." Physis was subse-quently degraded to "natura," and Logos became "reason," "dis-course," or "logic." This interpretation of ancient philosophy gave Heidegger some critical leverage in his encounter with Descartes and post-Cartesian philosophy; and it accorded well with his plan to col-lapse Being and Understanding in the same process, or at least to re-cover their original intimacy. Heidegger established new license to treat word and thing, syntax and process—the myriad relations of language and "world"—as identical themes, a seamless issue.

Derrida himself writes at one point that "Being is a grammar" (WD, 78), although it is never clear precisely how he intends this to be understood. It is the case, however, that he wishes to grasp com-plexity on a single level of determination, to argue against multiplici-ty: ". . . If the texts that interest us *mean* something, it is the en-gagement and the appurtenance that encompass existence and writing in the same *tissue,* the same *text*" (G, 105). And this attempt to elim-inate extralinguistic reference (*"Il n'y a pas de hors-texte"* [G, 158]) depends on Heidegger's ontological interpretation of the hermeneutic circle. The movement and meaning of Being and language are language and Being, the trace and différance, writing and the mark, spacing and supplement, gramme and greffe, "etc.":

There has never been anything but writing; there have never been anything but supplements, substitutive significations which could only come forth in a chain of differential references, the "real" supervening, and being added only while taking on meaning from a trace and from an invocation of the supplement, *etc.* And thus to infinity, for we have read, in the text, that the absolute present, Nature . . . have always already escaped, have never existed; that what opens meaning and language is writing as the disappearance of natural presence. (G, 159)

It is through Heidegger's resolution of Physis and Logos *at the ori-gin* that Derrida comes to grasp understanding of any process, per-ception, movement, act, force, feeling, possibility, creativity, desire, "touching-touched," will, mechanism, entelechy, telos, thing, or relation as a comment by language on the conditions and limitations of language, as a fold in différance; and to confuse language in gen-eral with a hyperstructural metalinguistic entity called "Western Metaphysics" (the Cluster of Alibis: "presence," "speech," "Idea," "etc.").

But Derrida himself is ambivalent about this model of thought. Its primary, Heideggerian structure provides that Being speaks—rather than people. With Heidegger, we know we are in the "presencing presence" of this speech, not when we hear something but when we enter into the circle of ritual repetition and pseudopoetic invocation that characterizes his work after *Being and Time*. In a profound sense, Derrida does not reject this view of language. He only rejects the assumption that Being's Word is copresent with a Truth, a transcendent meaning, a referent. When Being speaks to or through us (like Lévi-Strauss's myth), Derrida, unlike Heidegger, cannot hear Its meaning without anxiety and friction, cost, displacement, and loss of decipherment. But he clings to Heidegger's more profound reconciliation, in which language returns thought perpetually to the same question about itself. He only insists, against Heidegger, that this ontologia is not a speech, but writing.

In this curious refraction of Heidegger, everything still points back to an Origin, but it never gets there, by definition. For Derrida, to get outside of language means to return to an Origin. To cross "the limit that would pass between the text and what appears to overflow it" is to grasp at a "pre-text," "the anteriority of the 'thing' " (*Dis*, 49). In this perspective, reference is interpreted tendentiously as an attempt to posit an entity outside of any relation; and given such a premise, who could disagree that reference is impossible? But Derrida is not arguing that "meaning" is always a relation; he is saying that all meaning is a relation *internal* to language, that all external relations can refer only to an origin that is always (by definition) lost or fractured or "broached" in the attempt to articulate it; and that therefore there are no relations external to language.

Différance encompasses everything. The relativity of language, its volatile and insecure relation to the world, is "produced" from within language itself, as its own principle of movement. The heterogeneity of experience is resolved in the play of articulation; its syntheses and references devolve to the activity of the trace, on a planar network, or reflex arc, where tensions between different orders of concept are discharged instantly. The aura of dynamism in ambiguous words like cause, force, desire, function, mechanism, potential, telos, and will, the whole arena of notions about movement, unfolding, change, commotion, is swallowed up in a series of terms that normally express only what is already expressed, done, finished, over with: text, signifier, difference.

What Derrida has done is to translate a certain repertoire of more or less formal and sometimes expressive categories into dynamic principles, all of them expounding a metaphysics of autotelic production. What remains of the conceptual language inherited from philosophy is reduced to connotations of textual immanence. Everything outside language, everything to which language might on occasion refer, however clumsily, is conceived as *"force"*; but even this "force" is inconceivable except insofar as it is already prearticulated in the motion of différance (*SP*, 148), so that the ontologization of structuralist signification is complete. This is especially clear in one of Derrida's early formulations,[21] where we find a statement of "this strange movement within language."

To say that force is the origin of the phenomenon is to say nothing. By its very articulation, force becomes a phenomenon. . . . But in saying this, one must refer to language's peculiar inability to emerge from itself in order to articulate its origin, and not to the thought of force. Force is the other of language without which language would not be what it is. (*WD*, 27)

Oddly, what Derrida had wanted to avoid by saying this was "an energetics of pure, shapeless force" (*WD*, 25), by which he appears to have meant a merely Bergsonian critique of structuralism. But his success would be purchased at the price of confining the dynamism of the world to the structure of language.

When the range of available terms in dynamic and expressive modes has been reduced in this way to the single, overarching problematic of an absent Origin, the graphomorphic operation is complete. If there is no knowledge without the presence of the origin, we are confined to an internal networking of a code that defeats us at the outset. The effect is a tremendous, devouring opacity that Derrida will use to obscure or discredit any attempt to criticize technical reason. History and society are removed *tout court* from the grope of understanding, not to mention criticism, because they can never harmonize absolutely with the discrete *ratio* of our impulse to represent them. It is as if Derrida wanted to convert all thought to the unilateral tropism of an Original Code, a primeval program—literally, a Con-Template.

Ultimately, the success or failure of deconstruction would depend on Derrida's ability to mediate the tension between expressive and exponent concepts, perhaps by beginning to think about the connections between formal and substantive play. But, in a sense, the play of signifiers leaves everything else untouched. It is true that "writing" and "speech" are provisional concepts in his work; after reversing what he alleges to be the privilege of speech, Derrida seems to indicate the desirability of dialectizing this quasipolarity (e.g., *Pos*, 21-22). But the critical reversal is achieved only by enlarging the concept of writing, and subordinating a desiccated model of speech, shorn of its continuous features (the unrepeatability of its context, the interplay of heterogeneous levels of significance sustained by human interaction and not reducible to the "production" of difference). Derrida ends up stripping speech of its "presence," which is in fact a complex of mediations. Thus, while remaining within the abstraction of the opposition of speech and writing by "deconstructing" it, Derrida fails to see that he could move outside it by challenging *the structural model of language that establishes the privilege of the opposition itself*, and not just one of its terms.

In this larger perspective, logocentrism no longer appears simply as the repression of the lower term (writing) by the higher (speech). Rather, the lower term is made to function as the reduced model of the idealized other, and thus as its alibi. On this account, the theme of "presence" in speech is not the repression of writing, but of the transience and ambivalence of speech—in other words, the glorification of writing as an abiding presence in the flux. Contrary to Derrida, logocentrism has always been an attempt to exorcise the threats of speech by investing it with the apparent docility and certainty of the text. All communication is repressed in this metaphysics, not just writing, not just difference, not just formal play. But for Derrida, the player is identical with the game of language. Having jettisoned the possibility of an expressive, strange subjectivity, he cannot conceive how the player might submit himself to the rules of the game and its illusion of totality without being lost in it forever. In effect, Gödel's theorem is turned inside out. Thus, for Derrida, art is impossible. In principle, so is history, and so is critique.

In spite of his admirable "shaking" of the totality, Derrida, like Marx or Freud (privileged company), thinks he knows the infrastructures, the "economies," of his textual objects. The parody of Heidegger, the simulation model of Western thought, the Cluster of Alibis that gathers the history of philosophy into a simultaneous presence—this imposing apparatus establishes an identity between history and thought that functions like Spirit in Hegel or production in Marx or desire in some versions of Freud. Everything refers back to an infrastructure of rational signification, which means that Derrida can always conjure up and sanction the ideality of play, because the ontotheological *base* is always the same. Once it has been identified, it can be reduced, "in a remarkable relatedness backwards *or* forwards," to its "rational kernel," and defeated by play (or by the liberation of Spirit, production, or desire). Determination becomes unilateral, veridirectional, and therefore ahistorical, or transhistorical, in the name of Heideggerian historicity (or dialectic, "historical law," necessity).

Perhaps the most effective "logocentric" strategy has been to short-circuit the interplay of explanation and understanding, of infrastructure and levels, which can be accomplished by equating their concepts, or reducing them to a hypotactic series. But this does not result only in the metaphysics of presence and the totalizing subject. The controlling idea of the Logos is to objectify and order life through the power of abstraction, "without which," as Theodor Adorno once remarked, "the subject would not be the *constituens* at large at all."[22] This goes beyond any hermeneutics of the Voice and the Fall, to the structural projection of the "rational" concept and the reduction of the object, even "consciousness," to the fungible discreteness of the sign: ideas, impressions, traces—any graphomorphic representation. The fundamental operation of logocentric thought (established by Pythagoras as a repressive hermetic tradition), is to designate continuity as appearance and irrationality; only that which can be circumscribed and thus handled according to the law of equivalence ("ratio," cosmic harmony) is real.

Derrida's expansion of the logic of writing, i.e., the logic of the discrete sign (or its deconstruction—it no longer matters), is a fundamental rearrangement of this "metaphysic." It appears to accord, in the same "gesture neither witting nor unwitting" which he attributed to Rousseau, with the demands of a cybernetic rationality that wants to redefine sensibility and play (imagination) in terms that sever it from the body, to complete the separation of the body from its gestures, and of thought from the interplay of the analogue and the digital, in order to insert play in the nonreciprocal structure of networks and "reversible" circuitry. In fact, Derrida's most ideological statements envision a kind of bureaucratic utopia of chirographic control, in which everyone is always already working to rule:

As writing, communication (if we bother to retain this word) is not the means of transportation of meaning, the exchange of intentions and meanings, discourse or the "communication of minds." We will never witness an end of writing that will restore, following the ideological representation of McLuhan, a transparency or an immediacy of social relations. Rather, we are witnessing a more and more powerful historical deployment of a general writing of which the system of speech, of consciousness, of meaning, of presence, and of truth, etc., will only be an effect and should be analyzed as such. It is the positioning of this effect as a cause which I have described elsewhere as logocentrism. (*Marges*, 392)

This piece of social reasoning about the emergence of a homogeneous monoculture of writing may be unfortunately prophetic. After all, it describes a widely generalized experience. And perhaps Derrida is right to embrace McLuhan as his mirror image. McLuhan's optimistic dream of a cybernetic renaissance and Derrida's Baroque apologetics are distinguished only by "structural" kinds of difference, tactical reversals.

Deconstruction describes the transition from the polarity of the sign to the digitality of a kind of cybernetic space in which "the present becomes the sign of signs, the trace of traces, a function in a generalized referential structure" (*SP*, 156). It is, in short, a vision of the meaning of the triumph of the network over the hierarchy. How many times removed would this be from a much more desirable pluralism of communities? Both hierarchy and network oppose pluralism and community by redistributing them according to recursive rules of binary construction. Whereas the hierarchy abstracts the relational, the network autonomizes the aleatory. But the hierarchy contains a difference entirely effaced in the network: the difference of the horizontal and the vertical, the threat of rebellion. If the hierarchy makes structure abstract, the network dissolves it entirely in the name of a hyperstructure—a logographic dream in which, as T. S. Eliot described it, "the whole of the literature of Europe from Homer . . . has a simultaneous existence and composes a simultaneous order." If hierarchy is the foundation of an imperious subject, the network is the *unilateral construct* of a subject, albeit a self-effacing subject, a subject that orients and displaces itself at will. Only the community *challenges* with its unpredictable heterogeneity, for the community cannot be broken down in a sequential play of discrete encounters riveted on a uniform coefficient; and only the community can be challenged. But in the network, the subject, not necessarily a writer, can distance himself from the mediations of presence, and then disperse himself in a game of constellations. Derridean deconstruction is another gambit in the old philosophical game of deferring the danger of the world.

NOTES

1. Martin Heidegger, *Being and Time*, trans. John Macquarrie and Edward Robinson (New York: Harper, 1962), p. 194.
2. All references to Derrida's works will appear in the body of the text as follows:
   Dis: La Dissemination (Paris: Éditions du Seuil, 1972)
   G: Of Grammatology, trans. Gayatri Spivak (Baltimore: Johns Hopkins University Press, 1976)
   Marges: Marges (Paris: Éditions de Minuit, 1972)
   Pos: Positions (Paris: Éditions de Minuit, 1972)
   SP: Speech and Phenomena, trans. David B. Allison (Evanston: Northwestern University Press, 1973)

Spurs: Spurs: Nietzsche's Styles, trans. Barbara Harlow (Chicago: University of Chicago Press, 1978)

WD: Writing and Difference, trans. Alan Bass (Chicago: University of Chicago Press, 1978)

All references from French texts are translated by the present author.

3. Marjorie Grene, "Life, Death and Language: Some Thoughts on Wittgenstein and Derrida," *Partisan Review*, XLIII, 2 (1976), 274. See also *SP*, p. 17 f.

4. Note how both the question of a possible conceptual priority and, implicitly, the whole issue of *reference* are reduced here to the question of *temporal precedence*. This habit of Derrida's will be examined in the section of this essay entitled "The Administration of the Discrete."

5. Theodor Adorno, *Negative Dialectics*, trans. E. B. Ashton (New York: Seabury Press, 1973), p. 181.

6. "The concept of différance develops the most legitimate principal exigencies of 'structuralism' " (*Pos*, 39). "Différance is the production, if we may still call it that, of those differences, of that diacriticality which Saussurean linguistics and all the structural sciences taking it for a model remind us is the condition of all signification and all structure" (*Pos*, 17-8). "We are obliged to adopt, in a noncritical way, at least some of the implications inscribed in [Saussure's] system" (*Pos*, 29).

7. Soliciting—shaking of the totality (*WD*, 6). The concept is reminiscent of Jean Baudrillard's idea of seduction in *De la séduction* (Paris: Galilée, 1980). Sometimes it also sounds somewhat Samsonite.

8. "A historico-metaphysical epoch must finally determine as language the totality of its problematic horizon" (*G*, 6). See the argument below in the section entitled "The Political Economy of the Discrete" for the idea of language as totality, and as the absolute.

9. Claude Lévi-Strauss, "Introduction à l'oeuvre de Marcel Mauss," in Marcel Mauss, *Sociologie et Anthropologie* (Paris: P.U.F., 1950), p. xlix.

10. As Derrida himself admits, adopting a characteristic defensive posture: "the detours, phrases and syntax that I shall often have to resort to will resemble—will sometimes be practically indiscernible from—those of negative theology" (*SP*, 134).

11. Ferdinand de Saussure, *Course in General Linguistics*, trans. Wade Baskin (New York: Philosophical Library, 1959), p. 18.

12. Derrida refers to différance as a "productive and primordial constituting causality" (*SP*, 137), but adds, hedging his bets as always, that "the concepts of production, like those of constitution and history, remain accessories . . . to what is here being questioned" (*SP*, 142). Elsewhere he describes these accessory features of production as its "vaguely unnoticed . . . nuances of creativity, activity, formulation, presentation—its connotations of the formulation and presentation of manifest presence" (*Spurs*, 77). Derrida never seems to grasp that the essence of the meaning of the term "production" is abstraction, and that production is an abstraction of "creativity," "activity," "formulation," "presentation." It is an impersonal, authoritarian word that has always been associated with the rupture of the mutual responsibilities of social interconnectedness—it always implies a unilateral determination. Thus, although Derrida recognizes the sexist connotations of "production," he never notes the extratextual resonances of this connection, since "textuality" itself is our most refined metaphor of abstract production.

13. See Jonathan Culler, "Jacques Derrida," in John Sturrock, ed., *Structuralism and Since* (Oxford: Oxford University Press, 1979), p. 163.

14. "The place of continuous phenomena in linguistics has been a much disputed question," writes Jonathan Culler, "but the tendency has been to relegate them to a minor place if not to exclude them from *la langue* altogether. . . . Whatever the rights of the linguistic case, for the semiologist or structuralist concerned with the social use of material phenomena

the reduction of the continuous to the discrete is a methodological step of the first importance." *Structuralist Poetics: Structuralism, Linguistics and the Study of Literature* (London: RKP, 1975), p. 14. For a general theoretical analysis of the role of this reduction in
fashioning social life along logocentric lines, see Jean Baudrillard, *For a Critique of the Political Economy of the Sign*, trans. Charles Levin and Arthur Younger (St. Louis: Telos Press,
1981), especially ch. 8.

The importance of this reduction for structuralism cannot be overstressed. It is *the* basic
move of structuralism—its *sine qua non*. The privileging of the discrete also links structuralism to the major reductionist themes in classical and modern philosophy and explains why
Derrida is able to resurrect both *rationalist* and *empiricist* models with equal force and
equanimity.

15. We have only to think about the way this temporal problem is worked out in hermeneutic theory to see parallels in the time dimension of the trace and to realize that through
the trace Derrida is reintroducing consciousness, experience, or some kind of protoaware-
ness through the back door of the subtext. Hermeneutics is constantly dogged by conun-
drums about time and relativism and bridging temporal discontinuities. Is the past radically
other? Can it be made familiar or present, or be relived? Or should it be reinterpreted in
terms of the present time? And if the latter, what is the status of such an interpretation? In
spite of Derrida's strictures on structuralist synchronicity, the relationality of the trace seems
to be an attempt to furnish an analogue of synthetic consciousness by invoking a systemic
moment that transcends time. "This chaining is such that each element—phoneme or
grapheme—is constituted from the trace in it of the other elements of the chain or system.
This chaining, this tissue [nerve tissue?] is the *text* that produces itself only in the transformation of another text" (*Pos*, 38). The trace rejoins what has been separated by abstraction
from contextual time. The time dimension of the trace is therefore the mark of a theoretical connectedness (*episteme*), a constellation, congeries or *cluster*—"*un monde des signes
sans faute*" (*WD*, 292)—not a history with its lapses and moments of unforeseeing (recognition of which prevents interpretation from becoming a positive science, even when it
wants to be).

16. As Derrida himself writes, "every form is spatial" (*WD*, 20).

17. Drawing from Derrida's discussion of Bataille, one might describe symbolic exchange
as a "continuum [which] is not the plenitude of meaning or of presence, as this plenitude is
envisaged by metaphysics" (*WD*, 263). My use of the term "symbolic exchange " is derived
from Jean Baudrillard's critique of neocapitalist culture and semiolinguistics, especially the
aforementioned *For a Critique of the Political Economy of the Sign*.

18. In effect, Derrida reproaches Foucault for failing to grasp the origin or "pre-open-
ing" of rational discourse and the silence of madness (*WD*, 39). We have another circle and a
double standard. To invoke an origin is metaphysical. But in order to put metaphysics at a
distance, in order not to "abandon ourselves to this language with the abandon which today characterizes the worst exhilaration" (*WD*, 28), we must broach the *question* of the
origin.

19. See *Writing Degree Zero* and *Elements of Semiology* (Boston: Beacon Press, 1968),
part IV, and *Mythologies* (Frogmore, St. Albans: Paladin, 1973), especially "Myth as a
Semiological System."

20. "A sign is never an event. . . . A sign which would take place but once would not
be a sign. . . . A signifier (in general) must be formally recognizable in spite of, and through,
the diversity of empirical characteristics which may modify it. It must remain the *same*
. . ." (*SP*, 50). This regularity and mechanical familiarity is, of course, difficult to achieve
in speech, even in our highly documented monoculture. Moreover, the kind of rapt exclusive
attention to separate, discrete signifiers that Derrida's theory of interpretation calls for can
be a hindrance to speech.

21. I am referring to the article "Force and Signification" (1963), which tentatively advances Derrida's logographics, but short of the whole Cluster of Signifieds and Alibis. Derrida means by "sign" the (for him unfortunate) "natural predicament in which everything refers to the disposition of a contingent situation." But in all modern accounts of the sign, including Derrida's, what emerges is a metaphysics of discreteness, abstraction, and universality that is always explicitly opposed to any "contingent situation." And this rationalist metaphysics appears in the early essay as precisely what Derrida values in the graphocentric model: "By enregistering speech, inscription has as its essential objective . . . the emancipation of meaning—as concerns any actual field of perception—from the natural predicament. . . . It creates meaning by enregistering it, entrusting it to an engraving, a groove, a relief, to a surface whose essential characteristic is to be *infinitely transmissible*" (WD, 12) (emphasis added).

22. Adorno, *Negative Dialectics*, p. 177.

Chapter 12
Modernity in the Literary Institution: Strategic Anti-Foundational Moves
John Fekete

My work gets thought in me unbeknown to me. I appear to myself as the place where something is going on, but there is no "I," no "me." Each of us is a kind of crossroads where things happen. The crossroads is purely passive; something happens there. A different thing, equally valid, happens elsewhere. There is no choice, it is just a matter of chance.

Claude Lévi-Strauss

The North American Institution of Anti-Foundationalism

I propose to construct an argument that touches on five dimensions of the modern critical nexus: first, its quadrangular institution by way of speculative, critical, analytic-empirical, and pragmatic discursive elements. Second, the institution of attention to networks of objectified practices in which the subject-supports of idealism can be dissolved. This is the consequence of a commonly shared anti-idealist motif, entailing a turn from consciousness and its contents to practices and their procedures. Third, the institution of the language paradigm as the organizing principle of a structural model for articulating in difference, for schematizing, digitalizing, and relativizing these realms of objectified practices. Fourth, the institution of a restless movement of formalization as a dynamic method for assembling the field of attention as structured world, rationalized to the standards of an apparently autonomous order of commensurable meanings and values. And fifth, the institution of an anti-foundationalist ethos as a characteristic mode of justification and legitimation for a succession of theoretical adventures.

A parade of intellectual substitutions, critical theories, and methodological disputes, supported in a cultural network of new journals, publications, conferences, and pedagogical practices, suggests the convergence of various currents in North America over the past few decades within an intellectual institution in the process of formation that I would broadly characterize as an *anti-foundationalist language paradigm.* Semiotic rationalism and Wittgensteinian pragmatism — both nourished from European as well as Anglo-American sources — are currently perhaps the two main identifiable alternative routes into this paradigm, which interprets society, in *its* objective relations, on the model of language, in *its* objective relations. It comes to challenge classical transcendental foundations, at the same time that it also comes to deploy a series of alternative foundations. Liberation from one foundation appears to bring enslavement to another. In different words, we could say that anti-foundationalism — a valuable and salutary project, if a problematical and paradoxical one to the extent that it remains confined to the matrix of the language paradigm — struggles against or in the shadow of identity theory, which, if not the only interpretive scheme in Western culture, has nevertheless been dominant.

A sketch of the salient moves in modern North American literary theory might properly begin with the New Criticism. In 1939, John Crowe Ransom announced "The Age of Criticism" in the opening issue of *The Kenyon Review.*[1] What he meant was that a profession was being formed, that a critical and speculative revolution was dislodging the then dominant precritical forms of literary scholarship in favor of an interpretive scheme focused on "the structure and mode of construction of the object."[2] In other words, a New Criticism was being instituted whose rules would be developed, monitored, and enforced by a professoriate.

The important point here is that Ransom launches an anti-foundational program. Notwithstanding the strategic intra-institutional disputes in our own day with the New Critical proposition of determinate meanings inscribed in closed texts, in the very different context of the late 1930s and 1940s, Ransom's institution-forming strategy most plausibly had to be to separate the critical enterprise from what he called "the shapeless miscellany of all prior criticism."[3] By this he meant all the various historical, biographical, philological, editorial, sociological, and psychological enterprises that attended to the origin and end of literature, to everything but its literary specificity—that is, all the interests that would have reduced literature to foundations on which a literary institution could not have been built.

At the time, especially in the light of the dead end that I. A. Richards' practical reading experiments had reached, the famous trinity of the Intentional Fallacy, the Affective Fallacy, and the Heresy of Paraphrase offered probably the best protection racket availble. I suggest through this, partly, that the costs were high, the most important being the methodological isolation of formal procedures and humanist concerns from one another.[4] It would be anachronistic to argue that this was an "error" of the New Criticism; on the contrary, the exclusion of foundational factors extrinsic to the text is an important strategic move for formalization, and it is not until Michel Foucault that the question is seriously re-raised within a formalization that is by then firmly instituted and looking for sociopolitical density.

After the New Criticism, the impact of Northrop Frye's work was to deconstruct identity in the sense of singularity and to displace the literary work toward a cultural text structurally regulated by repeating conventional patterns. By stressing, in formal terms, "the sense of context," that is, "literature as an order of words,"[5] Frye contributes to a momentous institutional reorientation away from the subjectivity pole toward the other pole of the hapless romantic antinomy, a world dominated by conventions. The ideas of context and sign system have since differentiated considerably, but the impulse is continuous.

Even more important, in directing literary theory toward a schematic formalization of the whole of social communication through a concept of the "verbal universe,"[6] Frye's move to formulate a unified cultural language ordered by structural regularities that cut across empirical irregularities marks out the territory that semiotics and rhetoric today approach in quite different ways, but with a parallel interest in finding relationships between literature and other discourses. What I would emphasize is that Frye and his network instituted an impulse to integrate literature structurally as a decisive internal principle at work in Western civilization, at the same time that the speculative humanist dimension—the visionary idealism that Derrideans would today call Frye's logocentrism—was even further isolated from the ostensibly value-free critical theory and method than in Ransom, and employed only as a general legitimating frame for the institution of formalization.

It is left, then, to Marshall McLuhan, whom I described extensively in *The Critical Twilight* as the culminating figure in the Anglo-American tradition (although his contributions have yet to be appreciated in the literary institution proper), to introduce key mutations that were to become fixtures in the academic repertoire only through the recent French imports. These range from a pancultural "speaking/writing" opposition to a stress on difference, discontinuity, and the media of regulation. But the most salient aspect of McLuhan's influence arises from his thematization of the electronic cultural environment by way of a semiology of communications technology, and his arguments for putting literature to work in the "control tower of society"[7] as a cybernetic epistemological device to assist our adaptation to the domination of objectifications. It is here that the powerful lure of the object world first saturates the field of attention; and, correspondingly, that this cybernetic world is understood on the analogy of the digital language of the text and through regulatory metaphors of the media of communication. It is not difficult to observe, from a competing theory, how cravenly McLuhan embraced his culture after a certain point. Decisively, then, the speculative dimension of rationalism is not only completely excluded here from the formal reach of the theory, but also completely separated from the critical dimension of rationalism. It is blended with an idiosyncratic irrationalism, hopelessly compromised, and consequently lost to the tradition. This result is an effect of McLuhan's strategy for dissolving the subject-object dualism in a monism centered on cultural objectifications. The structuralist phase of institutional development continues to embrace that strategy, if in variant forms.

In the light of the recent antispeculative European influences, it seems important to remember that the North American literary institution is significantly (though not exclusively) shaped by writers who carry with them the entire baggage of Anglo-American literature and criticism from Blake to the present, that is, basically the romantic and modernist traditions of construction and deconstruction. There is an impulse here toward order, synthesis, criticism, *and* vision, though it is not univocal, and part of the family tree branches toward German idealist philosophy. The French rationalist graft, when it arrives, differs in important ways. It would be simplistic simply to prefer one or the other, or one against the other. Looked at differently, it seems entirely fortunate that French analytic rationalism should have a crack at transforming the native pragmatism, the English empiricism, and its own longtime German rivals, and that these in turn should have a chance to complement the epistemic flavors of the French import. The North American literary institution, in a critical ecumenical spirit, may become the site of a larger intellectual life. The crisis in contemporary intellectual practice suggests that such ecumenicism may prove the most radical strategy.

Structuralism: The Institution of the Analytic-Empirical Language Paradigm

If the Anglo-American tradition had been reworking its inheritance and moving from models of literature to models of broader language systems, in the 1970s it got a shot in the arm from continental currents that were moving from models of language systems to models of literature. Let me propose for now, as a general statement, that one major impact of the French arrival is to strengthen immeasurably the institution of the language paradigm as the frame around the space of literary discourse, that is, as that beyond which other fundamentals are to be considered transcendent. In a multidisciplinary movement, the language paradigm is naturalized with ever greater priority and scope of formalization—that is, linguistic inquiry as the model for inquiry procedures; linguistic structures and systems as the semiological models for any other relations (whether intersubjective, interobjective or subject-object) that can be drawn into a system of signification; language then as the measure of being, and then as the whole of reality. This naturalization of the language paradigm, in effect, could be taken to represent a reversal within rationalism of the dominant production paradigm that had peaked in the nineteenth century.

Within this complex, the geometry of invariant cultural universals that results from Lévi-Strauss's anthropological attempt to understand with universal validity the culture of others while using investigative tools from his own culture, Todorov's universal grammar coinciding with the structure of the universe, the structuralist presentation of Saussure as a closed system with fixed differential properties and fundamental oppositions (e.g., signifier/signified, *langue/parole*, synchrony/diachrony), the taxonomic semiologies with their diachronic displacements, and the transformational grammars with their universal deep structures, are all variants—important variants, but variants. The expressivist modeling endemic to structuralism so overstates the colonization of the event by the structure, and so fully enslaves meaning to the rule of an automatic system, that its fetish of universality makes it an easy target for Derridean critical rationalism, which, readily perceiving the speculative character of such analytic-synthetic imperialism, moves to destroy it. Universalism—here in its essentialist aspect—now begins to invite its own displacement from formalization, although this tendency will not mature in the literary institution until it is blended with the situationism of Stanley Fish and the American pragmatist sociology of knowledge.

Underpinning structuralism is a fundamental attitude: an antisubjectivism directed against the notion of a sovereign, autonomous, individual subject-consciousness, with the added proviso that intersubjectivity be understood only in objectified form, i.e., that the objectified interpersonal be regarded as the impersonal. One local version of this is the proposition that the concept does not precede in full plenitude its linguistic articulations; that is, the language system in which it is manifested is not a mere vehicle carrying independent, prior meaning. The general formula is to refer the subject, its practices and the phenomena of its experiences—in the form of functions or effects—to the system of relations of which they are manifestations or the conditions that make their existence possible.[8] The turn from idealism to practice is a turn here to conventions, to objectified practices.

This is not a deficiency in structural theory if one is satisfied to accept given oppositions as given and merely investigate the procedures by which readers read. But the choice of oppositions—why these differences and not others—is not accounted for in the structural investigation of synchronic or diachronic differences and changes, because that explanation, having to do with causal complexes and purposes, lies beyond structural consideration. In other words, the conditions necessary for *reading* signs are not conditions sufficient for their *existence* in the first place. But even the relative relevance or significance of this latter is undecidable within the autonomous formalization itself.[9]

Ironically, the habitual traditionalist attacks against structuralism are generally misdirected against the antisubjectivist imagery of such formalization when they might better question the particular (language) paradigm of the formalization and the power of its autonomization. Antianthropologism (or antihumanism) at its formal level arises from and at its polemical level serves to legitimate the language paradigm as its particular version of anti-foundationalist ethos. For structuralism, the objects of attention and formalization are objective states and processes, and what is resisted at all costs is the

234 □ JOHN FEKETE

reduction of the wealth of the objective world to secondary status with respect to a founding source in some allegedly autarchic, arbitrary, sovereign subject of rationalist idealism, Cartesian or Hegelian. Perhaps the many crimes attributable to historical voluntarism and individual egoism may account at least in part for the polemical excesses of antihumanism. If, by contrast, we say that possessive individualism is an episode, that bureaucratic planning is a correlative aberration, that a self-governing social individual within an intersubjective community mediated by the wealth of historical objectifications is both desired and therefore also possible, and that rationalism and humanism have redeemable value features in their ideal of a reason that surpasses instrumental rationality—all this is not to say that the language paradigm is inconsistent, but that it is severely limited, and therefore to call for modified or different theoretical parameters.

To accept, moreover, the best of the structuralist pathos, the valorization of respect for the objective world, is not yet to demonstrate that the latter cannot bear variable relations to the subjective world. In particular, to recognize that the subject cannot totally command the objective conditions of existence or that the writer cannot totally command the language, both of which currently seem beyond dispute in most interpretive communities, is not yet to indicate the manifold proportions that the subject-object relation can potentially assume. The point I am making is that the autonomization of language and the objective world must itself be accounted for, and the language paradigm cannot do that on its own because that is the premise it takes for granted. If one is interested in that question, one needs to step outside the language paradigm, i.e., into some other interpretive frame. Although both the regulatory proceduralism of structuralist relativism and the potentiating deconstructionism of post-structuralist relativism can serve to effect a certain anti-empiricist denaturalization of the phenomenal event, neither escapes the limiting—and, ultimately, the reifying—frame of the language paradigm, which excludes evolutionary, axiological, and praxical dimensions of human agency that are germane to the future of the human community with respect to real options at the levels of communication and social organization.

Post-Structuralism: The Institution of Cybernetic Criticism and Contextualization

Derrida says that one cannot step outside the language paradigm, the structuralist culmination of a long logocentric tradition, but that one can offer permanent criticism, keep it honest, as it were, by instituting a process of reversal in perpetual motion. This may recall to us McLuhan's cybernetic "reversal of the overheated medium."[10] Where McLuhan proposed that the sensory closures inevitably effected by the objective environment could be understood only by virtue of the anti-environments created by art, Derrida proposes that the inevitable logocentric closures of linguistic play in Western culture require the antilanguage of deconstruction. Criticism engages the power that is structured within an articulation. In both instances, critique interprets the blind spots of the system and, as a kind of cybernetic control device, keeps it from crashing into things, blowing up, or running down. In other words, curiously enough, deconstruction provides critical subsidies (supplements, grafts) for the system so that, since it cannot be surpassed, it may effectively move along. Critics like Hillis Miller who have wrestled with the opposition "host/parasite" have interpreted, though not surpassed, the paradox here.[11] For the moment, I would just note that Derrida adds to the absolute system of the language paradigm a second absolute principle, that of autoregulation.

His brilliant anti-foundationalist maneuver consists in a daring campaign within the language paradigm: a sweeping assault on the differential structure of the sign. Derrida observes that even if the work is not referred to some prior entity as its source, even if language is not referred to any nonlinguistic entity, thing, or consciousness, even if the sign is desubstantialized, it is still permitted by structuralist theory and practice to be totalized, i.e., to be founded in some central signified presence that limits the play of signifiers. His target then has to lie beyond the structuralist problem of the subject, and in the blind spot of structuralism, its epistemological foundation, the structure of representation.

What happens here is that the attack on representation articulates a valuable critical or anarchist impulse against stable essences, essences in the sense of ontological absolutes. At Johns Hopkins in 1966, in his interview with Julia Kristeva in 1968, Derrida's criticism of the signifier/signified structure for the sign is that it inherently accedes to the classical exigency of a transcendental signified, and therefore to the power entrenched through the assumption of concepts that might be present to thought independently of a relationship to a system of signifiers. The strategy is to exclude totalization around ontological foundations and to permit the movement of supplementarity, the free play of substitutions, the endless chain of signifiers, on the grounds that "every signified is also in the position of a signifier."[12] The structure of the sign is accordingly redefined as the *trace*, and all the familiar Derridean apparatus follows. The trace leads Derrida, Barthes, and others in time to the notion of the productive text in place of the representative text, that is, the text that plays with its semiological materials, deconstructs the linguistic system of representation, and functions as its own model without end or center, irreducibly plural, reaching to all the resources of language, an intertext traversed by cultural languages.

With respect to the shibboleths of New Criticism, the Heresy of Paraphrase is here dealt a final blow in a double sense. Its purpose and function as a doctrine are preempted, since there is said to be no self-sufficient, determinate signified that can be protected from paraphrase; and its antagonists are multiplied, since all there is said to be available to criticism in the deconstructive mode is an endless chain of periphrastic transformations. Here the critical, dynamic side of rationalism displaces its contemplative structural side but, having already suppressed its speculative side, risks entropic emptiness beyond the productive emptiness that the theory proclaims.

The *production* of differences in place of the *discovery* of differences within a given structure of representation is a far-reaching advance, although we should note that this is held *within* the text as language, as an activity simply of deployment. In principle, this antifoundational maneuver is a powerful opening to the wide world of language, to a formalization beyond the earlier limits, because it claims to incorporate and hold all available dynamic movement within the language system itself. To cite Roland Barthes's version of linguistic utopia: "the Text achieves, if not the transparency of social relations, at least the transparency of language relations. It is the space in which no one language has a hold over any other, in which all languages circulate freely."[13]

It is not difficult to see here a cybernetic, digitalized inversion of the metaphysical transparency of reconciliation and presence. Indeed, Derrida's move to theorizing fundamentals in the notion of *différance* comes to produce just as much a transcendent(al) first principle and prime mover as any first principle of his logocentric adversaries, and ultimately ontotheologizes the language paradigm itself. Critical rationalism here problematically generates its own nihilist metaphysics which, at its limits, takes us from the entropy of logocentrism to the entropy of randomness. In spite of itself, it invites an additional theory of boundaries.

In this regard, Michel Foucault's efforts to reject the consolations of a semiotic isolation of free play and to introduce some variable determinacy by conceptualizing boundaries of domination are particularly sharply focused in his debate with Derrida over a reading of Descartes: he is led to accuse Derrida of "the reduction of discursive practices to textual traces alone,"[14] i.e., of teaching that there is nothing outside the text, and is himself charged with a historicist pathos that superimposes an extrinsic organization on texts that are, instead, intrinsically organized by linguistic differences that precede historicity as its preconditions. What is intriguing is that, while both Derrida and Foucault respect the trace structure of the language paradigm, the implications of their positions diverge with regard to the linguistic autonomy and stability of texts.

Foucault's semiology of discursive practices calls for a hypothesis of extratextual determinations in the context of which textual strategies can be seen as directly social strategies. Yet Foucault is by no means a naive realist and takes care not to double the text in some transcendent exterior through a relationship of representation. In treating texts, with their gaps, constraints, and exclusions, as (discursive) social practices, which, on that account, can be analyzed through political concepts as one would analyze political forces, Foucault insists that the trace structure of a philosophical text is already inscribed by the political practice of philosophical discourse. At issue here are the torsions within a text that produce its boundaries, and Derrida is prepared to admit the torsions so long as they are said to be produced from within the language of the text. Foucault's proposition is a new opening within the order of discourse. Not through a metaphor of representation (of something anterior to the text), but through the objective relations among discursive formations, formalization is extended to include the point at which texts strategically deploy an extratextual politics through the use of their linguistic resources.

At the same time, if one takes account of the persistent and harsh antihumanist polemic in Foucault, the language of "transgression," the rehabilitation of the brutal Marquis de Sade, the view of life as saturated with violences installed in systems of rules within an endlessly repeated play of dominations, one finds an element of apocalyptic impatience that translates into an overpoliticization of discourse. This overstatement of domination can be characterized as the other side of the Derridean location of deconstructive critique in a perpetually subordinate position, doomed to serve, never to supervene, the host discourse. By contrast to both, if we not only accept that the play of the text is strategically oriented by the context of social practice it inscribes, but also resist the excessive political tropism of the argument, then we can conceptualize the trace structure of the text as a social practice as potentially seized of a variety of discourses (philosophical, political, sociological, economic, esthetic, cosmological, axiological, scientific, and so on). Salient extratextual context will not be transcendentally exterior to the text. At one level, the ostensible host discourse thus cedes its privilege of self-deployment to endless interdiscursive ploys; at another, the host discourse becomes itself a contextual strategic determination.

Inasmuch as what can be said about strictly philosophical discourse according to this theory of the text can equally be said about other discourses, including literature, the second of the New Critical shibboleths, the Intentional Fallacy, now comes under decisive (if still delimited) challenge, as the text is opened and interrogated as a verbal intention that bears the marks of extratextual determinations. Of course, there is no concession in Foucault to subjectivity or psychological intentionality. The emphasis is on a contextual *orientation* of the intertextuality and genealogy of the trace structure within a frame of objective interdiscursive relations. The place of the languages of criticism, meanwhile, is firmly assured, because they can be seen not as supplements but as necessities for the objective existence of the texts, that is, not exterior to the texts but veritable intertexts moved into the gaps within the texts.

By way of Frye and McLuhan, then structural semiology, Derrida and Foucault, from the object pole, and even more, as I shall argue, by way of the implications of pragmatist reception theory, from the intersubjective pole, the anti-foundationalist movement of the language paradigm systematically undermines the stability of the foundations on which it began to build its institution: i.e., the autonomous work of literature. In the end, neither the work nor the literary text nor literature as a whole are permitted stable autonomy; undoubtedly, the literary institution itself risks destabilization.

The strategic edge to this powerful development of formalization is immense. In general, the most significant result of the Derrida-Foucault modifications to the language paradigm would seem to be to open forms, of objective necessity, to other forms. The move is Gödelian: no form or system is complete; that is, neither can a form or system be founded on itself and establish its own noncontradiction, nor can it encompass its own metatheory and determine its ultimate foundation through its own resources. This move then provides both for local undecidability and for regional foundation, which, moreover, has the character of an interplay of social practices. Although we are still in the realm of the language paradigm here, the continuing deferral of foundation begins to implicate the closure of the language paradigm itself. A tension between anti-foundationalist formalization and the language paradigm begins to strain the paradigm.

Pragmatism: The Institution of the Customary Context

Stanley Fish's recent work collected in *Is There a Text in this Class?* involves theoretical moves of considerable significance for the literary institution in its reworking of the notion of context. This is the moment when Wittgensteinian pluralism and community-oriented American pragmatism come to provide an important supplement to the formulations instituted through variants of European rationalism. The intent is to make the endless epistemic dispersion unproblematical and practically workable in empirical interpretive practice. Northrop Frye and Marshall McLuhan had already shifted the focus of cultural attention and value away from the producer of literature to the consumer of literature, and the structuralist traditions, with their emphasis on literary competence, intertextuality, and the indispensable role of criticism, have helped to prepare the way for reception theory, a field which, through the works of Walter Benjamin, the Frankfurt School, and the tradition of Ingarden, Iser, and Jauss, has in any case been gaining prominence. But it is only with Stanley Fish that the third shibboleth of New Criticism, the Affective Fallacy, is now flatly rejected, and the site not only of meaning but of textuality itself is transferred from the domain of any science of signs to reception and its institutions.

Fish enters a battlefield, between the postmodernist proponents of the undecidability of texts and the traditionalist proponents of objective reading of determinate texts, with a consoling message: all the anxieties about the impositions of subjectivity, either violating free play (the post-structuralist anxiety) or performing idiosyncratically (the New Critical anxiety), are the effects of a pseudo-problem of subject-object relations, of a hopeless search for some relationship between two entities (reader/text) that are falsely assumed to be either autonomous or stable. The pivot of Fish's counterargument is *context*. Like Foucault, Fish refuses to permit any distance or doubling between context and sense or meaning. To be in a context or situation is to be seized of language as already meaningful, inasmuch as it is not the signs but the interpretive contexts, understood as objectified in conventional structures of norms and constraints, that determine meaning, including what will count as literature, or any of its subcategories, forms, contents, periods, genres, standards, canons, and so on.

This maneuver, then, both univocal (as concerns the individual interpreter, who is said to be as much a product or extension of his interpretive context or community as the meanings it enables him to produce) and plurivocal (as between the different interpretive contexts or communities), liberates interpretation from a series of transcendentals—the textual essence of the traditionalists, the universal commensurations of the structuralists, and the idiosyncrasies of the critical nihilists. Interpretation is thus a productive, meaningful, public, and pluralist institution of persuasion. Fish's sociology of knowledge rests on a gentle pragmatist emphasis on the world of practical rationality in which all participate. What tends to be unelaborated here is the nature of the intensely interested competition among these communities that amounts to each being defined against the other, therefore encompassing the other in its assumptions, from the start. This can matter to the extent that it implies questions about the boundaries of context (and thus rebounds on the issues at stake and the meaning of their resolution).

The argumentation is nonetheless compelling for several reasons. Texts and other human products indeed have their reality only as they are being realized, their openness or closedness only as they are being opened or closed, and their life only as they are being lived. The turn to reception theory is a major strategic contribution to literary understanding, and the contextual argument properly situates the individual interpreter in a community within the plural structure of the literary institution. The maneuver, as a whole, questions the status of the text and more than removes the last vestiges of parasitism or inferiority from criticism which, on its account, produces the very objects of its attention.

Yet, in the end, we have arrived here at some border country between the language paradigm and the paradigm of objective custom. Fish reintegrates different interpretive forms into the relative continuity of a linguistic and customary temporal constitution of the objective world of practical public intelligibility. Structures of assumptions, ineluctable "prejudices," are the perspectival horizons, the alterable articulations of the institutional domain. As in Gadamer, here the interpretive community, that is, intersubjectivity, is described as the thing itself.[15] Fish's paradigm deploys polemically its subject-object indifference. We belong to the structure of interpretation, not it to us.

There are a number of questions one would wish to pose, mainly about the relationships between individuals and communities, essentially to test the degree of porousness of the normative structures and to establish the contexts relevant to interpretation. For example, with reference to the place of individual contributions to the social, what is the contribution of the writer to the reading, particularly as there is an asymmetry between reader and writer in language capacity and intention and an asymmetry between their respective contextual roles? What is the site of an inquiry where this becomes relevant? Such questions are perhaps answerable from Fish's system or, at any rate, within its framework as it becomes further specified—and modified to take account of writers and their contexts.

The bigger problem would seem to be generally how we describe the scope of our "situation" and the limits of commensurability. Fish says that relativism is a position one can entertain but not occupy. In the practice of literary criticism, one inhabits one's context-bound internalized assumptions without reservation. At the same time that we are all living out a metatheory that proclaims a perspectivism of assumptions, the metatheory has no practical implications; our own interpretive contexts or communities provide for a full round of practical activities that we are always able to perform.[16] But does the individual always have an assured basis of action in everyday life, or perhaps only in relatively stable periods? In periods of crisis or decay, as the social norms fracture and disintegrate, that is, in periods of de-institutionalization, is there not an increasing distance between the norms and the interpretive acts they contextualize? As individual appropriation suffers, to what extent does disorientation mark even the everyday? Is it not possible that relativism may become a position that one *can* occupy at the practical level, and that relativism at what Fish calls the metatheoretical level may become a legitimation, rather than an inconsequential epistemological observation?

Of course, the problem has its own importance at the so-called metatheoretical, that is, institutional and societal level as well. The virtue of the notion of competing interpretive communities is that at least it lifts the relativism question to the cultural level. Several times Fish registers this *level* of questioning, only to dismiss it from consideration as beside the point for individuals. But is there no interrogation desirable about how competing situational normative structures might be adjudicated or addressed from the point of view of a culture or civilization? To be sure, the nature of the putative "subject" for whom or by whom such an adjudication would be carried out is by no means unequivocally clear, and certainly admits no final formulation. Indeed, such a subject ("interpretive community") and such an address may be virtually ruled out by the demands of pluralism. But what my questions target is the extent to which the boundary conditions of more or less automatic, unproblematical social reproduction tend to become paradigmatic and saturate the whole field of social reproduction, *mutatis mutandis*, at the two levels of ordinary, everyday life that Fish postulates. It seems that Fish confines the coordinates of discussion to the level of customary behavior, in effect leaving custom unquestioned and unjustified, indeed, exempted from requirements of justification.

It may be our current social situation that objective processes not only share but dominate us, the reproduction of society accounting for the structure of institutions and then interpretive communities, these in turn producing individual extensions and then meanings. We may be approaching the limit where these are automated, homeostatic cybernetic operations. It may be that conducting this entire analysis in the realm of everyday life, in the realm of ready-made institutions and pragmatic relations, is increasingly permitted historically, inasmuch as our self-conscious higher-level objectifications, art, science, and philosophy, for instance, appear to be losing—as modern theory indeed informs us—their ability to offer to our appropriation values that can be turned against the reproduction of customary valuations. But then again, perhaps this is not our natural condition and can be altered if we can consciously, practically, alter our relations to these dominating objective processes. *If* that is desired and practiced. On Fish's own argument, interpretive assumptions and beliefs act as objective forces. They define their objects. Why does the theorist then not wear emancipatory glasses and look for, and therefore define and orient, more free space?

Of course, this presupposes a modified paradigm: certainly not an asituational one that would interpret from a neutral, decontextualized, transcendent standpoint, but rather one that would be prepared to accept culture, civilization, and their development as value terms. It is possible to say, in what may be only a strategic variant of a more cautious and skeptical pragmatism, but an anti-foundational variant outside the language paradigm, that value axioms are prior to the practiced valuations and assumptions to which they are always attached and which derive from them. Therefore they play a role in the choice and organization of these assumptions, and in the scheme of justification within the theory-practice circle, and provide freer space for problematizing institutions and moving among alternatives. This is desirable. Indeed, as it is possible on this account to articulate value continuities moving retentively and protentively from the value axiom, it is possible also to articulate universal validity, and hence to target a future with greater scope for a practical emancipatory intent.

Also desirable. To be sure, such postulates carry only conditional objectivity, since the objective possibility they assume upon entering a public life by way of an interpretive community that shares them is conditional on their actual validation in history. Since value axioms require elaboration a posteriori in order to be practiced, their formulation at the level of theory is not mere epistemological mirroring, therefore, but itself a level of practice as well as a strategic device for being more persuasive. This too is desirable.

Anti-Foundationalism Revalued?

In general, the language paradigm is a cognitive practice that is seized of the world as always already prestructured in its inventory, rules, or processes, i.e., a cognitive practice with a deductivist character. Formalizations within this tradition are inflected with an analytic-empirical, contemplative, factualist epistemological attitude that neutralizes its varied and variably radical proclamations by attaching them to a universal standard of commensuration: the standard of linguistic structurality. The diacritical relational field of linguistic structurality is ontologized as the ground of phenomena, including the articulation of the object world, both making and being made, both decidability and undecidability, both subject and object, both the institution and the cognition of society. In the course of the structural reduction that "denaturalizes" phenomena, the world of human relations is, paradoxically, made "nature," though now at the level of our conventionally coded second nature, as *natura naturans* or *natura naturata*. It is stripped of alternativity posed as a problem for value as an underived category of human life. It is stripped of significance. It is stripped of purposive agency, and hence of history. And, as social "nature," it is stripped also of evolution.

It appears that the world allows itself to be described through the language paradigm and permits itself to be seized in modalities of structurality. My argument is that the world may be embraced as other and more than what such structural reduction institutes, if the appropriate practices and languages can be produced. The virtue of the language paradigm, finally, is that it places subjectivity and objectivity at the same ontological level within a single circuit. But whether the subject pole or the object pole is stressed at a given point, whatever dualism is presented is held at the surface and rapidly dissolved into a monism of the prior structuration. For all the anti-Hegelianism of the actual formulations, the most troubling distortion of the Hegelian system is preserved, if in inverted form: the unwillingness of the theory to distinguish between alienation and articulation per se. In Hegel, under the domination of the Spirit, in the language paradigm, under the domination of structurality, the immediacy of subject-object identity is established. There is only one dimension: in the modern framework, the rule of the instituted, of the always already digitalized, conventionalized relations. The quite acceptable proposition that conscious language choices cannot fully command the play of language is disproportioned to reduce or eliminate the possibilities of conscious, not already rationalized, relations to objective formations.

This unstable proportioning may be susceptible to displacement in different directions. It would seem to be the site of Habermas's not altogether successful attempts to establish a moment of epistemological self-reflection at the heart of interpretive theory.[17] This impulse toward expanding the site and role of self-consciousness remains important, even though pragmatism is unlikely to find the truth claims of self-reflective universals convincing on their own, since its entire corrective strategy with regard to the interrationalist wars is to remove meaning from the problem complex of objective universals, either systemic or nihilistic.

What, then, might assist the literary institution to make the best of its anti-foundationalist modernity? As a complement to self-reflection, one is drawn to attempt to secure nontranscendent foundations for interpretive theory and interpretive practice through a philosophy of value that proposes value as irreducibly both a priori and a posteriori.[18] Once we make room for competing interpretive communities and practices, we find, for example, that the *intention* of emancipatory praxis is prior to interpretive practice, a primary value axiom that is not derivable from actually practiced valuations or assumptions, although its possible forms can only be articulated in various levels of interpretive argument and attached to practical valuations and assumptions. By contrast, the variants of the language paradigm offer a definition of human life that invites us to be satisfied with the brute factuality of the multiplicity and serial succession of symbolic and institutional systems, whose significance we have no standards to evaluate and about which nothing can or need be done. Such a definition is not necessarily untrue, which is to say that, in a situation of competing views, only time and the play of historical practices will prove its truth or give it the lie. But meanwhile, like all interpretations, it acts materially as a self-fulfilling prophecy. It can be described, if not as false, then as either too pessimistic about the possible alternatives in this epoch or as too optimistic about the character of the customary life of the epoch.

In my argument, the modern literary institution can benefit from an ecumenical assimilation of its full heritage. The analytic-empirical attention to combinations of differences and relative stabilities is necessary for the basic organization of institutions of meaning and interpretive life; the critical dimension is a key to movement and choice, a protection from the false consolations of full presence, the metaphysical, linguistic, or customary closure of the game, and the uncritical doubling of the sign with congealed privilege. But the critical cannot on its own justify its value of free play; for this the pragmatic context, jointly with the speculative meta-empirical (but not metaphysical) conjecture are called on, as well as a hermeneutic of traditions to provide substance from the horizons of inherited traditions for the continuing renewal of a pluralist, rational, pragmatic, anti-foundational interpretive project. The interpreter can hold fast, moreover, to the ontological primacy of value as a dimension introduced into the complex anti-foundationalist paradigm. Value came into being with the beginning of society and will not disappear before its end. The subject, the object, man, the origin, the end, and the essence, all of which are properly rejected as having any transcendent claims, can all be preferred as values with a practical intent to redefine them provisionally, again and again, in the light of a value axiom and in value continuity with the choice of a future and a past, both inscribed with ends but no end. This is a project for shaping the present and robbing it of a false metaphysical plenitude.

It is just as clear that not every interpretive practice promotes a humane world as it is clear that there is no single formula for so doing. It will be left to a social history of ideas to decide whether the rise of grammatology, for instance, was implicated in a moment when European culture was dominated by a circulation of signs that occluded its links to a meaningful history or an animating project. It is always possible, however, for some interpreters to opt for a meaningful history through an animating project and to insert this project into the world as a value hinge between the *always already* and the *never yet*, shared objectively by those who are prepared to share it, the play of the hinge making the object world more or less problematically poised among alternatives, and thus further preferences and objectifying practices.

What is decisive for interpretive (paradigm) choice, then, is how we see our inherent possibilities and how we design our practical relation to our future. I am convinced that practical criticism is implicated in metatheoretical debate. The anti-foundationalist program, as it moves beyond the matrix of the language paradigm, can effectively embrace a value debate about the orientational features of discursive formations, the assumptions of critical practices, the values and implications inscribed in texts as we see them, and the stakes in play in the literary institution and at large. On this account, a multiparadigm anti-foundationalist program can best redeem Saussure's call to study "the life of signs" if to that study is attached a meliorist project to denaturalize, problematize, and revalue the signs of life with practical emancipatory intent. Within the current crisis in the production of knowledge and in the quality of critical conversation, this would appear desirable.

NOTES

1. John Crowe Ransom, "The Teaching of Poetry," *The Kenyon Review*, I (Winter 1939), 81.
2. "Mr. Tate and the Professors," *The Kenyon Review*, II (Summer 1940), 349-50. See also "Criticism, Inc.," *The World's Body* (New York: Charles Scribner's Sons, 1938), p. 347, and "Strategy for English Studies," *The Southern Review*, VI (Autumn 1940), 226-27, 235, particularly interesting in equating the critical and the speculative.
3. "Ubiquitous Moralists," *The Kenyon Review*, III (Winter 1941), 95. See also *The New Criticism* (Norfolk: Conn., 1941), p. 216; "Criticism as Pure Speculation," in Donald A. Stauffer, ed., *The Intent of the Critic* (Princeton, 1941), pp. 101-2; and "The Irish, the Gaelic, the Byzantine," *The Southern Review*, VII (Winter, 1942), 541.
4. For an extended discussion of these issues and developments, see John Fekete, *The Critical Twilight: Explorations in the Ideology of Anglo-American Literary Theory from Eliot to McLuhan* (London, Henley, and Boston: Routledge & Kegan Paul, 1978), pp. 43-103.
5. Northrop Frye, *Fables of Identity: Studies in Poetic Mythology* (New York: Harcourt, Brace & World, 1963), p. 127. Also, "The Critical Path: An Essay on the Social Context of Literary Criticism," *Daedalus, Journal of the Academy of Arts and Sciences*, XCIX (Spring 1970), 268.
6. *Anatomy of Criticism: Four Essays* (Princeton: Princeton University Press, 1957), p. 352.
7. Marshall McLuhan, *Understanding Media: The Extensions of Man* (New York and London: New American Library, 1964), p. 70.
8. With regard to cultural "things" or entities, structuralism thus recycles (in a different, antidialectical context) the metaphysical moves that took Heraclitus and Plato beyond the ancient metaphysics of self-contained thing-hood to a structure of oppositions. Cf. Alexander P. D. Mourelatos, "Heraclitus, Parmenides, and the Naive Metaphysics of Things," in E. N. Lee, A. P. D. Mourelatos, R. M. Rorty, eds., *Exegesis and Argument: Studies in Greek Philosophy Presented to Gregory Vlastos* (Assen, Netherlands: Van Gorcum, 1973), pp. 16-48. The antiempiricist Platonism of the structuralist intervention is an intriguing problem that remains to be explored.
9. For one powerfully elaborated discussion of such problems, see Cornelius Castoriadis,

L'Institution imaginaire de la société (Paris: Éditions du Seuil, 1975). In English, see an extended excerpt from this work, "The Imaginary Institution of Society," trans. Brian Singer, in the present volume.

10. McLuhan, *Understanding Media*, p. 45.

11. J. Hillis Miller, "The Critic as Host," in Geoffrey Hartman, ed., *Deconstruction and Criticism* (New York: Continuum, 1979), pp. 217-53.

12. Jacques Derrida, *Positions*, trans. Alan Bass (Chicago: The University of Chicago Press, 1981), pp. 19-20.

13. Roland Barthes, "From Work to Text," in Josue V. Harari, ed., *Textual Strategies: Perspectives in Post-Structuralist Criticism* (Ithaca: Cornell University Press, 1979), p. 80.

14. Michel Foucault, "Mon corps, ce papier, ce feu," in *Histoire de la folie*, 2nd ed., (Paris, 1972), p. 602. See also Derrida's essay on Foucault in *Writing and Difference* (Chicago: University of Chicago Press, 1978). Gayatri Spivak briefly discusses the controversy in the "Translator's Preface" to Derrida's *Of Grammatology* (Baltimore and London: The Johns Hopkins University Press, 1976), pp. lx-lxii. An elaborated and less partisan discussion of this controversy, Robert D'Amico's "Text and Context: Derrida and Foucault on Descartes," is included in the present volume.

15. See György Márkus, "The Paradigm of Language: Wittgenstein, Lévi-Strauss, Gadamer," in the present volume.

16. Stanley Fish, *Is There a Text in This Class? The Authority of Interpretive Communities* (Cambridge: Harvard University Press, 1980), p. 370.

17. See Jurgen Habermas, "A Review of Gadamer's *Truth and Method*," in Fred R. Dallmayr and Thomas A. McCarthy, eds., *Understanding and Social Inquiry* (Notre Dame and London: University of Notre Dame Press, 1977), pp. 335-63. See also *Knowledge and Human Interests*, trans. Jeremy J. Shapiro (London: Heinemann, 1972).

18. For one important attempt to develop such a philosophy of value, see Agnes Heller, *Towards a Marxist Theory of Value*, trans. Andrew Arato, in *Kinesis*, V, 1 (Fall 1972), published by Southern Illinois University at Carbondale (76 pp.).

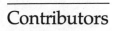

Contributors

Contributors

Marc Angenot was born in Brussels in 1941, graduated from the University of Brussels in 1967 with a Ph.D. dissertation on "The Rhetoric of Surrealism," and currently teaches French and comparative literature at McGill University in Montreal. He is co-editor of *Science-Fiction Studies*, an international journal established in 1974 and now the leading journal in that field. At present, Angenot is working on the theory of social discourse conceived as an encompassing whole of textual interactions in a given state of society. His publications in literary semiotics, the history of ideas, and the critique of ideologies and social discourse include:

Le Roman populaire. Montréal: Presses Universitaires de Québec, 1975. A survey of French popular literature, 1800-1914.

Les Champions des femmes. Montréal: Presses Universitaires de Québec, 1978. A historical approach to the concept of the superiority of women from the fifteenth to the eighteenth centuries.

Glossaire pratique de la critique littéraire. Montréal: Hurtubise, 1980. A glossary of literary criticism.

La Parole pamphlétaire. Paris: Payot, 1982. A contribution to the typology of modern discourses, mainly polemics and pamphleteering.

Jean Baudrillard teaches sociology at Nanterre. His radical intellectual project, his critique of Freud and Marx, and his commentary on contemporary culture have attracted increasingly significant interest since 1968. His publications include:

Le Système des objects. Paris: Gallimard, 1968.

La Société de consommation. Paris: Gallimard, 1970.

Pour une critique de l'économie politique du signe. Paris: Gallimard, 1972. Translated into English by Charles Levin and Arthur Younger, *For a Critique of the Political Economy of the Sign.* St. Louis: Telos Press, 1981.

Le Miroir de la production ou l'illusion critique du matérialisme historique. Tournai: Casterman, 1973. Translated into English by Mark Poster, *The Mirror of Production.* St. Louis: Telos Press, 1975.

L'Échange symbolique et la mort. Paris: Gallimard, 1976.

L'Effet Beaubourg: Implosion et dissuasion. Paris: Galilée, 1977. (Also in *Simulacres,* below). Translated into English by Rosalind Krauss and Annette Michelson, "The Beaubourg-Effect: Implosion and Deterrence," *October,* No. 20 (Spring 1982).

Oublier Foucault. Paris: Galilée, 1977. Translated into English as "Forgetting Foucault" in *Humanities in Society,* 3:1 (Winter 1980).

A l'ombre des majorités silencieuses ou la fin du social. Paris: Cahiers d'Utopie, 1978.

Le P.C. ou les paradis artificiels du politique. Paris: Cahiers d'Utopie, 1978.

De la séduction. Paris: Galilée, 1979.

Simulacres et simulation. Paris: Galilée, 1981.

Les Stratégies fatales. Paris: Grasset, 1983.

For discussions of Baudrillard in English, the reader may find helpful the following selected list, in addition to Mark Poster's and Charles Levin's introductions to the English translation of *The Mirror* and the *Critique* respectively.

Robert D'Amico, "Desire and the Commodity Form," *Telos,* No. 35 (1978), 88-122.

Robert D'Amico, *Marx and the Philosophy of Culture* (Gainesville: University of Florida Press, 1982).

Jean-Claude Giradin, "Towards a Politics of Signs: Reading Baudrillard," *Telos,* No. 20 (1974), 127-37.

Charles Levin, review of *De la séduction, Telos,* No. 45 (1980), 198-202.

Karlis Racevskis, "The Theoretical Violence of a Catastrophical Strategy," *Diacritics* (Sept., 1979), 33-42.

Marshall Sahlins, *Culture and Practical Reason* (Chicago: University of Chicago Press, 1976).

Cornelius Castoriadis was born in 1922 in Greece and studied law, economics, and philosophy in Athens. Under the Metaxas dictatorship, at the age of fifteen, he entered the Communist youth organization. After the German occupation of Greece, he founded, along with fellow militants, a group opposing the bureaucratic and chauvinistic policies of the Greek Communist Party, and then entered the Trotskyist organization led by Spiros Stinas, later also participating in the French Trotskyist party (P.C.I.) after his arrival in France in 1945. There he developed a critique of Trotsky's ideas about Russia and Stalinism; a faction built around this critique broke with Trotskyism in 1948. In 1949, Catoriadis cofounded the group and the journal *Socialisme ou Barbarie* and authored the main texts defining their ideas and orientations from the beginning to the end (1949-66). His writings from this period, along with some more recent, occasional pieces, have been collected in eight volumes published in Paris by Éditions 10/18, 1973-79:

La Société bureaucratique, 2 vols., 1973.
L'Expérience du mouvement ouvrier, 2 vols, 1974.
Capitalisme moderne et révolution, 2 vols, 1979.
Le Contenu du socialisme, 1979.
La Société française, 1979.

A few of Castoriadis's most important writings from *Socialisme ou Barbarie* have been translated into English by Solidarity Press in London, notably *Modern Capitalism and Revolution*, 1974. And two essays originally written to introduce some of the 10/18 volumes can be found in English translation in *Telos: A Quarterly Journal of Radical Thought*: "On the History of the Workers' Movement," No. 30 (Winter 1976-77), 3-42, and "Socialism and Autonomous Society," No. 43 (Spring 1980), 91-106.

After *Socialisme ou Barbarie*, Castoriadis's publications include three books of deeply theoretical work brought out in Paris through Éditions du Seuil:

L'Institution imaginaire de la société, 1975.
Les Carrefours du labyrinthe, 1978.
De l'écologie à l'autonomie (with Daniel Cohn-Bendit), 1980.

One of the essays from *Les Carrefours* has been translated as "From Marx to Aristotle and from Aristotle to Us," *Social Research*, No. 4 (Winter 1978).

Castoriadis also published two works of particularly conjunctural analysis:

Mai 1968: La Brèche (with E. Morin and C. Lefort). Paris: Éditions Fayard, 1968.

Devant la guerre, I. Paris: Éditions Fayard, 1980.

This last book is controversial. The English-speaking reader interested in these writings is advised to consult *Telos*: "The Social Regime in Russia," No. 38 (Winter 1978-79), 32-47; "Facing the War," No. 46 (Winter 1980-81), 43-61; "The Crisis of Western Society," No. 53 (Fall 1982), 17-28.

From 1948 to 1970, Castoriadis worked as an economist in the International Secretariat of the OECD in Paris. Since 1974, he has been a practicing psychoanalyst. In 1977, he was elected Director of Studies at the École des Hautes Études en Sciences Sociales in Paris, where he directs a seminar on the "Institution of Society and Historical Creation."

For useful discussions in English of Castoriadis's writings, the reader may turn to the entries listed under Brian Singer, below, as well as: "An Interview with C. Castoriadis," *Telos*, No. 23 (19750, 131-55.

Dick Howard, "Introduction to Castoriadis," *Telos*, No. 23 (1975), 117-31; and "Ontology and the Political Project: Cornelius Castoriadis," in *The Marxian Legacy* (New York: Urizen, 1977), pp. 262-301, 328-33.

John B. Thompson, "Ideology and the Social Imaginary: The Appraisal of Castoriadis and Lefort," *Theory and Society* (1982), 659-81.

For a Castoriadis bibliography, see also Gregory Renault, "Major Writings of Cornelius Castoriadis," in *Catalyst*, No. 13 (Spring 1979), 105-110.

Robert D'Amico is an associate editor of the journal *Telos* and teaches philosophy at the University of Florida. His most recent publication is *Marx and the Philosophy of Culture* (Gainesville: University of Florida Press, 1982), and he is currently working on a book about the relationship between critical theory and science.

John Fekete was born in Budapest in 1946. He settled in Canada following the 1956 Hungarian uprising, and was active in the global youth revolt of the 1960s. That experience remained with him as a deep formative impulse, and colors his voice in both scholarship and political life. Fekete currently teaches English and cultural studies at Trent University in Peterborough, with a particular interest in literary/critical theory and utopian/science-fictional narratives. He is a senior editor of *Telos*, an advisory editor of *Science-Fiction Studies*, and a consulting editor of *Cine-Tracts* (a journal of film and cultural theory). His current research is into the nature of the speculative imagination in modern culture, the discourse on technology, and the relationship between value and meaning. His publications include

The Critical Twilight: Explorations in the Ideology of Anglo-American Literary Theory (London and Boston: Routledge & Kegan Paul, 1978) and articles on literary theory and such figures as McLuhan, Frye, Ransom, Benjamin, Kermode, Graff, Le Guin, Delany, and Swift in journals such as *Telos, New Literary History, Criticism, Science-Fiction Studies, English Studies in Canada*, and the *Canadian Journal of Political and Social Theory*.

Arthur Kroker teaches political theory and contemporary cultural studies at Concordia University in Montreal. He is the founding editor and publisher of the *Canadian Journal of Political and Social Theory*, and is currently preparing a book on the discourse of power in Western society. His most recent publications in this area include a rethinking of Barthes and Baudrillard, "The Disembodied Eye: Ideology and Power in the Age of Nihilism," and a genealogy of the discourse of power, "The Arc of a Dead Power: Augustine/Baudrillard." In addition, he is engaged in a study of three major contributors to the Canadian discourse on technology: Harold Innis, Marshall McLuhan, and George Grant.

Charles Levin was born in London, England and grew up in Montréal. His M.A. thesis for McGill University was a study of Jean Baudrillard's work. He has published a translation of Baudrillard: *For a Critique of the Political Economy of the Sign* (St. Louis: Telos Press, 1981). Levin currently teaches English and humanities at Dawson College in Montréal. He writes fiction and was once a full-time musician. He is now absorbed in research on psychoanalytic psychology.

György Márkus was born in 1934 in Budapest, Hungary. He studied philosophy in Moscow at Lomonosow University, 1952-57, and then taught in the philosophy department of Budapest University, 1957-65. His doctoral thesis on Wittgenstein was accepted by the Hungarian Academy of Sciences in 1965. From 1965 to 1973 he was a research scholar at the Institute of Philosophy of the Hungarian Academy. Márkus belonged to the close circle of philosophers and sociologists around György Lukács called the "Budapest School." In 1973 he was removed from all academic positions for "hostile" and "anti-Marxist" theoretical and ideological activity, together with the other members of this circle. He remained unemployed in Budapest until, in 1977, he emigrated with his family from Hungary. Currently he teaches as Reader in the Department of General Philosophy, University of Sydney, Australia. His publications include: *The Epistemology of the Young Marx* (1960, in Hungarian; published also in German, Italian, Portuguese, and Japanese).

Language, Logic and Reality: On Wittgenstein's Tractatus (1964, in Hungarian).
Modern Western Philosophy (with Z. Tordai, 1964, in Hungarian).
Marxism and "Anthropology" (1965, in Hungarian; English trans. published by Van Gorcum, 1977; published also in German, Italian, Spanish, and Japanese).
Die Seele und das Leben. Studien zum frühen Lukács (with F. Fehér, Á. Heller, and S. Radnóti, Frankfurt, 1977; also in Italian).
Langage et production (Paris: Denoel, 1982).
Dictatorship over Needs (with F. Fehér and Á. Heller, Oxford: Blackwell, 1983; also in German).

John O'Neill was born in 1933 in London, England. Currently, he teaches sociology at York University in Toronto, and is an Affiliate of the Centre for Comparative Literature at the University of Toronto. In 1983 he was University Distinguished Visiting Professor at Ohio State University. He is coeditor of *Philosophy of the Social Sciences* and editor of Routledge & Kegan Paul's International Library of Phenomenology and Moral Sciences. In addition to translations of Maurice Merleau-Ponty, his publications include:
Perception, Expression and History, Evanston: Northwestern University Press, 1970.
Sociology as a Skin Trade. New York: Harper & Row, 1972.
Making Sense Together. New York: Harper & Row, 1974.
On Critical Theory (ed.) New York: Seabury, 1976.
For Marx Against Althusser and Other Essays. Washington: Center for Advanced Research in Phenomenology and University Press of America, 1982.
Essaying Montaigne: A Study of the Renaissance Institution of Writing and Reading. London: Routledge & Kegal Paul, 1982.

Brian Singer has just completed a Ph.D. in social and political thought at York University in Toronto. His publications include: "The Early Castoriadis: Socialism, Barbarism and the Bureaucratic Thread," and "The Later Castoriadis: Institution under Interrogation," in Nos. 3 and 4 (Fall 1979 and Winter 1980) of the *Canadian Journal of Political and Social Theory*.

Andrew Wernick was born in 1945 in Wolverhampton, England and was educated in history and economics at King's College, Cambridge, and in political theory at the University of Toronto after his arrival in Canada in 1967. Following a period of activity in the New Left, from 1971 to the present he has been teaching sociology and cultural studies at Trent University in Peterborough, where he is currently head of Trent's Peter Robinson College. He is a member of the editorial board of the *Canadian Journal of Political and Social Theory* and has published a number of articles on social theory. He is engaged in research on the ideological history of popular culture.

Index

Index

Abelard, 133
Adorno, Theodor, 223
Affective fallacy, 230, 239
Agency, xii, xiv, xix, 243
Albertus, 134
Althusser, Louis, xii, xiii, xxi, 130, 133, 139, 143, 144, 145, 151, 154, 161
Anagrams, 55
Angenot, Marc, xxiii
Anselm, 133, 134, 145
Anthropology, 24, 113, 232
Antifoundationalism, xxiv, 229-46 *passim*; language paradigm as, 238-39; in the literary institution, 244-46; in structuralism, 233-36
Apel, K. O., 108
Aquinas, Thomas, 134
Aristotle, xiv, 24, 32, 134, 135, 136, 137, 138, 140, 142, 144, 157
Augustine, 77, 133

Bacon, Francis, 135
Bad infinity, 80, 81, 99
Bakhtin, Mikhaïl M., 153, 154, 157; *Marxism and the Philosophy of Language*, 153
Bally, Charles, 152

Barthes, Roland, xiii, xxi, xxiii, 48, 78, 151, 154, 155, 161, 217, 236; écrivain/écrivant, 187-88; on failure of structuralism, 185; influence of Lacan on, 192; on language, 191, 196; on literary criticism, 195; on literature, 184; *Mythologies*, 154, 185-86, 193; on pleasures of the text, 192; on poetry, 191; on political commitment, 190; *On Racine*, 195; on style, 192; *Le Système de la mode*, 185; theory of the text, 188; on writing, 191; *Writing Degree Zero*, 187, 189, 191
Bataille, Georges, 78
Baudrillard, Jean, xvii, xix, xx, xxi, xxii, 46-52, 75, 80, 88, 89, 128, 152; on art and the estheticization of reality, 71-72; "Forgetting Foucault," 88; *Mirror of Production*, xxii
Benjamin, Walter, 63, 64, 239
Benoist, Jean-Marie, 46; *La Révolution structurale*, 46
Bentham, Jeremy, *Panopticon*, 85, 100
Biological metaphor, xxii, 75-78, 93-94, 98-99, 137-38, 139-41, 143, 144; bio-power, 77-79; body metaphor, 141, 193, 197-98; political biology, as source of structuralism, 79-80

261

Identitarian logic, 30, 31, 32, 35, 36, 37, 41
Identity, xv, 49, 58, 63, 136, 229, 230
Imaginary, The: and alienation, 14-19; central imaginary, 12-13, 43n10; complement to social order, 11; contact, 70; and individual imaginary, 27-28; Marxist view of, 15-18, 43-44n10; peripheral imaginary, 13; positive imaginary, 42n10; radical imaginary, xxi, 26, 42n4, 44n12 (a); and the real, 72; second imaginary, 12; signifiers/signifieds in, 25-26; social imaginary, 14; and the symbolic, xxiv, 9-10, 14, 25-30
Incest taboo, 20, 22
Indeterminacy, xvi, xvii, xviii, 49, 57, 60, 61, 65, 66, 67, 92, 216, 236-39
Ingarden, Roman, 239
Institution: autonomization of, 22; interpretation of, 14; as language, 113; literary, 239, 240, 244-46; of society, 32-41; and the symbolic, 19-23, 29
Intentional fallacy, 230, 238
Interpretation, 239-41, 242, 244-45; deconstructionist, 214; ecumenical project of, 245; Fish's view of, 242; foundation in philosophy of value, 244-45; as objective force, 242; as persuasion, 240; relevance of context to, 241; theories of, 165
Interpretive community, 240-41
Intertextuality, 184, 188, 238. *See also* Context; Language; Text; Trace
Irony, xv, 146
Iser, Wolfgang, 239

Jakobson, Roman, 153, 154
Jameson, Fredric, 162
Jaspers, Karl, 78
Jauss, Hans Robert, 239
Joyce, James, 187

Kant, Immanuel, 78, 79, 80, 92, 130, 136, 140, 211; "Copernican Revolution," 136; Kantianism, xi, xii, xvii, 77, 79, 105, 107, 109, 137, 139, 141, 145
Kenyon Review, The, 229
Kojève, Alexandre, 142
Kroker, Arthur, xxii
Kuhn, Thomas, 105

Lacan, Jacques, 151, 154, 157, 161, 183, 187, 188, 192

Langages, 152
Language, 202, 203, 204, 206; and art, 189-90; autonomization of, 234; and body, 189; body language, 192; catachresis as feature of, xv; and custom, xxii, 240; and deconstruction, 215, 217; and différance, 221; empiricist critique of, 211; as expression of identitarian logic, 36; and force, 221; and history, 203; ideal, 122, 198; institutions as, 113; and literature, 187, 232; Marxist view of, 126; and meaning, 49, 214, 217, 220, 239; and medium, 202; and metaphysics, 218; and myth, 187; natural, 122, 123; as object, 144; objectivations as, 110, 113; and play, 214; plurality of, 197; and political commitment, 190; and power, 80, 85, 90-91, 96-98; and presence, 215; productivity of, 191; realist view of, 191; and reason, 214; as representation, xv; as social activity, 110; as social fact, 113; and spirit, 122; and style, 193; as symbol, 6; as system of signs, 117; and trace, 203; transparency of, 124-25; and understanding, 119-20; violence of, 196; and world, 219; world-constituting character of, 117
Language games, 110-14 *passim*, 117, 122, 141, 222; and meaning, 118; as prerequisite for rationality, 117
Language paradigm, xiii, xiv, xvi, xxii, xxiv, 47-48, 50, 104, 125-27, 141, 228-29, 232, 233, 234, 235, 236, 237, 238-39, 240, 242, 243-46; as antifoundationalism, 233, 238-239; closure of, 238-39; as cognitive practice, 243; in Derrida, 236; in Derrida and Foucault, 238; indeterminacy and, 49; Marxist critique of, 127-28; naturalization of, 232; and paradigm of objective custom, 240; and paradigm of production, xxii, 128; and play, 121; rise of, 104-5; and subject/object relations, 243-44; universality of, 112, 117, 123; and value, 244-46; in Wittgenstein, Lévi-Strauss, and Gadamer, 105-28
Langue Française, 152
Langue/parole, 113, 115, 208, 210, 232
Le Bon, G., 159
Le Dantec, G., 159
Lefebvre, Henri, 162
Legein, 30, 31, 32, 34

Solicitation, 69, 206
Sollers, Phillipe, 154
Sophocles, 14
Smith, Adam, 77, 92
Speaking/writing opposition, 231
Speech, 210, 212, 217, 219, 220-22; and
  differences, 209; and fantasy, 214; and
  perception, 214; as presence, 203; and
  writing, 208, 218
Spencer, Herbert, 75, 76, 79, 80
Strawson, P. F., 160
Structural allegory, xi-xvii, xix-xx, 243-44
Structuralism: anti-empiricism of, xiii; anti-
  humanism of, 233-34; antisubjectivism
  of, 233; approach to social sciences, 164-
  65, 170; claim to universality, 115, 233;
  colonization of event by structure, 232;
  critique of, xiv-xv, 31, 45n26(a); as
  critique of humanism and historicism,
  xiv; and deconstructionism, 183-84;
  Derrida's revision of, 210-11; dissolution of subject/object dualism, 231; as
  expression of intellectual crisis, 132; fetish of universality, 233; Foucault's re-
  nunciation of, 77-78; as French episteme,
  156-57; impact on literary theory, xxiii,
  183, 232; lack of causality in, 233; philosophical defense of, 170; philosophical
  foundations of, xiv, 104-7, 130-46, 232-
  33; political biology as source of, 79; rationalist bias of, 25; as scientific method,
  115, 164-65, 170; and structurality, xviii;
  weakness of traditional critique of, 233
Style: and language, 193; in Barthes, 192-93
Subject/object, xii, 115-16, 120, 208, 231,
  234, 239, 240, 243-44; Derrida's critique
  of, 207; dualism dissolved into monism,
  233, 234, 243; indifference, 120, 240; in
  language paradigm, 243-44; in literary interpretation, 239; as logocentric metaphysics, 204; and meaning, 206; in reception theory, 239
Subjectivism, 104-5, 132; antisubjectivism,
  104-5, 233; Gadamer's critique of, 120
Subjectivity, 144, 230, 238; Derrida's rejection of, 222; intersubjectivity, 104, 220;
  move away from in literary theory, 230
Surrealism, 70, 71, 72
Symbolic/imaginary, 9-10; difficulty in distinguishing between, 24-25
Symbolic, The, 6-7, 54; and imaginary, xxiv;
  indeterminacy of, 22; overdetermination

of (symbolism), 22, 29; return of, 51;
  and semiosis, xvii; symbolic ambivalence,
  47; war on, 52
Symbolism, 29; autonomization of, 8, 22;
  importance of, 22-23; and linguistics,
  45n19, 45n25; and repression, 50; social constitution of, 7-8
Synchrony/diachrony, 113, 114, 210, 232
Syncretism, defined, 159

Tathandlung, 107
Tel Quel, 151
Teleonomic principle, 66
Text, 193, 198, 201, 207, 208, 216, 220,
  238; Barthes's theory of, 188, 195; and
  book, 201; boundaries of, 236-37; cultural forms as, 164-65; and desire, 218;
  and meaning, 219; pleasures of, 192,
  198; as productive model, 236; and psychic condensation, 215; and reader, 239;
  and reference, 213; and reversal, 215;
  status of, 179-81; theory of, 167, 170,
  172, 175-76, 178-80, 238; and trace,
  213
Todorov, Tzvetan, 151, 154, 160, 232
Tomaševskij, Boris, 153
Totemism, 47
Trace, xii, xiv, xviii, 202, 203, 206-7, 209,
  210, 211, 216, 217, 224, 235-36, 237,
  238; and language, 203, 206-7; and sign,
  235-36; and text, 213
Trubetzkoj, Nikolaj S., 153, 155
Tynjanov, Jurij, 153

Unconscious, 55, 56, 57; and imaginary significations, 28; as simulation model, 57;
  symbolic elaboration in, 26
Understanding, 118-21; as agreement, 118-
  19; and explanation, 223; limits of, 111
Utopia, xviii, 106, 107; linguistic, 236

Vacher de Lapouges, G., 159
Value, 30, 43n9, 55, 106-7, 242-46; autonomization of, 61; commodity, 56; commodity law of, 61, 62, 64, 69; creation
  of, 242-43; and deconstructionist interpretation, 214; and desire, 55; exchange,
  59, 60; floating, 57; and interpretation,
  244; and language, 59; law of, 54, 55
  56, 59, 61; loss of, 106; natural law of,
  61; and nonvalue, 45n29; philosophy of,
  244; and political economy, 56; primacy

of, 244-46; and production, 54; and
reality principle, 52; referential, 67;
revolution of, 56; in Saussure and Freud,
158; and simulation, 56; structural, 56;
structural law of, 61, 64; structural play
of, 60; tactical, 65; use, 59, 60
Verbal universe, 230
Vico, Giambattista, 109, 184, 194
Vienna Circle, 105
Vinogradov, V. V., 153
Violence: symbolic, structural, theoretical,
59, 237
Vološinov, V. N., 153

Walker, Evan Harris, xix
Warhol, Andy, 72

Warren, Austin, 160
Weber, J.-P., 154
Wellek, René, 160
Wernick, Andrew, xxii
Will-to-Will, xvii, xxiii, 82, 87, 91
Wilson, Robert Anton, xix
Wittgenstein, Ludwig, xxii, 104-28, 135,
229, 239; as continuation of German
classical idealism, 122; and language
paradigm, 112; *Philosophical Investigations*, 112; *Tractatus*, 112
Writing, 201-2, 210, 212, 216, 217, 218,
220, 221-22, 223; and history, 204; and
meaning, 204; and speech, 205, 208; as
representation, 207